Media Literacy

MEDIA
LITERACY

KEYS TO
Interpreting Media Messages

Art Silverblatt

Westport, Connecticut
London

Library of Congress Cataloging-in-Publication Data

Silverblatt, Art.
    Media literacy : keys to interpreting media messages / Art
Silverblatt.
        p.   cm.
    Includes bibliographical references and index.
    ISBN 0–275–94830–7 (alk. paper).—ISBN 0–275–94831–5 (pbk.)
    1. Mass media. I. Title.
    P90.S49   1995
    302.23—dc20   94–22004

British Library Cataloguing in Publication Data is available.

Library of Congress Catalog Card Number: 94–22004
ISBN: 0–275–94830–7
        0–275–94831–5 (pbk.)

First published in 1995

Praeger Publishers, 88 Post Road West, Westport, CT 06881
An imprint of Greenwood Publishing Group, Inc.

Printed in the United States of America

The paper used in this book complies with the
Permanent Paper Standard issued by the National
Information Standards Organization (Z39.48–1984).

10 9 8 7 6 5 4 3 2 1

To my two loves,
Margie and Leah Babette

CONTENTS

PREFACE

This text offers a critical approach that will enable students to better understand the information conveyed through the channels of mass communication—print, photography, film, radio, and television. Becoming media literate can best be described as a process of discovery. In some respects, you are already media experts. You are familiar with the channels of mass communications, media programming, and significant media figures. This text is designed to enable you to put your considerable media experience into meaningful perspective.

One of the principal goals of *Media Literacy* is to enable you to realize a healthy independence from the pervasive influence of the media and make up your own mind about issues. In the course of the text, I will be presenting some ideas and hypotheses about the media. I invite you to challenge these assertions and extend my arguments so that you can come to your own conclusions.

To be sure, media literacy requires a degree of energy and concentration. It initially may feel awkward to analyze films or television programs. However, as in any activity, the more you practice, the easier the process becomes.

Two questions invariably are raised by students in discussions with regard to media literacy: *Did the media communicator purposely add all of the complex layers of meanings contained in a media production, or are these interpretations simply imposed upon the content by overzealous critics?* Economy is a fundamental operating principle in the media industry: There is no space, money, or time to waste. Media professionals are judged on the basis of how well they can work within limits. Unfortunately, not all productions are carefully crafted, and some unwanted "fat" may be contained in a program. However, the audience *should* assume that all production elements are intended to contribute to a unified message or theme.

In addition, media communicators may operate on an intuitive level—selecting a particular color, angle, or word simply because it "feels right" or because it will ensure a profit. Media analysis can reveal and clarify meanings that may not have been formally articulated by the media communicator. Of course, it is irresponsible to ascribe meaning to a work without supporting evidence from the text. But it is certainly legitimate (and appropriate) to present an interpretation based upon systematic, concrete analysis of media content.

Finally, the collaborative nature of mass communications can result in unintended messages. For instance, a newspaper article must go through a reporter, copy editor, managing editor, and headline writer before it appears in print. As a result, messages contained in a story may simply be an unintentional result of this combined effort. However, the question of intention is ultimately irrelevant; the critical issue is how the public receives and interprets media content.

Are the media malevolent? Because media literacy analysis can uncover inaccuracies, deceptions, and manipulations, students may be left with the impression that "the media" are diabolical. However, the media are simply neutral channels through which information is conveyed to large groups of people. The media can be used for many purposes and either used well or badly, depending on the intention—and skill—of the media communicator.

ORGANIZATION OF THE BOOK

Part I presents a theoretical framework for the critical analysis of media text. Part II gives students the opportunity to apply this methodological framework to a variety of media formats: journalism, advertising, and American political communications. Part III consists of a brief consideration of mass media issues (violence in the media, media and children, media and social change, and global communications), as well as a discussion of potential outcomes once people have become media literate.

ACKNOWLEDGMENTS

Many thanks to Peter Coveney, my editor, whose support has meant so much to the successful completion of the book. I would also like to acknowledge the enormous contributions of my research associates Kurt Groetsch and Julia Smillie. Many thanks for your persistence, patience, and attention to detail. I also owe a great debt to various colleagues who provided constructive feedback and support: Rick Rosenfeld, Tripp Frohlichstein, Elaine Berland, Jane Squier, Alan Osherow, and Michael Burks. Ellen Eliceiri and the research staff at Eden-Webster Library were always helpful and professional. Barb Finan, program assistant in the Department of Media Communications at Webster University, deserves special mention for her help during the course of the project, along with Pat Bahlinger. Finally, I wish to thank several colleagues in the field of media literacy for their helpful suggestions: Renee Hobbs (Babson College), John Dillon (Murray State University), and Barbara Osborne (California State University at Northridge).

CHAPTER 1

INTRODUCTION TO MEDIA LITERACY

When children 4–6 were asked in a survey, "Which do you like better, TV or your daddy?," 54 percent said "TV." [1]

The media have assumed a large role in the lives of the average American family. For instance:

- Only 59 percent of adults talk with other family members during the course of an evening.[2]
- Only 34 percent of parents spend time with their children during the evening.[3]
- The average American married couple spends only four minutes a day in "serious" conversation.[4]

At the same time:

- Watching TV is the dominant leisure activity of Americans, consuming 40 percent of the average person's free time as a primary activity.[5]
- In the average American household, the television set is on for over seven hours per day.[6]
- Children between the ages of two and five watch an average of 31 hours of television per week.[7]

And remember, television represents only *one* media system.

The traditional definition of *literacy* applies only to print: "having a knowledge of letters; instructed; learned." However, the principal channels of mass media now include print, photography, film, radio, and television. In light of the emergence of these other channels of mass communications, this definition of literacy must be expanded. The National Telemedia Council defines media literacy as "the ability to choose, to understand—within the context of content, form/style, impact, industry and production—to question, to evaluate, to create and/or produce and to respond thoughtfully to the media we consume. It is mindful viewing, reflective judgment."[8]

At the National Leadership Conference on Media Literacy, sponsored by the Aspen Institute in December 1992, the group's representatives settled on a basic definition of media literacy: "It is the ability of a citizen to access, analyze, and produce information for specific outcomes."[9]

This author's definition of media literacy builds on the preceding ideas but emphasizes the following elements:

1. An awareness of the impact of the media on the individual and society. The media have revolutionized the way we think about ourselves, each other, and our world. We develop brand loyalties that have little to do with the quality of the product. We vote for candidates on the basis of "gut reactions" to political spots devised by clever political media consultants. We take the word (or pictures) of journalists to provide us with a clear understanding of the events of the world. The media have become a pervasive force in contemporary society, which is why the need for a media literate public is so acute. As Bill Moyers observes, "At stake is our sense of meaning and language, our sense of history, democracy, citizenship and our very notions of beauty and truth."[10] Media literacy promotes the critical thinking skills that empower people to make independent judgments and informed decisions in response to information conveyed through the channels of mass communications.

2. An understanding of the process of mass communication. Media literacy requires an understanding of the production, transmission, and context of interpretation involved in the mass communication process. Chapter 2 discusses the elements involved in the process of media communications.

3. The development of strategies with which to analyze and discuss media messages. In order to become discerning consumers of media, individuals must develop strategies for the systematic analysis of media content. Part I, "Keys to Interpreting Media Messages" (see pages 128–131 for a concise summary of this material), offers a theoretical framework that can be applied to provide insight into *media messages* (i.e., the underlying themes or ideas contained in a media presentation). These keys also provide a framework that can facilitate the discussion of media content with others—including children, peers, and the people responsible for producing media programming.

4. An awareness of media content as a "text" that provides insight into our contemporary culture and ourselves. As we will see in Chapter 3, *media presentations* (e.g., films, newspapers, television programs, or advertisements) can provide insight into the attitudes, values, behaviors, preoccupations, patterns of thought, and myths that define a culture. Conversely, an understanding of culture can furnish perspective into media messages.

5. *The cultivation of an enhanced enjoyment, understanding, and appreciation of media content.* A well-produced media presentation can provide audiences with enormous pleasure. Media literacy should not detract from your enjoyment of programs. Indeed, critical interpretation should enhance your enjoyment and appreciation of media at its best: insightful articles, informative news programs, and uplifting films.

OBSTACLES TO MEDIA LITERACY

One would think that the evolution of mass communication would eliminate the traditional barriers to media literacy. After all, one must be educated in order to read. On the other hand, all that is required to watch television is a strong wrist to operate the remote control.

However, universal access to the media should not be confused with media literacy. Despite the pervasiveness of the channels of mass communications, media illiteracy remains a problem for several reasons.

Elitism

In 1980, a study was conducted in which people were asked: "To what degree does the media have an effect on society?" Eighty percent of those who responded "Strongly Agreed" that media had an effect on society as a whole. However, only twelve percent "Strongly Agreed" that media had a personal impact on them.[11]

The implications of this study are both intriguing and disturbing. Participants in the study apparently had no difficulty seeing the influence of the media on others. However, these same people were unable to recognize the impact of the media on their own lives. And the more that people deny the personal influence of mass media, the more susceptible they are to media messages.

Significantly, an updated study found that education was not a significant variable in this wide disparity between perceptions of effects of the media on others and on their own lives.[12] One possible explanation for this finding is that educated people are embarrassed to admit that, like everyone else, they watch "The Love Connection" and scan the *National Enquirer* while standing at the checkout counter. And as a result, well-educated people (in the traditional sense) may be as susceptible to the influence of media messages as the general population.

Therefore, a first step in media literacy involves an awareness that you receive numerous messages daily through the media and that these messages can affect your behavior, attitudes, and values.

Affective Nature of Photography, Film, Television, and Radio

Imagine glancing up from this text and gazing out the window. Suddenly, you spot a small, unattended toddler wandering into the street. Your immediate reaction might include:

- Experiencing a sudden jolt as your nervous system carries this information to your brain.
- Feeling a tightening sensation in your stomach.
- Breaking out in an immediate sweat.
- Struggling to translate these feelings into words and actions to help the child.

In contrast with print, visual and aural stimuli initially touch us on an emotional, or *affective,* level. In his discussion of the impact of the visual image, art historian E. H. Gombrich observes:

The power of visual impressions to arouse our emotions has been observed since ancient times. . . . Preachers and teachers preceded modern advertisers in the knowledge of the ways in which the visual image can affect us, whether we want it to or not. The succulent fruit, the seductive nude, the repellent caricature, the hair-raising horror can all play on our emotions and engage our attention.[13]

Because of the affective nature of visual and aural media, it may seem more natural (and considerably easier) to simply "experience" a song or film rather than undertake the arduous task of conceptualizing, articulating, and analyzing your emotional responses.

But please don't discount your emotional responses. One effective strategy for the interpretation of media messages involves using your feelings as a starting point for analysis by asking *why* you reacted as you did while watching a program.

Audience Behavior Patterns

In the communication process, audience members select the most pertinent bits of information to store and assimilate into meaning. However, audiences are often engaged in competing activities while receiving media messages. Because your primary attention may be focused on other activities (driving while listening to the radio, for instance), you may be susceptible to subtle messages that can affect your attitudes and behaviors. In addition, when you answer the phone or leave the room for a portion of a telecast, the text of information from which to select has been altered. As a result, you may be receiving an altogether different message than was originally intended by the media communicator.

Audience Expectations

After a long, stress-filled day at school, you may turn on your television to wind down and put the day's events into perspective. This form of "electronic meditation" also may signal to others that you are not in the mood for conversation. As a result, you may not feel particularly inclined to analyze media content. And the only way to discover media messages is to *look* for media messages.

Indeed, individuals may cling to media content as a retreat from reality. Ian Mitroff and Warren Bennis contend that the complexities of modern society have intensified the individual's need for order and meaning: "As reality became more complex, so complex that no one single individual could understand all the forces and patterns unleashed, we retreated more and more into the invention and proliferation of self-contained worlds of unreality over which we could maintain the illusion of control." [14] In response, media programming has created an alternative reality—an unreality—that is simplistic, entertaining, and satisfying.

At the same time, people tend to underestimate the effort required to comprehend certain media—most notably television. Gavriel Salomon and Tamar Leigh observe:

[Children] have learned that print materials, so highly prized in school and elsewhere, are indeed more difficult to process, whereas TV can be processed for pleasure without much effort. However, this argument pertains only to the minimum effort needed for the satisfactory processing of materials; it says nothing about the amount of additional effort one *could* expend in processing televised material if one aimed at a deeper understanding of it. [15]

Nature of Programming

The American media system is a market-driven industry predicated on turning a profit. Feature films, popular music, and newspapers must attract and maintain an audience in order to remain in business. To illustrate, journalists are now feeling pressured to present the news in an entertaining fashion. This trend toward "infotainment" can severely compromise the content of a news story or broadcast.

Nevertheless, programs that were never intended to instruct the public *do* educate us. These programs convey messages about how the world operates, provide models of acceptable and unacceptable behavior, and reflect cultural definitions of success and failure.

Credibility of Media

Audiences are often predisposed to believe what is presented in the mass media. One particularly dangerous media message is that information presented on television or in the newspaper must be true simply because it appears in the media. To illustrate, a recent Times-Mirror poll found that up to 50 percent of those who watch crime re-creation TV shows such as "Rescue 911" regard the programs as news footage even though a disclaimer appears at the bottom of the TV screen stating that the program is a dramatic reenactment of a crime.[16]

However, a great deal of fragmented, contradictory, and false information appears in the media. Audiences must learn to look at information presented through the media with a healthy skepticism and determine for themselves whether the content is accurate.

Complexity of the Language of Media

As mentioned earlier, for a person to be considered literate in the traditional sense, a certain amount of education is mandatory. However, media literacy also requires an understanding of the sign and symbol system of media. David Considine and Gail Haley observe that audiences may underestimate the complexity of media messages: "Most Americans still perceive the media image as transparent, a sign that simply says what it means and means what it says. They therefore tend to dismiss any intensive explication as a case study of reading too much into it."[17]

Mass communicators have learned to manipulate the "language" of the media to influence the audience. A familiarity with various production elements (i.e., editing, color, lighting, shot selection) therefore should enhance the audience's understanding and appreciation of media content. Chapter 5 discusses how production elements can be used to communicate media messages.

LEVELS OF MEANING: MANIFEST AND LATENT MESSAGES

Manifest messages are direct and clear to the audience. We generally have little trouble recognizing these messages when we are paying full attention to a media presentation. For instance, have you ever noticed how many commercials *tell* you to do something?

- "American Express: Don't Leave Home Without It"
- "Beat the '92 Price Increase Now!" (Toyota ad)
- "Insist on Blue Coal" (Radio broadcast, 1947)

Latent messages are indirect and beneath the surface and consequently escape our immediate attention. Latent messages may reinforce manifest messages or may suggest entirely different meanings. For example, "G.I. Joe" commercials promote their line of war toys. However, the latent message of the G.I. Joe ad glorifies war and equates violence with masculinity.

Latent messages can be conveyed through *affective strategies, embedded values,* and *cumulative messages.*

Affective Strategies

As mentioned earlier, media communicators can influence the attitudes and behavior of audiences by appealing to their emotions. For instance, advertisers often sell their products by appealing to emotions such as guilt or the need for acceptance.

The visual and aural media (photography, film, television, and radio) are particularly well suited to emotional appeals. Production values such as color, shape, lighting, and size evoke emotional responses that can convey messages.

Embedded Values

Media content may reflect the value system of the media communicator as well as widely held cultural values and attitudes. Embedded values may appear in the text through such production techniques as editing decisions, point of view, and connotative words and images.

Cumulative Messages

Cumulative messages occur with such frequency over time that they form new meanings, independent of any individual production. Consistent messages recur in media presentations with regard to gender roles, definitions of success, and racial and cultural stereotypes. For instance, taken by itself, *Rambo* is simply an action-entertainment film. However, when depicted in countless other media presentations, this macho image can send an aggregate message about the ideal of manhood.

MEDIA LITERACY

Media literacy is an established field of study within the international academic community. Thanks in large measure to Barry Duncan and John Pungente, Canada has emerged as a leader in the development of this discipline. Australia, Chile, India, England, Scotland, France, and Jordan have also made significant inroads into the field of media literacy.

Significantly, the United States has lagged behind these other countries in the media literacy movement. The National Leadership Conference on Media Literacy, sponsored by the Aspen Institute in December 1992, noted:

It is ironic and also understandable that the United States is the premier producer of international mass media, but that media literacy is only beginning in this country. The United States has a culture fascinated with individualism and with the potential of technology to solve social problems. Its culture is also pervaded with commercialism . . . that simultaneously produces a "culture of denial" about the cultural implications of commercialism. Media literacy is thus an especially difficult challenge in the U.S.[18]

However, in recent years the media literacy movement has gained momentum in the American academic community as well. A number of professional associations promote media literacy in the United States, including the Center for Media Literacy in Los Angeles, Strategies for Media Literacy in San Francisco, the National Telemedia Council in Madison, Wisconsin, and Citizens for Media Literacy in Asheville, North Carolina.

U.S. educators have begun to recognize the value of media literacy education. In March 1993, New Mexico launched a National Media Literacy Project, a statewide initiative designed to incorporate media literacy across the secondary curriculum. Institutions of higher education are also becoming involved in the field of media literacy. For instance, an Institute in Media Education was held at Harvard University in August 1993. This week-long institute brought together 100 educators, scholars, and media professionals to discuss issues in media literacy, to design curriculum, and to develop implementation plans for integrating media literacy concepts into existing curricula. Renee Hobbs, director of the Harvard Institute, declares, "I am convinced that media literacy will ultimately fuel a reform movement in higher education, as communication departments rethink their responsibilities to broadly educate citizens in our media age."[19]

NOTES

1. Berkeley Pop Culture Project, *The Whole Pop Catalog* (Berkeley: Avon Books, 1991), 547.

2. Joe Schwartz, "Is There Life Before Bed?" *American Demographics* 12 (March 1990): 12.

3. Ibid.

4. NBC, 1991.

5. Schwartz, "Life Before Bed?" 12.

6. James D. Harless, *Mass Communication: An Introductory Survey,* 2d ed. (Dubuque, IA: Wm. C. Brown, 1990), 3.

7. John P. Murray and Barbara Lonnborg, *Children and Television: A Primer for Parents* (Boys Town, NE: Communications & Public Service Division, Father Flanagan's Boys Home), 2.

8. "The National Telemedia Council," *Telemedium* 38 (1992): 12.

9. Presented at the Aspen Institute's National Leadership Conference on Media Literacy, Queenstown, MD, December 7–9, 1992.

10. Bill Moyers, "The Public Mind: Consuming Images," Public Broadcasting Service, November 8, 1989.

11. James Tiedge, "Public Opinion on Mass Media Effects: Perceived Societal Effects and Perceived Personal Effects" (paper presented at the Speech Communication Association Convention, Minneapolis, 1980).

12. James Tiedge, Arthur Silverblatt, Michael J. Havice, and Richard Rosenfeld. "The Third-Person Effects Hypothesis: Scope, Magnitude, and Contributing Factors," *Journalism Quarterly* 68 (Spring–Summer 1991): 141–54.

13. E. H. Gombrich, "The Visual Image," in *Media and Symbols: The Forms of Expression, Communication, and Education,* publication of the National Society for the Study of Education, vol. 73, pt. 1, ed. David R. Olson (Chicago: University of Chicago Press, 1974), 244.

14. Ian I. Mitroff and Warren Bennis, *The Unreality Industry* (New York: Oxford University Press, 1989), 38.

15. Gavriel Salomon and Tamar Leigh, "Predispositions About Learning from Print and Television," *Journal of Communication* 34 (1984): 129–30.

16. Thomas B. Rosensteil, "Viewers Found to Confuse TV Entertainment with News," *Los Angeles Times,* August 17, 1989, I17.

17. David Considine and Gail Haley, *Visual Messages: Integrating Imagery into Instruction* (Englewood, CO: Teacher Ideas Press, 1992), 3.

18. Aspen Institute, Leadership Conference.

19. Renee Hobbs, director of the Harvard Institute, interview by author, St. Louis, MO, September 22, 1993.

PART I

KEYS TO INTERPRETING MEDIA MESSAGES

How do you interpret messages that are presented through the media? Manifest messages, by their very definition, are rather easy to spot. However, it is trickier to identify latent messages. As we will see, media communicators are extremely sophisticated in their ability to communicate messages.

The keys to interpreting media messages provide you with an approach for the systematic analysis of media-carried "text." The keys, outlined on pages 128–131, are also intended to enhance your enjoyment and appreciation of media programming, whether it is a television documentary, soap opera, or MTV.

Think of these keys as a series of lenses. Each lens will provide you with fresh insights into media-carried content. Not all of the keys are necessarily appropriate for every media presentation. Obviously, the production element of movement would not be relevant to an analysis of newspapers. Use only those keys that will be most applicable to the particular media format.

CHAPTER 2

PROCESS

OVERVIEW

In order to become media literate, you must first develop an understanding of the communications process. Communication is an active, dynamic experience that demands your fullest attention and energy. The moment that someone approaches you and initiates a conversation, you become engaged in a rapid sequence of activities:

- Receiving a message
- Selecting relevant information
- Forming appropriate responses
- Responding to the message

Immediately after you have formed the appropriate response, the roles are reversed: You shift from audience to communicator, and vice versa.

For people to communicate effectively, a relationship of mutual trust and respect must be established. The communicator and audience form a communication contract that governs their conduct. Both parties agree to abide by the rules. For instance, people should maintain a comfortable distance from one another during conversations (neither too close nor too far away). There is also an unwritten understanding that one person should not dominate a conversation by talking for an exhaustive period of time. Any violation of these agreements results in an instant breakdown of the social contract. To illustrate, if you feel that the person with whom you are conversing isn't really listening to you or doesn't respect what you have to say, then the conversation is doomed.

People typically engage in three types of communication. *Intrapersonal communication* takes place within ourselves. It is the basis of all forms of communication, because until we know what it is that we want to say, we will not be able to communicate effectively with other people. *Intrapersonal communication* is based upon face-to-face interaction with another person. In *mass communication,* messages are communicated through a mass medium (e.g., radio or television) to a large group of people who may not be in direct contact with the communicator.

The basic *communications model* consists of the following elements:

- The *communicator* is the person who delivers the message.
- The *message* is the information being communicated.
- The *channel* refers to the passage through which the information is being conveyed. For example, you use your voice, eyes, and facial expressions as channels for interpersonal communication. In mass communication, the media—newspapers, photographs, film, radio, and television—serve as channels for the communication of information to large groups of people.
- The *audience* consists of the person or people who receive the message. The more familiar the communicator is with the audience, the more effectively he or she can tailor the message to the listener.

Two elements are critical to the communications process: *feedback* and *interference.*

Feedback

Feedback provides an opportunity for the audience to respond to the communicator. Listeners may ask questions or comment in order to better understand what the communicator is trying to say. Feedback also reassures the communicator. When listeners nod their heads, smile, or repeat key phrases, they are letting the communicator know they are alert and involved in the conversation.

Interference

Interference refers to those factors that can hinder the communications process. Interference can occur at all points of the communications model. *Communicator interference* is a result of the communicator obstructing the message. Sometimes people have difficulty expressing themselves clearly. Or perhaps the communicator does not know exactly what he or she wants to say. In this instance, the communicator might ramble on until the listener eventually loses interest. Communicator interference also takes place if the communicator is not self-aware. For instance, you may be angry at a friend but are unwilling to admit it—even to yourself. As a result, you may be sending mixed messages, denying that you are angry at the same time that you are acting gruff and abrupt.

Channel interference occurs when a glitch in the channel distorts the message. For example, if you have laryngitis, your audience may be unable to understand you. In mass communications, channel interference arises when the television picture suddenly goes blank or the sound becomes inaudible.

Channel interference can also result from using an inappropriate channel to send a particular type of message. As we will discuss later in this chapter, each medium is uniquely qualified to carry specific types of information. For instance, corporations may spend enormous amounts of money on promotional videos when in reality the detailed information they are trying to convey would be more suitable in print. Corporations sometimes commit to an expensive media presentation when a one-to-one (interpersonal) conversation would be more effective and cost-efficient.

Environmental interference refers to distractions within the setting in which the information is received. For example, we have all attended movies in which the people behind us have talked throughout the picture, or have had our view blocked by the people seated in front of us.

Audience interference occurs when the audience obstructs the communication process. Several principles can affect the ways in which the audience receives and interprets information:

- *Selective exposure* refers to the audience's program choices, based on his or her personal values and interests. People seek out information that offers a perspective with which they agree and avoid communication that offers a different orientation. This principle also applies to mass communication. Sports fans will watch ESPN, while people indifferent to sports will tune in something else. Audiences are selective about the people who appear in the media as well. If you are a Jack Nicholson fan, you will make an effort to see his movies. If not, you will make an effort to avoid films starring Nicholson.

- *Selective perception* is the phenomenon in which people's interpretation of content is colored by their predispositions and preconceptions. To illustrate, several years ago this author attended a preview of "The Day After," a television drama about the effects of a nuclear war on a town in Kansas. Asked about his reaction to the program, an air force colonel replied that he felt that the program was "excellent" in its dramatization of why America needed to beef up its nuclear arsenal to prevent sneak attacks from Russia and to preserve "peace through strength." A nuclear freeze activist also agreed that the program was "excellent," although she came away from the program with an entirely different message: The devastation depicted in the program illustrated why America and Russia needed to eliminate nuclear arms. In this case, both parties saw the program as supporting the points of view that they held going into the preview.

- *Selective retention* occurs when a person selectively remembers (or forgets) information. We tend to tune out conversations when we are exposed to subject matter in which our interest level is low. For instance, if you decide to talk about a subject I know nothing about (e.g., nuclear physics), I will focus my attention elsewhere, where I am more comfortable. An individual's recall of information may be influenced by a number of other factors as well: whether the person was distracted at the time, a sense of nostalgia (reconstructing past events so that they appear more positive), or the impulse to minimize unpleasant thoughts or experiences.

• *Audience attention span* may also be a factor in interference. As mentioned earlier, communication is an active process that demands concentration and energy. Occasionally we'll just take a brief rest and tune out the speaker. This option is particularly tempting when we are presented with information outside of our frame of reference.

• Finally, audience members often filter messages through their *egos*. That is, they focus on those aspects of a conversation that relate to them, ignoring the rest of the message. During conversations, audience members are not always paying strict attention to the speaker. Instead, they may be busily engaged in the process of forming their responses or are anxiously awaiting their chance to talk.

Differences Between Interpersonal and Mass Communication

While the principles discussed above apply to all forms of communication, some significant differences exist between interpersonal and mass communication:

Communications Model. When Marshall McLuhan declared, "The medium is the message," he was suggesting that the media have reconfigured the traditional communications model. The channels of mass communications have now assumed a primary role in determining content, choice of communicator, and the audience (see Figure 2.1).

A useful illustration can be found in the world of broadcast news. The medium of television often dictates the choice of communicator: Anchorpeople must be attractive, likable, and convincing. Indeed, journalistic ability is often subordinate to performance skills. The message is also affected by the characteristics of the medium. Television news emphasizes events rather than issues in order to take advantage of the visual capabilities of the medium. (Further discussion on comparative media will follow later in the chapter.) Broadcast news content also must be entertaining and dramatic to maintain the attention of the audience. Stories must be brief to fit into the structure of a newscast.

Finally, the choice of medium has a significant impact on the audience. To illustrate, the majority of Americans find television to be the most credible source of news (Table 2.1). And half of the American population relies solely on television for its news (Table 2.2).

Feedback in Mass Communications. Without immediate contact with the audience, the media communicator has only one opportunity to convey

Figure 2.1
Communications Models

Interpersonal Communications Model	Mass Communications Model
Communicator	Channel
○	○
Message	Communicator
○	○
Channel	Message
○	○
Audience	Audience

a message. As a result, media presentations must be carefully planned in order to anticipate any ambiguities or questions raised by the audience.

Indeed, the media communicator has no way of knowing whether the audience is truly involved in the communication process. Studies indicate that half of the audience leaves the room at least once during the course of a TV show—while the media communicator is "talking" to the audience. And approximately one third of the audience typically abandons an hour-long program before it is over, switching to another channel or turning off the television.[1]

Table 2.1
Most Credible News Source—Roper Poll

	1959	1986	1988
Television	29%	55%	49%
Newspapers	32%	21%	26%
Radio	12%	6%	7%
Magazines	10%	6%	5%
Don't Know	17%	12%	13%

Source: The Roper Organization, America's Watching: Public Attitudes Toward Television 1991 (New York: The Network Television Association; Washington, D.C.: The National Association of Broadcasters, 1991), p. 21. ·

Table 2.2
Which Medium They Relied Upon Most

	1959	1963	1967	1971	1974	1980	1984	1988
Television	51%	55%	64%	60%	65%	64%	64%	65%
Newspapers	57%	53%	55%	48%	47%	44%	40%	42%
Radio	34%	29%	28%	23%	21%	18%	14%	14%
Magazines	8%	6%	7%	5%	4%	5%	4%	4%
Other People	4%	4%	4%	4%	4%	4%	4%	5%
Don't Know	1%	3%	2%	1%	----	----	----	----
No Answer	----	----	----	----	----	----	----	----

Source: The Roper Organization, *America's Watching: Public Attitudes Toward Television 1991* (New York: The Network Television Association; Washington, D.C.: The National Association of Broadcasters, 1991), p. 22.

Audiences do have a number of feedback opportunities as part of the mass communication process:

Participatory response occurs when individuals respond directly to programs through laughter, anger, and even personal boycotts of programs and products. In addition, audience members may also participate in the production of a program through call-ins, community productions, and the like.

Media content (e.g., advertising, political spots, and certain kinds of religious programming) often have very specific cognitive, attitudinal, and behavioral response objectives for the audience (e.g., buy this, or vote for this proposition). Of course, these messages do not necessarily mean that the content is manipulative or harmful. Information on AIDS or other public service messages can be very helpful to the public.

Since immediate responses are not observable, most mass communications feedback is delayed and cumulative. Media organizations depend on the following *indirect feedback mechanisms:*

Ratings

Revenue generated
  • How many people attend a movie or buy a newspaper.

Delayed audience response
  • Examples of audience response include letters to the editor, petitions, or phone calls.

Audience research
  • Surveys, focus groups, mechanical devices such as the audimeter used by the A. C. Nielsen Co. to measure television use.

Critical response
- Oscars, movie reviews.

Saturation of the Mass Media. In interpersonal communications, the speaker enjoys direct, personal access to the audience; however, the size of this audience is limited. On the other hand, a media communicator can reach a vast audience simultaneously with the same, undistorted message. For example, it took nearly two months for news of the signing of the Treaty of Ghent (officially ending the War of 1812) to reach America. In contrast, within one hour of the assassination of John Kennedy in 1963, 90 percent of the adults in the United States had heard of the major events connected with the shooting.[2] As a result, the mass communicator is in a position to influence a wide range of people at one time.

But while mass communications is unrivaled at providng a breadth of information, there are limits to the depth of information it can furnish. Clearly, some media are more limited than others. But whether it is a five-minute news report or a two-hour documentary, media presentations operate within distinct limits that may or may not meet the needs of the audience.

Ability to Preserve a Message. In interpersonal communication, information is exchanged on an informal basis. Because nobody is recording our conversations, we may forget precisely what we said. Or we may choose to reinterpret the conversation on the basis of what we meant to say—particularly if we said something silly or embarrassing.

In contrast, messages presented through the channels of mass communication (e.g., newspapers and videotapes) may be scrutinized and reexamined by the audience. Consequently, mass communicators are highly accountable for the material that they produce and must be prepared to accept responsibility for their work.

Media as Collaboration. In contrast with interpersonal communications, the production of a newspaper, news broadcast, or ad campaign is a collaborative process requiring the input of numerous people. For example, a Hollywood film production requires a large crew:

- The producer is the chief business executive, responsible for the business arrangements (e.g., financing, business planning, insurance, contracts, and personnel).

- The script writer develops the script. He or she may be responsible for the original treatment; however, writers are frequently brought in to revise a script that has been obtained by a producer or studio.

- The director is the film's principal creative authority, responsible for the presentation of the script on screen.

- First and second assistant directors assist with cast and crew management, crowd control, and coordination of the schedule.

- People in the continuity department are charged with making sure that the props, clothing, and makeup remain consistent, since scenes are often filmed out of sequence.
- The cast includes the stars, supporting players, bit players, and uncredited extras. Additional cast members consist of stunt doubles, who perform dangerous shots, and stand-ins, who work with the crew to set up the proper camera positions and lighting for the performers.
- The cinematographer is responsible for the artistic and technical quality of the film, including lighting, framing, and color values.
- The production designer, or art director, is responsible for set design.
- The editor assembles, arranges, and selects the footage, often in concert with the director.

Other crew members include a gaffer (chief electrician), best boy (gaffer's assistant), grips (who haul heavy lights), costume designer, music director, sound editors, and publicity teams.[3]

Because members of the crew may hold different opinions about content and approach, compromise is a large part of the decision-making process. As a result, the messages contained in the final presentation may be unclear or confusing.

Media as Industry. Media programming is extremely expensive to produce; for example, *Jurassic Park* (1993) cost $60 million. As a result, many decisions are made on the basis of their financial implications, as opposed to any artistic consideration. Producers often are afraid to take risks, relying instead on "bankable" stars and stories. Studios are pressured to produce only what audiences *want* to see. As a result, they may opt for gimmicks like violence, sex, and flashy music rather than risking loss of profits by challenging the audience.

KEYS TO INTERPRETING MEDIA MESSAGES

The first key to interpreting media messages—process—consists of the following elements:

- Function
- Comparative media
- Media communicator
- Audience

Function

A simple communication activity may be motivated by many purposes, or *functions:*

- One common function of communication is *expression*. In these situations, speakers inform the listener of their frame of mind—what they are thinking at that moment, how they are feeling, or their attitudes toward people and issues.

- A communicator can also provide *description*—including details, elaboration on general statements, or concrete examples. As E. H. Gombrich observes, "A speaker can inform his partner of a state of affairs past, present or future, observable or distant, actual or conditional."[4]

- *Instruction* refers to occasions in which the purpose is either (1) to inform someone about a subject with which he or she is unfamiliar or (2) to furnish additional information about a subject with which the audience is already acquainted. Examples include giving someone directions to the airport or watching the evening news on television.

- *Information exchange* occurs in interpersonal communication when all parties benefit by sharing knowledge.

- The ultimate purpose of *persuasion* is control. The communicator's objective is to promote a particular idea or motivate you to action. For example, advertising attempts to persuade you to think positively about a product and, more important, to purchase that brand.

- A surprising proportion of our communication is devoted to *entertainment*. Jokes, stories, and gossip divert us from the more serious and pressing matters of the day. Humor is also a social mechanism that brings people together. Speakers often begin their talks with an amusing anecdote as a means of making the audience feel comfortable. Sharing laughter is a time-honored way to break down traditional barriers.

- Artists often regard their work as a form of *creative expression*. Novelists, painters, or experimental videographers express themselves through their art and share their artistic vision with the audience.

- Sometimes a communicator is not clear about what he or she wants to say but is merely involved in *exploration*. Stalling techniques (like interspersing "uh" and "you know" between words) give us a bit of space to figure out where we are going next. However, we still say things that we wish we could take back. Mass communicators generally present polished information that has been prepared in advance. However, media communicators are sometimes subject to slip-ups when they work without a script.

- As it pertains to communication, a *ritual* is a verbal or written exchange that has a social significance beyond the surface. European friends have expressed some bewilderment over Americans' habit of greeting people with, "How are you?" and then moving on without waiting for a reply. What my friends have mistaken for superficiality is, in fact, a ritual in which people are making a formal connection with one another. "Small talk" is another ritual that makes social situations more comfortable.

- *Performance* is also a major communications function. Think of the dynamics that occur in singles bars. A fellow may be talking about his job, his astrological sign, or telling an amusing story, but the underlying purpose of the conversation is to create a favorable impression. This function also carries over into the world of mass media. As we'll learn in Chapter 5, production values should reinforce the theme, mood, or message of the presentation. All too often, however, media communicators may include dazzling special effects and elaborate camera movements in order to impress the audience with their expertise.

- *Emotional catharsis* includes spontaneous expressions of love, passion, anger, pain, happiness, or the release of tension. These expressions may not be coherent or planned—What did you say the last time that someone dented the fender of your car?—but your speech can be startlingly clear and graphic. Media figures— whether they are interviewers or interviewees—are trained to control these revealing outbursts. However, restraint is not always possible when people are under constant media scrutiny. These moments provide brief but candid glimpses behind the images that have been so carefully cultivated for public view.

- *Disengagement* applies to situations in which the objective is to discourage extended conversation. Perhaps you are in a hurry and find yourself in an awkward or tedious conversation. In this instance, you might adopt strategies designed to terminate discussion—by responding in monosyllabic answers or furnishing verbal cues intended to accelerate the conversation (e.g., "And then . . . ?").

- The underlying function driving the American media industry is *profit*. Of course, advertising and commercial television are geared to generate income. However, journalists may be torn between serving the public's right to know and making a profit. As Allen Neuharth, chairman of the Gannett newspaper chain has noted, "Wall Street didn't give a damn if we put out a good paper in Niagara Falls. They just wanted to know if our profits would be in the 15–20 percent range."[5]

Complicating Factors. The process of identifying communications functions can be complicated by a number of factors: multiple function, latent function, undefined function, and false function.

Multiple function refers to a communications exchange that serves more than one function at a time. To illustrate, we have all participated in conversations during which the function shifts from entertainment to serious discussion. While these functions are often compatible, at other times they may be in conflict. For instance, the functions in advertising include (1) promoting the sale of goods or services and (2) serving the customer. However, when these functions are in competition, the advertising agency's principal allegiance is to its client—sometimes at the expense of the public. As an example, an ad for Newport cigarettes emphasizes the gratification associated with smoking through their slogan "Alive with pleasure." The slogan is ironic, however, given the health hazards of cigarette consumption. The prime beneficiary of this ad is obviously the cigarette company—not the consumer.

Latent function refers to instances in which the media communicator's intention may not be immediately obvious to the audience. In fact, it is astounding to discover how frequently the manifest function of a communication exchange is irrelevant—or at least subordinate—to other, latent purposes, like impressing the audience, nurturing relationships, or expressing emotion. For instance, we have all been involved in conversations in which it becomes clear that the other person is not really interested in your opinions but instead is intent on converting you to his or her point of view. In this case, the latent function is persuasion.

Humor can also fulfill a variety of latent functions. For instance, humor has been a very effective advertising technique for persuading an audience. Humor can also be a subtle means of attacking a person or undermining an opponent's position.

And while the principal function of children's programming may be to entertain or educate, children may be unaware that its underlying purpose is to generate sales of products. This latent function was further camouflaged by the practice, subjected to regulation in 1990, of having the animated characters featured in children's programs appear in commercials as well, pitching products.[6]

Stuart Ewan observes that this latent commercial function ultimately undermines the meaning initially ascribed to images: "All people make images sacred as a way of commenting on their world and ascribing meaning to culture. Now this has been transformed into merchandise—the general meaning is lost."[7]

An excellent example of how the commercial function can co-opt meaning can be found in the case of Jim McMahon, the pro quarterback who developed a reputation on the field as a nonconformist and a rebel. However, he then began to parlay this attitude into a commercial image, serving as a spokesperson for Taco Bell—and in the process becoming the very conventional, corporate type he ostensibly rebelled against.

Undefined function occurs when the media communicator does not have a clear intention in mind. This lack of definition can result in a muddled, directionless presentation. For instance, we have all attended movies in which it seems the director could not make up his or her mind whether the film should be a comedy or tragedy. And as a result, it is neither.

However, undefined function can sometimes be used as a vehicle to attract audiences. For instance, Rush Limbaugh's radio and television programs are informational and persuasive. At the same time, the program is intended to be entertaining; Limbaugh's tongue-in-cheek manner verges on self-parody. Finally, Limbaugh unabashedly promotes his book (and himself) in the course of the program. As a result, there is something for everyone. The Limbaugh shows are "camp," or satire, for liberals and gospel for conservatives.

False function refers to media programs that may offer the appearance of serving one function while actually fulfilling other purposes. For instance, "infotainment" TV programs like "Entertainment Tonight" and "A Current Affair" are entertainment programs presented in a news format, complete with anchorpeople, newsroom set, and journalistic style. As a result, people mistakenly may look to these programs as a source of legitimate news, when their predominant functions are to amuse and titillate.

Finally, media productions sometimes attempt to fulfill several *competing functions* simultaneously, which undermines the effectiveness of the presentation. For instance, in order to remain competitive, broadcast journalists are pressured to present information in an entertaining fashion. However, these functions are frequently in conflict with one another. Some information is complex and difficult (if not tedious) to understand. However, journalists often feel compelled to dress up these reports, changing the content in the process.

Comparative Media

The effective media communicator takes advantage of the unique properties of each medium to convey media messages. For instance, radio obviously cannot employ visuals in transmitting information. However, the radio producer can appeal to the imagination of the listener through creative use of words and sound. The media communicator must decide which medium can best accommodate the message and use the language of that medium to reach the intended audience.

Considerations in assessing the characteristics of a medium include:

• The senses involved in receiving the information
• The pace of the presentation
• The environment in which the medium is received
• The dissemination schedule of the presentation
• Audience use and expectations

Print. Print is a tangible medium. Books are bound, collected, and passed from generation to generation. Although the primary sense used in reading is sight, you can hold printed material in your hands, smell the paper, and in the case of newspapers, feel newsprint rubbing off on your hands. Even newspapers, which have an active life of one day, must be physically removed from your home. This material can be reread and examined in depth. And because writers' names generally appear in their published work, they are accountable for the accuracy of their statements.

To all outward appearances, you may be simply lounging about with a book in your hands at this moment. However, reading is a physical activity that demands an intense level of concentration and energy.

Print lends itself to the detailed presentation of information and discussion of complex issues. For example, research associate Kurt Groetsch conducted a cross-media analysis of the coverage of the Peruvian government's capture of rebel Abyel Guzman in 1992. The *New York Times* printed three related articles: an account of the capture, a biographical sketch of Guzman and how the capture might affect U.S.-Peruvian relations, plus a timeline history of the conflict. All told, the stories amounted to more than 3,000 words. In contrast, ABC News' coverage of the story amounted to fewer than 300 words, accompanied by graphic visuals of the event itself.

Print also enables the author to describe internal states of consciousness: not merely what people are doing but what they are thinking as well. For instance, Henry James's novel *Portrait of a Lady* looks into the very soul of Isabelle Archer and the principal inhabitants of her world. James focuses on the interior life of the various characters and the complex motives behind the actions of the characters. The following passage (detailing a chance meeting between Isabelle's husband Osmond and the nefarious Madame Merle) offers James the opportunity to examine the subtext behind a simple, everyday encounter:

In the manner and tone of these two persons, on first meeting at any juncture, and especially when they met in the presence of others, was something indirect and circumspect, as if they had approached each other obliquely and addressed each other by implication. The effect of each appeared to be to intensify to an appreciable degree the self-consciousness of the other. Madame Merle of course carried off any embarrassment better than her friend; but even Madame Merle had not on this occasion the form she would have liked to have—the perfect self-possession she would have wished to wear for her host. The point to be made is, however, that at a certain moment the element between them, whatever it was, always leveled itself and left them more closely face to face than either ever was with anyone else. This was what had happened now. They stood there knowing each other well and each on the whole willing to accept the satisfaction of knowing as a compensation for the inconvenience—whatever it might be—of being known.[8]

In print, the author clearly establishes the *pace* at which the material is received. Pace refers to the rhythm or rate at which information should be assimilated. The density of information and sentence structure requires a particular reading rate. As you doubtless noticed, Henry James's style is characterized by long, complex narrative prose with frequent interpolations. James's novels demand careful attention. On the other hand, the spare writing style and colorful graphics of *USA Today* encourages readers to skim the paper.

However, the reader does exercise a degree of control over the pace. If you decide to put this text down now, there is very little that this author can do about it. If you decide to read more rapidly or skip entire paragraphs, that is ultimately your choice.

Print also has a distinctive *environment*. Environment refers to the physical surroundings that can affect communication. Print is a portable medium. You can take your book with you anywhere—the library, in the park, or on the subway. The major factor in location is adequate lighting.

Reading is generally a primary experience. Unless you are reading a story to a small child, you tend to read silently, by yourself. Reading requires relative solitude. Try reading this textbook while engaged in other activities (driving or talking on the phone, for instance). Then see if you can clearly summarize the major points in the chapter. One activity or the other will surely suffer. However, the simplified information and colorful graphs characteristic of publications like *USA Today* enable readers to participate in other activities simultaneously.

The *dissemination schedule* for print is comparatively deliberate. The dissemination schedule refers to the amount of time that it takes for information to reach you through a particular medium. Newspapers are published on a daily basis. If you do not get the opportunity to read your morning paper at breakfast, it may well be "old news" by the time you pick it up in the evening. Magazines may come out once a week or even bimonthly. It may take a year or more for a book to be written, edited, published, and distributed. However, publishers will scramble to release a book on a popular subject before interest in the subject subsides. To illustrate, *OJ Simpson: American Hero, American Tragedy* (written by Marc Cerasini and published by Kensington Publishing) was in the bookstores 12 days after the murders of Nicole Brown Simpson and Ronald Goldman took place.[9]

Photography. We live in a photo environment. Photographic images are pervasive. We see billboards in crowds, wear images on our clothes, and leaf through magazines in a variety of public places as well as at home. Although photographs have a distinct feel and smell, the principal way in which we apprehend photographs is through the sense of sight. As mentioned earlier, we tend to respond to visually oriented media in an affective, or emotional, way.

Photography has become a primary means of documenting family history. The family photo album furnishes an important record of who we are and where we came from. Photos keep a record of significant rites of passage in the family, such as birthdays, holidays, graduations, and weddings. A household with children is more likely to have at least one camera than a household in which there are no children.[10] Pictures have become particularly precious in a time when the extended family is no longer in close proximity. The dissemination schedule for photographs varies, from immediate (or one-hour) photo processing to a delay of several days.

A photograph possesses an almost mystical quality. People achieve a measure of immortality through photographs. Examine a picture from your childhood. Although you have changed, your image remains forever young. And looking at your photo book stirs memories that bring the past into the present.

In its ability to instantaneously preserve a moment of time in space, photography creates the illusion of *verisimilitude,* or lifelike quality. We must remember, however, that photographs present only an image of reality. A photograph can capture only a brief instant, without the context that gives it meaning.

Not only can a photograph be an unreliable record of our world, but it can actually alter the reality it was intended to capture. Consider the typical wedding. The photographer does not hesitate to interrupt the proceedings and whisk the newlyweds away from the celebration. Like trained seals, the bride and groom strike the conventional poses: holding the rose, cutting the cake, and standing in formation with assorted relatives. The entire occasion is transformed into a photo session to be enjoyed later, when the couple leaf through the photo album.

In photography, the pace is primarily determined by the audience. The viewer determines how much time he or she chooses to devote to a photograph. And the viewers' own expectations or frames of reference can influence how they "read" a photograph. As E. H. Gombrich observes: "The information extracted from an image can be quite independent of the intention of its maker. A holiday snapshot of a group on a beach may be scrutinized by an intelligence officer preparing for a landing, and the Pompeiian mosaic might provide new information to a historian of dog breeding."[11]

However, the skilled photographer may exercise considerable influence in the communication process. The photographer can direct the attention of the viewer through the selection and arrangement of the subject matter. In addition, the image maker can use the visual tools at hand to create a mood that subtly conveys media messages. (For further discussion, see Chapter 5.)

Film. In the United States, more than 20 million people per week go to the movies. Movie attendance has increased over the last 20 years despite the competition of other media, the decline in average disposable income, and reduction in leisure time in the United States during the 1980s. Between 1969 and 1989, ticket sales increased by 62.5 percent. To put this figure in perspective, the U.S. population increased by 22.8 percent over the same period.[12]

Film combines sight with sound. As with photography, film is an affective medium that initially stirs the emotions. Another distinctive characteristic of film is motion. The illusion of movement makes the image appear more lifelike than still photographs. However, like photographs, film can create a false reality. The audience's attention is confined to the space within the frame. We can only see what the director wants us to see. For instance, we cannot detect what is happening behind the camera. What appears to be an intimate or spontaneous moment on screen is actually the result of intense planning by a large staff and a multitude of film equipment (cameras, lights, microphones, etc.).

Because film is more action-oriented than print, epic stories featuring strong narratives like *Robin Hood* and *Lethal Weapon* play particularly well on screen. On the other hand, Henry James's *Portrait of a Lady* would not translate easily from novel to film since most of the visuals would depict the characters standing around, deep in thought. However, a film that consists only of car chases also fails to take full advantage of the medium. Film at its best uses plot to furnish insight into character and theme.

Watching a film is a primary experience. In contrast with other media, you must travel to a designated area—a movie theater. One of the attractions of the movies is simply getting away from the pressures and routines of home. The theater is dark and comfortable. The sound and images on the large screen are overwhelming.

At the same time, attending a movie can be a social occasion. Who can forget their first date at the movies—the tension about whether to hold hands, sharing popcorn, and what to talk about after the show. The members of the audience are involved in a communal experience—responding to the program at the same moment. At times, the audience can be a major distraction (e.g., the loudmouth in the row behind you).

The pace of film is determined primarily by the filmmaker. We cannot stop the film to buy popcorn or visit the restroom. Movies are intended to be viewed in their entirety, in one sitting. The audience may be bored or overwhelmed by the pace of a film, but they have very little choice in the matter, other than leaving the theater.

The dissemination schedule for film is the most deliberate of all media. Because of the collaborative nature of the media, a Hollywood film project can take over three years from conception to exhibition in theaters. This process consists of four distinct stages:

Preproduction includes all the preliminary creative, developmental, and planning stages, including the writing of the script, the negotiation for film rights, casting the film, contract negotiations with the performers' agents, building of studio sets, and deciding on locations. According to Richard M. Gollin, "This stage generally extends between three months and two years." [13]

Production involves shooting the basic acted film footage, with accompanying recorded dialogue. This phase normally lasts between 30 and 80 days, "each long day covering perhaps 3 pages of script and generating perhaps two or three minutes of final used footage." [14]

Postproduction includes reshooting of specific scenes, editing, dubbing voices, sound mixing, creating and adding the musical score, addition of special effects, studio previewing, and general fine-tuning. This stage can take from three months to an additional year.

Promotion of a film consists of distribution, exhibition, and publicity. Many films never make it to this stage and are never released.

This arduous process handicaps a media communicator in several respects. Due to the time involved, it is difficult for a filmmaker to gauge whether a film will be topical by the time it is released. The content is likely to undergo many transformations in the process, so that it may not even resemble the original screenplay. And as Gollin notes, this elaborate system also reduces the chances that a film will actually be released.

Radio. Radio has emerged as an integral part of our everyday experience. The clock radio puts people to sleep and wakes them up. Radio is continuous and accessible 24 hours per day. Radios are found wherever people congregate: 95 percent of all American cars have radios, 58 percent of bedrooms have radios, 67 percent of our living rooms have radios, 50 percent of the kitchens have radios, 9 percent of dining areas have radios, and 7 percent of people's bathrooms have radios.[15]

The invention of the car radio and the transistor has transformed radio into a very portable medium. Radios accompany us everywhere; by 1990, there were over 131 million radios in cars.[16] The most popular time periods are the two "drive times" (between 6:00 and 9:00 A.M. and between 3:00 and 7:00 P.M.). As a result, radio has assumed a remarkable personal significance in our lives. We associate particular songs with specific places, experiences, and people in our past.

Radio relies entirely upon the listener's sense of hearing. We must use our imaginations to envision what is being described over the air. On one level, this can be liberating—enabling us to project our own mental pictures onto the events. Old-time baseball announcers, who relayed Western Union accounts of the action over the radio, learned to take advantage of the imaginative possibilities of the medium. Rather than simply announce the progress of the game, they embellished the report with fictitious details, sweeping emphasis, and the artificial crowd noise to dramatize the action.

In radio, the pace of the presentation is controlled entirely by the communicator. Because we are restricted to processing information aurally, it is sometimes difficult to assimilate complex information and intricate sentence structure. As a result, the radio announcer is trained to speak slowly and distinctly, with a pleasing modulation of tone. News broadcast on radio must be clear and concise. The content should be kept general because people tend to get confused when they simply hear a litany of facts and figures.

Although radio remains separated in space from its audience, it operates live, in "real time." Morning radio is geared to helping you wake up and getting you to work on time. Most stations strive to ensure that their weather information, news, and traffic reports are current and timely. As a result, the dissemination schedule for radio is immediate; as soon as radio broadcasters become aware of a story, they can put it on the air. This, combined with the pervasiveness of radio, makes this medium a primary source of information in times of crisis.

Radio is distinctly local in nature. The disc jockey takes dedications from fans and makes references to local celebrities, events, and landmarks. As a result, radio audiences develop intense loyalties to particular stations and radio personalities. (It should be noted, however, that satellite transmission and syndication have begun to transform radio into a broader, national medium.)

Finally, radio is often a secondary activity. That is, the radio may serve as background, as a mood enhancer or as a companion while we are engaged in primary activities at home, school, or work. While the car radio is on, our principal attention is (or should be) to keep the vehicle on the road. Because the radio audience is focusing its primary attention elsewhere, they may not be vigilant with regard to media messages conveyed through radio broadcasts.

Television. Television has emerged as the dominant leisure activity in the United States. TV is easily accessible; more than 98 percent of homes in the United States have TV sets.[17] Television is free. Anyone with a television can tune in. Television is continuous. Broadcast television is on for a minimum of 18 hours per day, 365 days per year (cable television is on the air for 24 hours per day).

Television is episodic in nature. The standard format for TV programming is the series, which can last anywhere from 13 weeks to 20 years. In contrast, film focuses on one final product (although the popularity of the sequel does extend this production into a miniseries of sorts). Episodes focus on a succession of small events (e.g., "Murphy Brown has a baby") or an installment in a much longer, more complex story (e.g., a soap opera or the news).

The episodic nature of television contributes to a unique personal dynamic between the characters and audience. For instance, much of the hoopla surrounding Johnny Carson's retirement in May 1992 can be attributed to the audience's *parasocial relationship* with the TV talk show host (i.e., the appearance of a personal relationship). After all, he was a guest in our living rooms on a nightly basis for 30 years. Indeed, in some cases he was an individual's most constant form of human contact. We watched him grow older and celebrated holidays (Christmas, New Year's, and anniversaries of the show) with him. Carson assumed an "interpersonal" communication style, sharing inside jokes and winking at the audience. Much of the humor of "The Tonight Show" derived from our familiarity with Johnny's personal life.

TV is an ideal medium for showing events in the process of unfolding, such as the 1991 Soviet coup attempt. Thanks to the advent of videotape and communications satellites, the dissemination schedule for television is immediate. Television news was able to show dramatic footage of the ill-fated Soviet coup. However, television was less successful in its ability to present the context, interpretation, and implications of the incident.

Like film, television combines sight, sound, motion, and color. TV hits us on an affective level, presenting images that move us emotionally. Television is a very intimate medium. The image on your television set in a fraction of the size of the screen in the movie theater. Instead of showing vast exteriors, television most effectively presents interior sets. As Herbert Zettl notes, television is an expressive medium that is well suited to focus on relationships: "Film derives its energy from landscapes as well as people; in television, it is primarily people with all their complexity who power a scene, while the landscape aspects take a back seat."[18]

Television utilizes many more closeups than film. In the soap opera, for example, the significance is not so much on the action but on the reaction of the characters. Soaps devote much of their attention on the effects of various events on relationships between characters and on the larger soap opera community. This emphasis on facial expression means that television subjects must maintain their composure. An inappropriate smirk, twitch, or tear can speak volumes to an audience.

Television is primarily an in-home experience, shared by a single individual or small group. Watching television can be either a primary or secondary activity. Complete darkness is not essential for viewing, allowing people to engage in other activities. The television set has been incorporated into the interior design of the home, much as the medium has become integrated into our daily activities. Think about the primary television viewing area in your home. The furniture is arranged around the television set; indeed, it is often difficult for people to face one another without craning their necks. Television has emerged as a prominent member of the family.

Television must compete with other programs, rival media, and assorted home activities for the attention of its audience. As a result, the pace of television is rapid. TV producers must also be sensitive to the time constraints of the medium. Networks compress as many as 13 stories into the 23 minutes allotted for the evening news. Through technology, television audiences have indirectly assumed a major responsibility for the pace of its programming. In 1992, almost 75 percent of American homes contained a VCR.[19] The audience can stop a tape or review a portion of a program that has been videotaped. In addition, the advent of the remote control enables the individual viewer to quicken the pace by flipping between programs.

Television is now increasingly shot in videotape, which has several advantages over film. First, videotape does not have to be processed in a lab, so that the director can immediately critique the footage and reshoot if necessary. In addition, video can be available for presentation without delay.

However, the production quality of videotape is noticeably different from film, which affects how the information is presented:

- The contrast in videotape is less distinct, reducing the range between light and dark areas.
- Videotape uses edge enhancement, which increases the separation between the subject and the background.
- Colors tend to be supersaturated, creating an artificial effect.
- Videotape produces a narrower range of light values (light intensities), reducing shadow detail in a shot.
- Videotape has less resolution—hence offering less detail in a shot.

Hybrid Media. As media technology has evolved, existing media systems have begun to overlap, creating hybrid channels of mass communications. One example is the VCR, which now presents film on television. Many of the characteristics of film have merged with television, resulting in an altogether unique viewing experience. For instance, the audience controls the pace; you can stop the tape whenever you want a break, freeze a "frame," or replay the tape. However, watching a movie with epic landscapes (e.g., *Dances with Wolves*) on the smaller TV screen can diminish the impact of the visuals. Other examples of hybrid media include electronic mail (mail on the computer) and MTV (radio on television).

Media Communicator

In interpersonal communications, the communicator and audience are in immediate contact. In contrast, the media communicator is separated both in time and space from the audience. An old movie that you watch on television may have been made 40 years ago by someone you never met, who lived in another part of the world.

As a result, the media communicator is often unknown to the audience. However, identifying the media communicator can provide significant insight into the content and outlook of the media production.

For example, the hit TV series "Beverly Hills 90210" focuses on the problems and concerns facing teenagers in contemporary culture. A student in a media literacy class, when asked to analyze the program commented, "This show presents situations, values, perspectives, and characters with which preteens and teens can identify. These values and experiences include coping with life as a teen, dealing with one's parents, and trying to find or maintain a romantic relationship." [20]

But while the show is produced for teens, it is produced by adults. As a result, "Beverly Hills 90210" offers a version of teenage life filtered through an adult perspective. On one level, the program provides direction to the teenage audience about the preparation for adulthood. On another level, however, the teenage characters function as surrogates for the adult writers. Indeed, the teenagers in the show function as adults, free of supervision by parents. In one episode, Brenda languishes in bed, reflecting on the recent events in her life. Her brother Brandon drops by to inquire whether Brenda is "thinking about going to school." Brenda declares that she is too preoccupied to attend. The parents are nowhere in sight.

The teenagers in "Beverly Hills 90210" deal with issues that remain a concern for the adult writers. For instance, in one episode, a teenage couple find themselves attracted to other people and reflect about how to deal with these impulses after they are married. Dylan observes that he hopes that although he will "feel flattered" if a woman finds him attractive, he will respect his commitment to his wife.

MEDIA LITERACY TIPS

MEDIA COMMUNICATOR

The following questions are useful in considering the role of the media communicator:

√ Who is responsible for creating the media production?

√ What are the demographic characteristics of the media communicator(s)?
- Age
- Income
- Race/ethnicity
- Gender

√ How do these characteristics affect the content and outlook of the media production?

Audience

Reception Theory: How Audiences Receive Media Messages. Reception theory refers to a school of thought that recognizes that the audience assumes an active role in interpreting the information they receive through mass media. According to this construct, audiences may arrive at entirely different constructions of meaning than the "preferred" reading. Different groups make sense of content in different ways. For instance, women may be more sensitive to messages about female stereotypes in film than men. Reception theory also addresses the issue of taste—why certain people derive pleasure from particular media presentations.

Some of the variables that affect how an individual receives media content include:

Background
- How much does the audience already know about the subject?

Interest level
- How interested is the audience in the subject? How attentive is the audience?

Predisposition
- What is the attitude of the audience toward the subject (positive or negative) going into the conversation?

Priorities
- What issues are of particular concern to the audience? Why?

Demographic profile
- National origin
- Gender
- Race
- Ethnic origin
- Age
- Education
- Income

Psychological profile
- Self-concept
- Primary relationships
- Significant life experiences
- Ways of relating to others
- Ways of dealing with emotions
- Personal aspirations

Communications environment
- What is the size of the audience?
- What are they doing while they are receiving the information?

Stage of development
- Have you ever reread a novel and reacted differently than you did the first time? The content did not change, but you did. As people grow older, their experiences influence their perception of what they see. In addition, the maturation process alters how people interpret their world—including media content.

Audience Identification. Audience identification is perhaps the most pressing challenge facing a media communicator. Media communicators devote enormous resources to developing a clear sense of audience. Different sectors of audience have distinct, identifiable interests and look for specific objectives or gratifications in media programming, based on their stage of life. For instance, fans of "oldies" radio stations fall between the ages of 35 and 44. Fewer than 5 percent of the audience for oldies stations are teenagers. Horst Stipp, director of Social and Development Research at NBC, observes, "The connection between age and popular music is so strong that a fan's age can be predicted from his or her favorite oldies." [21]

The variables cited above (background, interest level, predispositions, priorities, demographic profile, psychological profile, and communications environment) are critical to audience identification. This audience profile enables the media communicator to develop *communication strategies* that capitalize on the audience's interests, concerns, and preoccupations. For example, the Michelin tire advertising campaign featured a picture of a cute infant sitting in one of its products, accompanied by the slogan, "Because so much is riding on your tires." This ad appeals to parents' protective instincts by offering the product as a way to alleviate their concerns about the safety of their children.

The effective media communicator also adapts the *style* of the presentation to the audience. For example, advertisers for children's products must be acquainted with the latest trends, music, slang, and fashion in order to relate to the target audience. Television commercials must be slick and up-tempo to engage the attention of the young audience.

Audience identification even affects the *content* of media presentations. Material is selected specifically to respond to the interests of the intended audience. For instance, the preponderance of films dealing with the trials and triumphs of adolescence can be attributed to the makeup of theater audiences, which consist primarily of people between 16 and 24. In this case, film projects have been selected and developed only after the audience has been defined.

Audience identification, therefore, can provide perspective on how messages have been developed and presented to reach the intended audience. Significantly, one way to identify audience involves working backward: What does the communication strategy, content, and style of a media presentation tell us about the intended audience?

One cue to identifying the intended audience involves examining the advertising that accompanies media presentations. For instance, Saturday morning cartoon programs feature a preponderance of commercials for toys and cereals. Afternoon programming includes many ads featuring women involved in household chores. When looking at ads, ask the following:

- Which products are being advertised?
- Which group is depicted in the ad?

However, media programming may be targeted simultaneously at both a manifest and latent audience. Saturday morning commercials, for instance, obviously are directed at children. However, the target audience also includes parents, who are pressured to purchase the products featured in the commercial for their children.

SUMMARY

Communications is a very complex activity. This process is even more challenging in mass communications because the communicator is removed in time and space from the audience. However, in both cases, the successful communicator:

√ Understands the communication process.

√ Understands the purpose of the communication.

√ Is self-aware.

√ Understands the message (knows what he or she wants to say).

√ Understands the characteristics of the channel that he or she uses.

√ Can identify his or her audience.

√ Uses feedback to ensure that the audience comprehends the message.

Keys to Interpreting Media Messages: Process

Applying the following questions related to *process* can provide insight into media messages:

A. Function
   1. What is the purpose behind the production?
   2. Does the media communicator want you to act in a particular way as a result of receiving the information?
B. Comparative media
   1. What are the medium's distinctive characteristics?
   2. In what ways does the choice of medium affect:
      a) The content of the message?
      b) The presentation of information?
      c) The role/choice/effectiveness of the media communicator?
      d) The ways in which the audience receives the information?
C. Media communicator
   1. Who is responsible for creating the media production?
   2. What are the demographic characteristics of the media communicator(s)?
   3. How do these characteristics affect the content and outlook of the media production?
D. Audience
   1. For whom is the media presentation produced?
   2. Is there more than one intended audience?
   3. What values, experiences, and perspectives are shared by the audience?

4. How do the experiences and perspectives of the *individual* audience member affect his or her interpretation of the presentation?

5. How does the choice of audience influence the *strategy, style,* and *content* of the media presentation?

6. Do the strategy, style, and content provide insight into the intended audience(s)?

NOTES

1. Study conducted by Television Audience Assessment, Inc., 1983.

2. Joseph R. Dominick, *The Dynamics of Mass Communication,* 3d ed. (New York: McGraw-Hill, 1990), 33.

3. Richard M. Gollin, *A Viewer's Guide to Film* (New York: McGraw-Hill, 1992), 9–20.

4. E. H. Gombrich, "The Visual Image," in *Media and Symbols: The Forms of Expression, Communication, and Education,* publication of the National Society for the Study of Education, vol. 73, pt. 1, ed. David R. Olson (Chicago: University of Chicago Press, 1974), 242.

5. Ben Bagdikian, *The Media Monopoly,* 3d ed. (Boston: Beacon Press, 1990), xxi.

6. Barbara Gamarekian, "Ads Aimed at Children Restricted," *New York Times,* October 18, 1990, D1.

7. Bill Moyers, "The Public Mind: Consuming Images," Public Broadcasting Service, November 8, 1989.

8. Henry James, *Portrait of a Lady* (New York: Modern Library, 1966), 239.

9. Karl Vick, "Immediacy Plus: Book on O.J. Takes Six Days," *St. Louis Post-Dispatch,* July 1, 1994, 10D.

10. Photo Marketing Association International, *PMA Consumer Photographic Survey* (Jackson, MI: PMA International, 1993), 2.

11. Gombrich, "The Visual Image," 249.

12. Tessa Horan, "Trivial Pursuits: F.Y.I.," *Premiere,* July 1989, 17.

13. Gollin, *Guide to Film,* 2.

14. Ibid., 2–3.

15. Radio Advertising Bureau, *Radio Facts for Advertisers 1990* (New York: Radio Advertising Bureau, 1990), 3, 6.

16. Ibid., 6.

17. Nielsen Media Research, "Nielsen Television Information," Summer 1992.

18. Herbert Zettl, *Sight, Sound, and Motion: Applied Media Aesthetics* (Belmont, CA: Wadsworth, 1990), 95.

19. Nielsen Media Research, "VCR Penetration Reaches 73.9%; Pay Cable Households at 28.1%," *Neilsen Media Research News,* May 1992, 1.

20. In-class assignment, November 8, 1992.

21. Horst Stipp, "Musical Demographics," *American Demographics,* 12 (August 1990): 49.

CHAPTER 3

CONTEXT

- Historical context
- Cultural context
- Structure

Context refers to those surrounding elements that subtly shape meaning and convey messages.

HISTORICAL CONTEXT

We are all products of the historical events going on around us. Media communicators produce work that derives its significance from the events of the day. Obviously, the primary goal of the journalist is to record occurrences that have political or social significance. But while print journalism lends itself to detailed analysis, space limitations often prevent dailies from furnishing the historical context necessary for a comprehensive understanding of events.

Broadcast journalists generally do not have the time to furnish a full historical perspective on stories during a newscast. In addition, this background information does not come across easily in this visual medium. As a result, Ian I. Mitroff and Warren Bennis declare that TV news often presents information in isolation, without the historical context that provides meaning:

With very few exceptions, most issues on network television news are presented in a completely ahistorical context of no context whatsoever. Most news issues, especially local items, merely appear; they drop in from out of the blue. . . . The overall effect is one of dazzling confusion. Little or no attempt is made to present a larger view in which the issues could be located in a coherent framework.[1]

Entertainment programming and advertising also are shaped by current events. For instance, the popular film *Suspect* (1987) is a mystery in which the prime murder suspect is a vagrant. The scene of the crime is located in an area near the Potomac River frequented by the homeless. The film is not a documentary about homelessness but simply uses this setting as a new twist in the conventional entertainment/suspense genre. However, the very fact that this condition is accepted as the premise reflects the degree to which homelessness has become entrenched as a fundamental social problem in America.

Historical references are often subtle. Satirists often deal with controversial topics by working with fictional characters or distant settings. For instance, the cold war era film *Invasion of the Body Snatchers* (1956) was a thinly disguised allegory about communism. The story focused on an invasion of pods from outer space. These pods descended on a rural American community and assumed the identities of citizens once they fell asleep. These inhuman creatures had no souls and felt no emotion. Like ants, they operated within a collective mentality. However, these pods were easily destroyed once they were discovered. Thus, as with the communist threat, the primary defense against these creatures was eternal vigilance.

Another approach to historical context involves examining significant figures, events, and trends in the evolution of a particular medium (e.g., radio, television, or newspapers). This historical analysis can provide insight into the present state of the medium, as well as providing a context for anticipating future developments in the industry. In the same way, looking at the evolution of a genre such as the soap opera can provide perspective into corresponding changes in the culture. To illustrate, 1950s soap operas may have alluded to "the other woman" (accompanied by the single, sinister note of an organ). Today, entire programs are dedicated to "the other woman," signaling the culture's more permissive sexual mores, as well as society's preoccupation with sex. (For more discussion on genre, see Chapter 4.)

Tracing the history of one program or presentation can also provide insight into shifts in cultural attitudes and concerns. To illustrate, graduate student Lilli Ruggeri analyzed issues of *Cosmopolitan* magazine from 1886 to 1993 and noted changes in cultural attitudes toward women:

The 1886 *Cosmopolitan* women were women of prosperity. They did not have to work outside the home. Success to women in that era was having a nice home. They took pride in their cooking and appearance. Examples of articles include: "Clear Starching and Ironing," "Draperies in Our Home," and "The Art of Cake Making." The subjects included in the magazine were not (at the time) considered demeaning to women but rather an indication of what success meant to them.

Compared to the *Cosmopolitan* of 1886, the content of the 1923 version changed considerably. A consciousness of style, appearance, and image begin to emerge. A whole new woman is created in the 1920s—a woman who appears strong and in control. For instance, in one article, a young woman describes her dilemma of not wanting to marry a man she considers perfect. This may mark a continued change of attitudes among women: an attitude enlisting women as free thinkers and in control of their own destiny. However, these new freedoms are not without resulting problems. For instance, readers now learn to expect marital problems.

A remake of *Cosmopolitan* is seen in the '70s, consisting of a new audience, function, editorial, and advertising content. The entire format of the publication is revamped to satisfy women's obsession with appearance and changing lifestyle. Added are special sections: Dieter's Notebook, Your Body, Q & A About Your Health, and an Analyst's Couch. Quizzes have also been added as a part of self-evaluation: "Should I be single?" "How do you feel about your body?" The addition of these special sections suggests that women do have problems and reinforces the notion that they are not in control.

The '70s is a "what can you do for me" society. The editorial content reflects a decline in institutional values but an increase in sexual freedom and individualism. Marriage is out, living together is in. Success is being on your own and sexually active.

The '90s see a confused *Cosmo* woman. *Cosmo* is sending mixed messages. On the one hand, Cosmo symbolizes a strong, independent woman, in control of her destiny. On the other, the publication is telling women what she is doing wrong, telling her she has an imperfect body and face, and why she fails at relationships and careers.

Compared to their counterparts of 1886 and 1923, the '90s woman is weak, insecure, unstable, and unsure of her destiny. Articles from 1990s *Cosmo*s include: "You still get to his heart through his tummy," "How to make him like you as much as you like him," "Your man, his friends, where do you fit in?" and "Timing is everything—he can barely commit to dinner next week, you're already planning a wedding—be patient."[2]

Examining a media program from a different era can also furnish a cultural perspective into the period in which it was produced. For instance, many old films feature women in subservient roles. One striking exception was *City for Conquest* (1940), starring Jimmy Cagney and Ann Sheridan. In this movie, Peggy Nash (Sheridan) is a dancer who is forced to choose between a career and her boyfriend, Danny Kenny (Cagney). Mesmerized by ambition, Peggy deserts Danny and, within the context of the film, betrays herself in the process. It is only when she gives up her career and devotes herself to Danny that she again becomes a "whole" woman. However disturbing to a modern audience, this film provides a useful glimpse into the gender politics of the times.

Finally, the phenomenon of the "remake" can also furnish perspective on the interests, preoccupations, and values that characterize different

In *City for Conquest* (1940), Murray Burns (Anthony Quinn) is an unscrupulous dancer who appeals to the ambitions of Peggy Nash (Ann Sheridan) in order to come between her and Danny Kenny (Jimmy Cagney). © 1940 Turner Entertainment Co. All Rights Reserved.

eras. A useful illustration can be found in the two versions of the film *Cape Fear* (produced in 1961 and 1992). The plot of both films is essentially the same. The hero, Sam Bowden, is a lawyer who was responsible for the successful prosecution of Max Cady in a brutal rape case. Having served his sentence, Cady returns to Georgia, seeking revenge on Bowden and his family. At first, Cady stalks the Bowden family, cunningly remaining within the law. Finally, he leaps into action, and in both films he ultimately is vanquished.

In the 1961 version, the distinctions between good (Bowden) and evil (Cady) are clear. The threat to the Bowden family is clearly external, in the form of psychopathic Cady. Jenny Diski observes:

[The 1961 version of *Cape Fear*] shows decent values under threat. The Bowden family is untouched by suffering, and as nice as the apple pie Peg Bowden undoubtedly makes for Sam and their cutely precocious daughter, Nancy. They're wealthy, though not outrageously so, and they're happy together in a simple, enviable way that's as remote from passion as it is from divorce. There are no doubts and no clouds in the lives of the the Bowdens. . . . It's simple. You know where you are: the bad guy's come along, and the family—The Family—is under threat.[3]

Martin Scorcese's 1992 remake features a much more ambiguous moral landscape than the original. The distinction between good and evil is far from absolute in this film. In this version, Sam Bowden had served as Max Cady's public defender and, in the course of the trial, had withheld evidence to ensure that his client (Cady) was convicted. In this 1990s world, a distinction is drawn between justice and the law. Bowden, convinced that Cady was guilty, broke the law to see that justice was done.

As a result, the primary threat in the modern version of *Cape Fear* is not Cady but Bowden's own corruption. Diski remarks, "Thirty years earlier, there were no questions to be answered; no uncertainties, only inexplicable forces that attacked from outside. Since then, it seems we've learned that bad things are often shadows of ourselves."[4]

CULTURAL CONTEXT

What can we learn by studying a media presentation as cultural "text"?

Anthropologists study ancient civilizations by unearthing artifacts in order to reconstruct a portrait of the society. In the same way, the study of popular culture has a *hermeneutic,* or interpretive, function, furnishing a means of understanding culture.

Russel B. Nye offers a comprehensive definition of *popular culture:*

Popular culture describes those productions, both artistic and commercial, designed for mass consumption, which appeal to and express the tastes and understanding of the majority of the public, free of control by minority standards. They reflect the values, convictions, and patterns of thought and feeling generally dispersed through and approved by American society.[5]

Nye traces the origin of popular culture in the Western world to the industrial-democratic revolution of the eighteenth century. Democratization, urbanization, education, increased income and leisure time, and industrialization contributed to the emergence of an educated, affluent middle class (predominantly white and male), with identifiable needs and interests.

The emergence of this middle class created a new market for popular art. Nye observes, "This mass society had leisure time, money, and cultural unity; it needed a new art—neither folk nor elite—to instruct and entertain it."[6] Popular artists discovered that they could make a living by attracting a large enough audience to ensure a profit. In this sense, popular art became a type of consumer product, not unlike a pair of shoes or a new rug. These new market considerations also altered the traditional relationship between the artist and the audience. As a way of illustration, imagine novelist James Joyce jogging around a track with a group of his admirers. If the audience is unable to keep up with Joyce, they are out of luck. Indeed, in works such as *Ulysses* and *Finnegans Wake,* Joyce is contemptuous of his audience, regarding them as incapable of appreciating the complexities of his work.

Now imagine filmmaker Steven Spielberg running the track with his fans. If he pulls ahead of the pack, he . . . *slows down.* In popular art, the burden of understanding is shifted to the artist. Successful mass communicators can anticipate the interests and concerns of the audience and offer content that is interesting and challenging, without being so far afield that they lose their audience entirely. This relationship between media communicator and audience might best be characterized as reciprocal. Clearly, media presentations are beyond the immediate control of the audience; in that sense, the media is prescriptive. However, because the media is a market-driven industry rooted in popular culture, media communicators must be responsive to the needs and interests of their audience. Gifted media communicators intuitively sense what people are interested in and have the ability to anticipate potential questions and concerns.

The development of media technologies in the nineteenth and twentieth centuries provided an essential avenue for the dissemination of information and entertainment to a mass audience. Threatened by this loss of cultural control, members of elite culture historically have dismissed the media as legitimate channels of information and culture. In the eighteenth century, women were advised not to read novels for fear that it would make their brains soft. In 1859, poet Charles Baudelaire warned, "By invading the territories of art, this industry [photography] has become art's most mortal enemy."[7] More recently, educator Allan Bloom has decried the influence of popular music: "It ruins the imagination of young people and makes it very difficult for them to have a passionate relationship to the art and the thought that are the substance of liberal education."[8]

Of course, as a channel for information and education, the media also carries elite art as well (e.g., operas, plays, and PBS specials). According to Nye, *elite art* is defined by the following characteristics:

- *Exclusivity*. Elite art is intended to be enjoyed by a select few.
- *Aesthetic complexity*. Technical and thematic complexity is regarded as a virtue.
- *Historical context*. Elite art is part of a larger artistic tradition.
- *Experimental*. Elite art is unconventional and exploratory.[9]

Though useful, Nye's distinction between elite and popular art is far from absolute. For instance, popular artists William Shakespeare, Charles Dickens, and Mark Twain were elevated to elite status after their deaths when it became evident that their popularity was in many respects due to the elite characteristics of their work. To further confuse the issue, some productions within a popular genre become "classics," which have endured over time because the artists were able to work so skillfully within the accepted formats. Examples would include the western *Shane*, detective novel/film *The Maltese Falcon*, or the situation comedy "I Love Lucy."

However, it can be said that the majority of the content carried by the channels of mass communication meets Nye's definition of popular art.

Media and Popular Culture

The term *popular* connotes acceptance, approval, and shared values among large numbers of people. We admire the popular set because of who they are (attitudes and values) and for what they do (behaviors). This notion of popularity also applies to media presentations. People only watch programs that meet their approval. If we are truly offended by a violent program, we won't watch it. And in the market-driven media industry, programming with low ratings quickly disappears. In this sense, popular culture reflects the attitudes, values, behaviors, preoccupations, and myths that define a culture.

A recent example of this connection between popular media and society can be found in reporter Michael MacCambridge's contention that the Los Angeles riots of May 1992 were anticipated by messages contained in urban rap music:

To a remarkable degree, the fallout from the Rodney King verdict was presaged in the socially conscious rhymes of Public Enemy, the hard core gangster rap of Ice

Cube (himself a product of South Central Los Angeles), the new wave of black film making by Spike Lee and even the recent explosion of stand-up comedy.

Certain themes continue to pop up in the hard-core, street-level rap of Public Enemy, Ice-T, Boogie Down Productions, Ice Cube, Digital Underground, and others. Among these are a powerful sense of disconnection from America's most hallowed icons and institutions. Rap music, described by Chuck D (of Public Enemy) as "CNN for black people," devotes considerable attention to the feeling that the black community has been excluded from the American system of justice. . . . [The] violence in LA seems less surprising when one considers that the verdict simply confirmed the worst fears of blacks, expressed for years by rappers, film makers and comedians alike.[10]

Media-carried text can also reveal *cultural preoccupations*—that is, the relative importance that a culture places on particular issues. For instance, a perusal of an average week of television programming reveals that sex and violence are areas of tremendous fascination in American culture.

Popular media programming frequently centers around issues of cultural concern. For instance, episodes of "Beverly Hills 90210" focused on problems of alcoholism among teenagers. In "Roseanne," characters have struggled with the effects of unemployment in a troubled economy. And children's books like the *Berenstein Bears* series discuss issues such as talking to strangers, eating junk food, and watching too much TV.

Media content may also disclose *cultural myths*. Cultural myths are sets of beliefs that may not be true but nevertheless tell us about ourselves and our culture. For instance, popular song titles often pay homage to a cultural myth that might be entitled "The All-Sufficiency of Love." According to this cultural myth, a person's identity is totally dependent on a partner (as opposed to self):

- "There's No Living Without Your Loving"
- "All You Need Is Love"
- "You Are My Sunshine"
- "You Are My Everything"
- "All I Wanna Do (Is Keep on Loving You)"

According to this cultural myth, romantic love is a mysterious, mystical force that leads to loss of control ("I Can't Help Myself"). Thus, while romantic love is dangerous ("Devil with the Blue Dress on"), it is essential for survival.

Within this context, it's easy to understand the sense of urgency involved in finding romance ("It's Now or Never"). The end of a relationship has ramifications beyond the loss of your partner: You lose your identity, your self-esteem, and your reason for living.

Over time, cultural myths (such as the all-sufficiency of love) can assume a *mythic reality* as people buy into it. The danger presented by mythic realities is that people sometimes make decisions on the basis of these myths. For instance, an individual might react to the all-sufficiency myth by marrying someone out of fear of being alone.

Popular culture not only reflects but also reinforces cultural attitudes, values, behaviors, preoccupations, and myths. What does it mean to be a success in this culture? How should men and women relate to each other? These cumulative messages are reinforced through the countless hours of media that repeat, directly or indirectly, the cultural script.

Worldview

When you watch television or read the newspaper, what kind of world is depicted? Popular artists construct a complete world out of their imaginations. The premise, plot, and characters of fictional narratives are based on certain fundamental assumptions about how this world operates. Even when we watch nonfiction content like the news, we receive overall impressions about worldview. Consequently, considering worldview is a key to discovering manifest and latent messages contained in media programming.

Cultural Ideologies. What kind of culture or cultures populate the world of a media presentation? *Ideology* refers to the manner or the content of thinking characteristic of an individual group or culture.

Television generally presents a worldview reflecting a traditional, male-dominated ideology. For instance, a 1993 study conducted by George Gerbner found that the TV audience tuned into a world in which men outnumbered women three to one during prime time. White males in the prime of life constituted 40 percent of all prime-time characters. In children's programming, the ratio of men to women was four to one.[11] Eve Simson has found that most female television parts were "decorative," played by pretty California women in their twenties. As presented on television, the most frequent occupation for women was prostitution.[12]

Critical theorists like Stuart Hall argue that the worldview presented through the media does not merely reflect or reinforce culture but in fact shapes thinking by promoting the dominant ideology of a culture. We all had to receive messages for the first time. In this sense, the media also plays a role in inculcating, or educating, us in regard to cultural values, attitudes, behaviors, and preoccupations.

This imposition of an ideology within a culture is referred to as *hegemony*. Alan O'Connor declares that the media serve as "processes of persuasion in which we are invited to understand the world in certain ways but not in others."[13] Hall asserts that the media largely present the ideology of the dominant culture as a means of maintaining control. In that sense, the media can create (or *re-create*) representations of reality that support the dominant ideology.

To illustrate, George Gerbner and Nancy Signorielli identified the groups most frequently victimized by violence on prime-time television (in order):

- Women of all ages (particularly young adult and elderly women)
- Young boys
- Nonwhites
- "Foreigners"
- Members of the lower and upper class[14]

The group conspicuously absent from this list consists of white, middle-class/upper-middle-class males—the people primarily responsible for producing media programming. One can almost imagine these men sitting around a Hollywood pool vicariously killing off these other subgroups.

In reality, the groups most victimized by crime are (in order):

- Young black males. In 1988, approximately 40 percent of black males who died were victims of homicide. At greatest risk among this group were lower-class black males.
- White males/black females (18- to 24-year-olds). These groups fell roughly into the same levels, depending on the type of crime.
- White females statistically were victimized far less frequently.[15]

Another example of cultural re-creation can be found in media messages about women. In her book *The Beauty Myth*, Naomi Wolf observes that the cumulative media messages about female sexuality cause young girls "to absorb the dominant culture's fantasies as [their] own."

The books and films [young girls] see [are] from the young boy's point of view his first touch of a girl's thighs, his first glimpse of her breasts. The girls sit listening, absorbing . . . learning how to leave their bodies and watch them from the outside. Since their bodies are seen from the point of view of strangeness and desire, it is no wonder that what should be familiar, felt to be whole, becomes estranged and divided into parts. What little girls learn is not the desire for the other, but the desire to be desired.[16]

Wolf points out that much mainstream media content has assumed a pornographic, sadomasochistic orientation. Films like *Dressed to Kill, Tie Me Up! Tie Me Down!*, and *Blue Velvet* feature scenes "in which a female is stalked from the first person perspective, encouraging identification with the killer or rapist."[17] Wolf also cites examples from advertising: "In an

ad for Obsession perfume, a blond woman trussed in black leather is hang-
ing upside down, screaming, her wrists looped in chains, mouth bound.
. . . In an ad for Erno Laszlo skin care products, a woman sits up and
begs, her wrists clasped together with a leather leash that is also tied to
her dog, who is sitting up in the same posture and begging." [18]

Many music videos contain sadomasochistic overtones as well. For example, Motley Crue's videos depict women as sexual slaves in cages. Rick
James's videos portray him in the act of raping his girlfriend. And in Michael Jackson's "The Way You Make Me Feel," a gang stalks a lone
woman.

According to Wolf, the cumulative messages are clear: "The woman
learns from these images that no matter how assertive she may be in the
world, her private submission to control is what makes her desirable." [19]
Susan G. Cole warns that these messages can have disturbing repercus-
sions:

In spite of hopes to the contrary, pornography and mass culture are working to
collapse sexuality with rape, reinforcing the patterns of male dominance and female submission so that many young people believe this is simply the way sex is.
This means that many of the rapists of the future will believe they are behaving
within socially accepted norms. [20]

Media and Subcultures. Other scholars look at the media as a representation of *multiple realities* that compete for attention in our society. James
Carey observes:

Culture . . . is never singular and univocal. It is like nature itself, multiple, various, and varietal. It is this for each of us. . . . The analysis of mass communication will have to examine the several cultural worlds in which people simultaneously exist—the tension, often radical tension, between them, the patterns of mood
and motivation distinctive to each, and the interpretation among them. [21]

This multicultural perspective coincides with the media industry's shift
from *broadcasting* to *narrowcasting*. In the early days of American media,
the overall audience was limited. Consequently, the mass communicator
had to appeal to the broadest possible audience to generate a profit. To
illustrate, in the early days of television, producers had to lure everyone
who owned a set. This led to a "vaudeville" approach to programming—
a variety show format offering something for everyone within one program. For instance, the "Ed Sullivan Show" routinely featured puppet
shows, comedians, opera singers, and rock stars in the course of one hour.

Over time, the media market has become so large that it is now profitable to direct messages at specialized interests, tastes, and groups. For example, if you turn your radio dial, you will find AM stations geared to
African Americans, young people, and country music lovers. Cable TV has

been largely responsible for the narrowcasting of television. Channels are now dedicated to special interests (e.g., movies, sports, weather, religious programming, and home shopping). As a result, the media can serve as a text by which we can learn about the values, concerns, and priorities of various subcultures in American culture such as women, adolescents, and gays.

Narrowcasting enables the media to respond to the background and interests of particular subgroups; however, at the same time, this trend can also have the effect of further insulating individuals. Unfortunately, audiences can become locked in to this demographic straitjacket and, consequently, are not exposed to perspectives of other groups. An essential aspect of media literacy involves looking beyond the materials that have been directed at your particular demographic group, in order to get a broader perspective. For instance, magazines like *Ebony, Essence,* and *Jet* provide insight into the African American community. Other subgroups like Asian Americans and Hispanics have developed their own specialized media. Similarly, it is also important to become exposed to media presentations with different ideological perspectives. For instance, the *Nation* and the *Progressive* are magazines with a liberal orientation, while the *National Review* and *U.S. News and World Report* are examples of publications that provide a conservative perspective on events.

Media Stereotyping. A stereotype is an oversimplified conception of a person, group, or event. This term is derived from the Greek word *steros* ("hard" or "solid"), which underscores the inflexible, absolute nature of stereotypes.

Stereotype is an associative process; ideas about groups are based on a shared understanding about a group. For example, take a moment to picture a "typical" scientist. Now, compare your profile to the following version of the stereotypical scientist, compiled through a *New York Times* survey: "A scientist is a short, unattractive, old man who is bald, has few friends, is clumsy, silly, and is hard to understand. In some cases, he is dangerous."[22]

If there is a general consensus of opinion, then we have a working stereotype.

Stereotyping is a natural coping mechanism. People make decisions based on generalizations in order to function on an everyday basis. If you look outside and see dark clouds forming, you automatically take an umbrella with you. However, while prejudging can be a useful device (it can prevent you from getting wet, for example), prejudice is a reductive principle that interferes with people's ability to recognize individual differences. According to William B. Helmreich, this grouping principle is often inaccurate, negative, and dangerous: "Approximately one third of stereotypes can be said to have a good deal of truth to them, and that the accurate stereotypes are predominately positive, whereas those that seem highly inaccurate tend by and large to be negative."[23]

The media industry is particularly suited to stereotyping. Media communicators often do not have the time to develop a unique set of characters and consequently take advantage of the principle of *cumulative experience;* that is, the audience recognizes a character who appears on screen because they have seen him (or a character like him) dozens of times before in other similar programs.

Media communicators sometimes may rely on stereotypes as a result of their own shortcomings. For instance, a documentary on broadcast journalism, *Race Against Prime Time,* reports that during the Miami riots of 1980 white journalists were reluctant to venture into the black sections of the city. As a result, broadcast coverage of the riots reflected only a general, stereotyped understanding of the African American community.

Stereotyping Techniques. Media stereotyping techniques are often very subtle. Word choice often contains embedded values that reinforce stereotypes. For instance, the *Boston Globe* carried the following review of Susan Monsky's novel *Midnight Suppers:*

Monsky tells the story in a soft-spoken Southern accent which doesn't quite seem to go with her Semitic features and intellectual-looking wire-rimmed glasses.[24]

On close inspection, this passage invites questions about several stereotypes:

- What are "Semitic" features?
- Why would Monsky's Semitic appearance contrast with her "soft-spoken" accent?
- And doesn't this review suggest that southern women are not intellectual?

Editing decisions—what to omit or include in a media presentation— may also reinforce stereotypes. The problem is not so much that a particular stereotypical behavior is shown in the media but that this characteristic is the *only* dimension presented. It may appear harmless to depict a black man as silly and confused; after all, these qualities are central to comedy— and certainly it is easy to find similar examples of buffoonery among white performances. However, if this character trait appears repeatedly in black characters, and if this is the only way that he is presented, this characterization perpetuates cultural stereotypes.

Over the past decade, shows such as "Murphy Brown," "The Cosby Show," and "Golden Girls" have broken through many of the stereotypes perpetuated through the media. However, many television programs continue to reinforce traditional stereotypes. George Gerbner conducted an analysis of media characterization over the past ten years and observes, "We all have the impression things are improving. But they are not. . . .

Not only do white male roles predominate, the parts written for everyone else are more often obsolete stereotypes than reflections of real life." [25]

Gerbner's study contains the following findings:

- Mature women are usually witches or crazy.
- The mentally ill are evil.
- Blacks, Hispanics, and poor or foreign-born are victims.
- Women play only one of three roles in prime-time television and one in four in children's programs.
- Elderly in both sexes are generally underrepresented and seem to be vanishing instead of increasing, as in real life.
- Blacks account for fewer than 11 percent of prime-time roles and Hispanics for 1 percent. Asian Americans and Indians are almost absent.
- The 43 million disabled Americans are represented by only 1.5 percent of the roles in prime time.

Contemporary programs often present the *appearance* of transcending stereotypes. For instance, the lead character in "Murphy Brown" is a strong, independent, and assertive woman. However, the supporting females in the cast revert to stereotypical characteristics (e.g., the "dumb blonde" Corky).

A useful approach for identifying media cultural stereotypes involves outlining a profile of each character:

- What do we know about the characters as presented on the program?
- What does this tell us about the cultural stereotype of this group?

MEDIA LITERACY TIPS

CONTENT ANALYSIS

One way to identify media stereotypes is by conducting a content analysis of media content. Content analysis employs quantitative techniques to look for patterns, messages, symbols, language, art forms, and potential biases in print and electronic media.

Conducting a content analysis consists of the following steps:

- Defining the categories to be studied.
- Tabulating and summarizing the data.
- Making inferences—that is, drawing conclusions from the patterns you have identified.

It must be noted that content analysis can be conducted on many levels, ranging from simply tabulating types of occurrences (as outlined here) to sophisticated computer-assisted analysis of media content.

Professor Linda Holtzman has developed the following content analysis tally sheet for the analysis of media stereotypes:

MEDIA LITERACY TIPS CONTINUED

Content Analysis Tally Sheet

1. Name of program
2. Type of program
3. Name of character viewed
4. Male or female
5. Was this character *the main character* in the episode? (Judge by number of minutes on air)
6. Type of job
   a) Student
   b) Unemployed
   c) Unskilled labor
   d) Skilled or trained labor
   e) Job requiring at least a college degree
   f) "Prominent" or highly visible position
   g) Other
7. Level of education
   a) Grade school or under
   b) High school
   c) College
   d) Other
8. Race
   a) African American
   b) White
   c) Asian
   d) Latino
   e) Native American
   f) Biracial
   g) Other
9. Marital status
   a) Single
   b) Married
   c) Divorced
   d) Widowed
   e) Living with "significant other"
   f) Other
10. Age (approximate)
    a) 0–5 years old
    b) 6–12 years old
    c) 13–18 years old
    d) 19–25 years old
    e) 26–35 years old
    f) 36–50 years old
    g) 51–65 years old
    h) Over 65 years old
11. Number of children
    a) 0
    b) 1

MEDIA LITERACY TIPS CONTINUED

      c) 2
      d) 3
      e) 4
      f) Over 4

12. Appearance
      a) Attractive by traditional standards
      b) Glamorous
      c) Unattractive by traditional standards
      d) Average by traditional standards
      e) Other (please indicate)

13. Body type
      a) Slender or thin
      b) Average
      c) Voluptuous
      d) Athletic
      e) Heavy or above average weight
      f) Other (please indicate)

14. Personal characteristics (check as many as apply) displayed by the character in the episode:
      a) Nurturing
      b) Abrupt
      c) Devious
      d) Straightforward
      e) Flirtatious
      f) Sarcastic
      g) Emotional
         (1) Cries
         (2) Laughs
         (3) Yells
         (4) Whines
         (5) Other (please indicate)
      h) Physically affectionate
      i) Sexual
      j) Intelligent
      k) Other (please indicate)

As you conduct the content analysis, keep in mind the following:

√ Obviously, some of these categories are subjective. It is important, however, to strive for clarity and consistency in categorization.

√ Categories should be identified through behavior (e.g., patting a person on the head as evidence of nurturing behavior).

√ You must fill out one tally sheet for *each* character.

√ To complete the analysis, tabulate the results, and then draw your inferences, or conclusions.

√ It must be noted that the size of this sample is too limited to yield conclusive results. However, this type of limited study can provide a useful indication of stereotypes, as well as making you more sensitive to the portrayal of groups in the media.[26]

Romantic Ideal. The worldview reflected in popular media presentations often reflects a *romantic ideal*. As Richard Harter Fogle observes, this ideal presumes an ordered universe: "The center of romanticism . . . lies in a new and different vision, in which everything is alive, related, and meaningful."[27] In this ordered universe, nature is a microcosm of heaven. Within this context, the individualism that characterizes romanticism is celebration of the divinity in humankind. In "Song of Myself," Walt Whitman declares,

> I celebrate myself and sing myself,
> And what I assume you shall assume,
> For every atom belonging to me as good belongs to you.[28]

This heaven-on-earth is an optimistic world defined by an absolute value system:

- Truth
- Love
- Beauty
- Faith
- Justice

These values are unified and interchangeable; one virtue cannot exist in isolation from the others. Beauty is merely the external manifestation of the other, less tangible virtues. Justice ultimately prevails. Love triumphs, the truth is revealed, and faith is rewarded. Even in action/adventure films, violence is a necessary means to restore and preserve this ideal order.

An important issue in the romantic worldview is *control*. Our heroes either assume responsibility for their lives or willingly relinquish control to another person or a benevolent supernatural presence. A standard plot in entertainment programming consists of the protagonist assuming control despite overwhelming odds. Control is a central issue in other mass communication formats as well. For instance, no matter how catastrophic the news, the broadcast anchor is trained to present the information in a measured—and controlled—fashion.

Significantly, however, women in media frequently inhabit a world in which they have no control. They live in fear of the elements, of men, and of their own natures. Their only chance for happiness is through male benevolence and protection.

To be sure, we are exposed to worldviews both in entertainment and in informational programming that depart from this romantic ideal. The horror genre presents a world of evil and chaos, in which human beings are powerless and vulnerable. This genre explores concerns that are fundamentally terrifying to humans: fear of death, of demons, of worlds beyond our understanding, and of our own Promethean delusions that are manifested in the creation of genetically engineered monsters (the dinosaurs in *Jurassic Park,* for instance). However, order generally is restored at the conclusion, which reestablishes this romantic ideal—at least until the sequel is released.

Definitions of Success. What does it mean to be a success in American culture? Identifying the kinds of behavior that are rewarded in American media programming can provide insight into definitions of success in this culture. By examining cumulative media messages, it is possible to construct a composite of the various perspectives on success in American culture.

As reward. In *The American Myth of Success,* Richard Weiss traces the roots of the American myth of success to our Puritan tradition. According to the Puritan doctrine of predestination, God foreordained all things, especially the salvation of individual souls. This doctrine also provided an elaborate rationale and justification for personal achievement. Material success on earth was regarded as a sign that a person was predestined to go to heaven.[29]

A secular version of Puritanism translated easily into the American democratic and capitalistic definitions of success. A very subtle system of morality justifies the system. Those who succeed are somehow deserving; those who fail are unworthy.

As path to immortality. The notion of "upward mobility" suggests a heaven on earth, beyond worldly cares and concerns. Successful people attract public attention and adulation; and fame makes them appear bigger than life. Truly successful people leave a legacy that lives on after their deaths.

As an act of will. Striving for success is often portrayed as a test of personal resolve, requiring discipline, sacrifice, and commitment. In an 1888 instructional book on success, entitled *Road to Success; a Book for Boys and Young Men,* the Reverend Aaron Wanner declares that success is not for the frail: "A weak, sickly body is a great impediment in the way to one's success. It is like a broken, leaky roof, which subjects everything in the house to injury."[30]

As self-determination. Successful media figures are in control, free to determine their own fate. They are also in a position to assert their individuality. For instance, in the *Lethal Weapon* film trilogy, Officer Martin Riggs (Mel Gibson) is part of the system. Yet he dresses in street clothes, wears his hair long, drives his own car, and breaks the rules when it suits him. Riggs possesses a clear sense of identity. He is confident, possesses self-knowledge, and knows what direction in life he wants to pursue.

As standards of beauty and physical skills. Movie stars like Tom Cruise and Julia Roberts are adored for their good looks. Sports figures like Michael Jordan and Jackie Joyner Kersee are revered for their athletic prowess.

As a sport. Success is a game that people can learn to play. Successful competitors (e.g., Donald Trump, Michael Milken, and J. R. Ewing) understand the rules and devise strategies to come out on top. Popular books portray success as a matter of technique:

- *Winning Through Intimidation,* Robert Ringer
- *Nonverbal Communication for Business Success,* Ken Cooper
- *The Psychology of Effective Living,* Roger C. Bailey

As American dream. The Horatio Alger myth maintains that anyone can succeed through hard work. If you believe hard enough in your dream, it will come true.

As image. Media content promotes the notion of success by association. Through some sort of consumer transmutation, we become what we purchase. If we *look* successful, we *are* successful.

As affluence. For some, wealth is the ultimate measure of success. This sensibility is lampooned in the popular bumper sticker declaring that "The one who dies with the most toys wins."

Values Hierarchy. How can you identify the value system operating within the worldview of a media presentation? Milton Rokeach defines the notion of values as "[a]n enduring belief that a specific mode of conduct or end-state of existence is personally or socially preferable to alternate modes of conduct or end-state of existence." [31]

Personal values are interwoven within the larger value system of the dominant culture, which then provides order and meaning for that culture. To add to the confusion, we also belong to a number of subcultures based on gender (male/female), ethnic/racial identity (e.g., African American, Jewish), stage of life (college student), and class—all of which may operate according to separate value systems. Thus, in order to identify a value system operating in a media production, it is of paramount importance to define its culture (or subculture).

Some strategies for identifying the values hierarchy operating in a media presentation include the following:

Look for embedded values. A close examination can uncover many value-laden words that have been incorporated into the text. For instance, in NBC radio's March 11 coverage of the 1992 "Super Tuesday" primary, reporter Barbara Porter's reference to "Pat Buchanan's *renegade* campaign" contains a clear value judgment. Other production values such as editing and images (see Chapter 5, this volume) also send messages about the value system operating in the media production.

In addition to the manifest value system, there may be a latent value system as well. Malcolm Sillars suggests that in value analysis it is often fruitful to list both the positive and implied negative values contained in the presentation.[32] For instance, Patrick Buchanan's 1992 presidential campaign theme of "America First" conveys positive values of patriotism and focused priorities. However, this slogan also reflects subtext of latent values—isolationism, divisiveness, and racism.

Analyze the characters appearing in the production. Characters can be considered personifications of values. Heroes and heroines epitomize those qualities that society considers admirable. Heroes generally prevail in media entertainment programming because they embody the ideal virtues of truth-love-beauty-faith-justice. For instance, Superman is committed to "truth, justice, and the American way." Often the very source of the hero's courage and strength is rooted in these ideal values. Western heroes like "Gunsmoke's" Matt Dillon adhere to a strict moral code: Never draw first or shoot a man in the back. The clear implication is that any violation of this code would mean his downfall.

Villains generally represent negative values that threaten this world. Villains are not bound by the moral constraints to which heroes must adhere. They are free to draw first, lie, and cheat. However, these momentary advantages are not powerful enough to contest the moral order of the universe. They are inevitably brought to justice—for their crime and, in a broader sense, for their moral transgressions.

Even nonfictional heroes who are presented through the media, such as Albert Einstein, Ronald Reagan, and Vanna White, are celebrated because they possess these ideal romantic virtues. However, few people can in reality fulfill these expectations. Public figures like Gary Hart fall from grace once their indiscretions have been exposed by the media—almost as though the public cannot forgive them for being human.

Examine the conclusion of the production. As the protagonists and villains engage in conflict, the values that they personify are also in opposition:

- Good versus evil
- Justice versus injustice
- Truth versus falsehood
- Love versus hate
- Internal satisfaction versus material acquisitions
- Immediate satisfaction versus delayed gratification

The resolution of a production establishes a hierarchy of values, as the protagonists struggle to restore order at the conclusion. The culminating gun duel in "Gunsmoke" dramatizes the conflict between good and evil. The good guy wins. Happiness is restored. The conclusion of a presentation, then, reaffirms values in this media-created world.

STRUCTURE

Ownership Patterns

Who were the most influential media figures of the 1980s? Bruce Springsteen? Dan Rather? Clint Eastwood?

In 1989, *Vanity Fair*'s list of the most influential media figures of the 1980s included:

- Al Neuharth (founder, *USA Today*)
- John Fairchild (chair, Fairchild Publications)
- Steve Ross (Cochair and co-CEO, Time Warner Inc.)
- Michael Ovitz (president, Creative Artists Agency)
- David Geffen (chairman, David Geffen Company)

While these people may not be household names, they are behind-the-scenes executives who exercise enormous influence over content we receive through the media. Commenting on Steve Ross, *Vanity Fair* observes, "[H]e own[s] Warner Brothers *(Batman)*, a chunk of MTV, Lorimar *(Dallas)*, and the biggest record conglomerate of them all (Madonna, U2)."[33] The magazine points out that "[Ross] sweetens deals for his friends,"[34] which means that he can influence what projects are accepted and brought to the attention of the public through a combination of clout and financial resources.

These important media figures not only determine what appears but who appears as well. For instance, Michael Ovitz is the consummate agent: "In Hollywood he's the dealer—the others are players. . . . He can deliver winning hands of writers, producers, directors, and stars from a pack including, for example, Cruise, Hoffman, and Levinson. Result: *Rain Man*, the [1989] Oscar Jackpot."[35]

Without agents like Ovitz, writers, actors, and musicians would labor in complete anonymity.

Ben Bagdikian has identified a disturbing trend involving the narrowing of control in the American media industry. In 1981, 46 corporations owned or controlled the majority of media outlets in the United States. However, by 1992 that number had shrunk to 23:

1. Bertelsmann, A. G. (books)
2. Capital Cities/ABC (newspapers, broadcasting)
3. Cox Communications (newspapers)
4. CBS (broadcasting)
5. Buena Vista Films (Disney; motion pictures)

6. Dow Jones (newspapers)

7. Gannett (newspapers)

8. General Electric (television)

9. Paramount Communications (books, motion pictures)

10. Harcourt Brace Jovanovich (books)

11. Hearst (newspapers, magazines)

12. Ingersoll (newspapers)

13. International Thomson (newspapers)

14. Knight Ridder (newspapers)

15. Media News Group (Singleton; newspapers)

16. Newhouse (newspapers, books)

17. News Corporation Ltd. (Murdoch; newspapers, magazines, motion pictures)

18. New York Times (newspapers)

19. Reader's Digest Association (books)

20. Scripps-Howard (newspapers)

21. Time Warner (magazines, books, motion pictures)

22. Times Mirror (newspapers)

23. Tribune Company (magazines)[36]

Bagdikian projects that by the mid-1990s "a half-dozen large corporations will own all the most powerful media outlets in the United States."[37]

Bagdikian contends that these ownership patterns can have a significant impact on media content. "The lords of the global village have their own political agenda. All resist economic changes that do not support their own financial interests. Together, they exert a homogenizing power over ideas, culture, and commerce that affects populations larger than any in history."[38]

To illustrate, on May 22, 1992, NBC radio devoted part of its news broadcast to a story on Johnny Carson's farewell appearance on the "Tonight Show" (which airs on NBC television). On May 25, NBC radio followed up by covering the premiere of Jay Leno as new host of the "Tonight Show." Finally, on May 26, they filed a third story, reporting that Leno had garnered a "38% share" of the ratings on his first night. This sustained coverage, though highly suspect from a news perspective, had considerable promotional value for the NBC executives.

But while it is true that the modern media conglomerate requires considerable capital, new technologies have provided some opportunity for people without significant resources to send their messages through the media. Using desktop publishing software on personal computers, small companies can produce inexpensive, professional-quality publications to reach both internal and external audiences. Video and audio equipment are becoming more affordable, allowing individuals to produce materials without significant costs. Still, the corporate, mainstream media conglomerates are responsible for a significant number of messages that reach the mass audience.

Media and Government Regulation

Every country maintains a policy on the content and dissemination of information through the channels of mass communication. This relationship between a media system and government regulatory policy plays a role in shaping the quality and diversity of media messages.

In the United States, the First Amendment to the Constitution declares that "Congress shall make no laws abridging the freedom of speech, or of the press." Over the years, the term has been expanded to include any governmental body, local or federal. The First Amendment was established on the premise that the United States is a marketplace of ideas. All forms of ideas should be expressed, and each individual must be able to make his or her own decision about what is right and appropriate.

However, the Supreme Court has concluded that certain categories of speech are not protected by the First Amendment: obscenity, false advertising, "fighting words" inciting to riot, and defamation. It must be noted that speech falling within these categories can appear in the media unless laws are passed specifically restricting its existence.

Legislating restrictions on speech is a complex and delicate matter. For instance, what people consider to be obscene changes over time. The original conception of obscenity referred to material that aroused "impure thoughts." Further, the definition of obscenity is subjective; what is obscene to one person may not be to another.

A community may pass laws declaring material obscene, but it must clearly define what constitutes obscenity. Obscene material must be judged on the basis of the following criteria:

- "The material (taken as a whole) depicts or describes in a patently offensive manner sexual conduct specified by state or local law." However, the minimum standard of what is "patently offensive" is obscure.

- "An average person, applying a contemporary community standard, looking at the work taken as a whole, determines that it appeals to the prurient interest." In this case, the jury applies a local, not a national, community standard, which means that a work of art could be obscene in Little Rock but protected by the First Amendment in Chicago.

- "The material taken as a whole lacks serious scientific, political, literary, or artistic value." [39]

A legal precedent has been established (*Pope v. Illinois*, 1987) that a jury must use what a reasonable person under the circumstances would consider to have scientific, literary, or artistic value as its guideline.

For material to be declared obscene, it must meet all three criteria. For example, in 1989, the city of Cincinnati charged the Cincinnati Museum of Art with six separate obscenity law violations for displaying a collection of photographs by photographer Robert Mapplethorpe. While the jury found that the photos met the first and second criteria, they ruled that the material did have artistic value, and accordingly, the case was dismissed.

Unlike print media, broadcasting over the airwaves is regulated by the Federal Communications Commission (FCC). The rationale often given for allowing the government to regulate (and license) this form of speech is as follows:

Scarcity of the airwaves. Because only a limited number of broadcast frequencies are available, a formal procedure for licensing and use of the airwaves is necessary.

Public ownership. The airwaves are owned by the people. Broadcasters therefore are entrusted with using the airwaves, so long as they serve the public interest.

Characteristics of broadcast media. The broadcasting media (radio and television) are pervasive. Because broadcast programming comes directly into the home, the public needs protection from misuse.

As a result, broadcast stations have an obligation to serve the public interest. In their study of the historical foundations of the First Amendment, Dwight L. Teeter, Jr., and Don A. Le Duc observe:

In essence, the [Supreme Court] held that by accepting the privilege of using the limited and valuable public resource of spectrum space, each broadcast licensee also assumed an obligation to exercise this privilege for the benefit of the public; an obligation the FCC had the authority to enforce on behalf of the public.[40]

However, this imperative to serve the public interest is often in conflict with the pressure on stations to generate profits.

In order for stations to operate, they must be awarded a license from the FCC (the duration of a TV license is for five years; a radio license is good for seven years). The criteria for acceptance are as follows:

Threshold. All applicants must meet minimum criteria for citizenship, character, and financial and technical ability.

Comparative licensing. Consideration is given to applicants who can provide the best service, as well as to groups that reflect cultural diversity.

When a frequency becomes available, the FCC must hold public hearings to consider applications. However, there is generally an expectancy of renewal, giving the current license holder the advantage.

Although the FCC is prohibited from censoring content, they are charged with maintaining the following programming standards:

Obscene or indecent programming. Under current regulations, this type of programming is absolutely prohibited.

Personal attack and editorial. The FCC establishes parameters for public debate on controversial issues and makes a distinction between personal attacks and political debate.

The development of new media technologies is redefining the philosophical basis for the regulation of broadcasting content. Unlike broadcast technology, cable television (as well as cable radio) can carry considerably more channels. In addition, cable television is a service that the audience purchases; we invite cable into our home, as opposed to the more pervasive nature of traditional broadcast technology.

Attorney Michael Kahn contends that these technological changes are having an impact on the content of the broadcast media:

The whole intellectual framework for regulating radio and traditional television is based on radio and television technologies that are more than fifty years old. While the public may own the air, the cable companies own their cables. These days, it's cheaper to operate a local cable station than a local newspaper. As a result, reasons given for limiting the reach of the First Amendment in the regulation of radio and traditional TV don't easily transfer to cable TV. This is all good news for both consumers of news and producers of media, in that the basic First Amendment freedoms should be given more breathing space through cable technology than under the old regulation scheme of the FCC.[41]

Internal Structure

The *internal structure* of a media organization consists of the following elements: the resources of the production company, the organizational framework (i.e., different departments, lines of responsibility), and the process of decision making. These organizational factors have an impact on day-to-day decisions as well as on much of the long-range planning.

Case Study: Television News Operation. To illustrate, consider the organizational structure of a television news operation. Local television stations range from skeletal one-person news departments to sophisticated operations with $30 million budgets. In the case of television news, organizational factors to consider include:

The resources of the station. The resources of a news operation can have a dramatic effect on a station's ability to gather the news. Big-budget items include subscriptions to several news services, satellite transmission, and sophisticated minicams. The size of the staff (writers, reporters, and video-grapher) can also have a bearing on the depth and quality of news coverage.

The organization of the newsroom. The typical organization of a TV news operation is shown in Figure 3.1. Three little-known but vital positions in the newsroom are the general manager, business manager, and news director.

As the chief operating officer of the television station, the general manager is primarily responsible for the overall operation of the station, including long-term planning, community service, programming, and budgetary considerations. The general manager ordinarily is removed from the day-to-day activities in the newsroom; however, if he or she becomes enamored with a pet project for the news, it usually finds its way on the air.

The business manager is responsible for all financial aspects of the news station. As such, he or she monitors the entire operation from a fiscal point of view, including costs associated with the news broadcast. The recommendations of the business manager on the purchase of news-gathering equipment and salaries for writers, reporters, and anchors can have a significant impact on the quality of the newscast.

The news director is directly responsible for the station's daily newscasts. However, according to Jim Willis and Diane B. Willis, the news director's mission to produce the news often is compromised by the pressure to maintain strong ratings:

Often the quality that the news director would like to have in the newscasts is deemed too expensive to produce by owners and upper management. One key reason this is true is that too many upper-level managers tend to look at newsroom expenses as costs rather than investments that will pay dividends later in a quality news product. . . . Often, too, the kind of patience a news director would like to exhibit to give his or her staff a chance to shine is cut short by the demands of upper management and owners to produce first-place newscasts sooner rather than later.

These tensions often cause news directors to leave their position and move on to other markets. The average length of employment of many news directors at any single station is often less than two years.[42]

The decision-making process in the broadcast newsroom. The organization of the broadcast newsroom also can have an impact on the selection and presentation of information. For instance, while the assignment editor is generally the person responsible for assigning stories to reporters, in larger stations the initial gatekeeper may be a person in an entry-level position. This person opens the mail and answers the phones, only passing along the information he or she considers newsworthy.

Figure 3.1
Broadcast News Organizational Chart

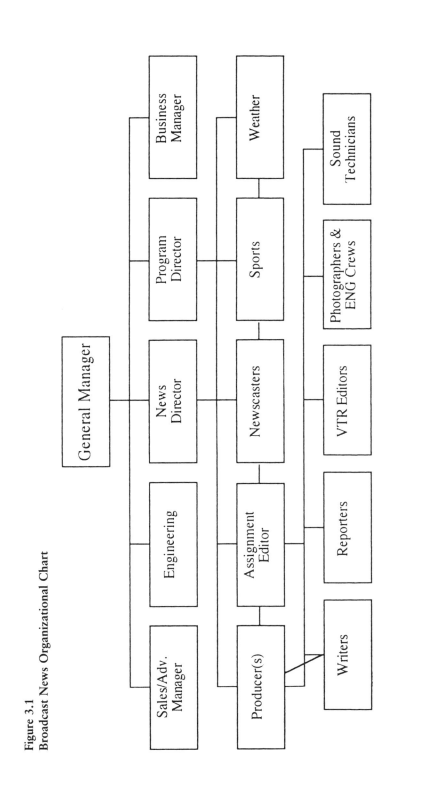

The decision-making process in broadcast journalism involves the following considerations:

- What are the criteria for the selection of stories?
- Is the process of news selection arbitrary (one person) or consultative?
- Is there an appeal process?
- How is it determined which crews (reporters and camerapeople) are assigned to a story?
- How are deadlines for stories determined?

SUMMARY

Context refers to those surrounding elements that shape meanings and convey messages. Historical context, cultural context, and structure affect the content and style of a media presentation and thus provide keys to interpreting media messages.

Keys to Interpreting Media Messages: Context

Applying the following questions related to *context* can provide insight into media messages:

A. Historical context
   1. In what ways has the media presentation been influenced by the events of the day?
      a) When was this media production first presented?
      b) What prior events led to the climate in which this media presentation was produced?
      c) How did people react to the production when it was first presented? Why?
         (1) How do people react to the production today?
         (2) How do you account for any differences in reaction?
      d) In what ways does an understanding of the historical context provide insight into the media messages contained in the presentation?
   2. What does the media production tell us about the period in which it was produced?
   3. What can be learned about shifts in cultural attitudes and concerns by tracing the evolution of a particular medium, genre, or presentation?
B. Cultural context
   1. *Media and popular culture:* In what ways does the media presentation reflect, reinforce, inculcate, or shape cultural:
      a) Attitudes
      b) Values
      c) Behaviors
      d) Preoccupations
      e) Myths

2. *Worldview:* What kind of world is depicted in the media presentation?
   a) What culture or cultures populate this world?
      (1) What kinds of people populate this world?
      (2) What is the ideology of this culture?
   b) What do we know about the people who populate this world?
      (1) Are characters presented in a stereotypical manner?
      (2) What does this tell us about the cultural stereotype of this group?
   c) Does this world present an optimistic or pessimistic view of life?
      (1) Are the characters in the presentation happy?
      (2) Do the characters have a *chance* to be happy?
   d) Are people in control of their own destinies?
      (1) Is there a supernatural presence in this world?
      (2) Are the characters under the influence of other people?
   e) What does it mean to be a success in this world?
      (1) How does a person succeed in this world?
      (2) What kinds of behavior are rewarded in this world?
   f) What is the *hierarchy of values* that appears in this world?
      (1) What embedded values can be found in the production?
      (2) What values are embodied in the characters?
      (3) What values prevail through the resolution?

C. Structure
  1. What are the ownership patterns within the media industry? How do these ownership patterns affect media content?
   a) What are the ownership patterns within the media industry?
   b) What are the ownership patterns within the particular media system you are examining (e.g., television, film, radio)?
   c) Who owns the production company that has produced the presentation you are examining (e.g., television station, newspaper, film company)?
  2. How is the media industry regulated? How does government regulation affect media messages?
  3. What is the internal structure of the media organization responsible for producing the media presentation? How does this internal structure influence content?
   a) What are the resources of the production company?
   b) What is the organizational framework of the production company?
   c) What is the process of decision making in the production company?

NOTES

1. Ian I. Mitroff and Warren Bennis, *The Unreality Industry* (New York: Oxford University Press, 1989), 13.

2. Lilli Ruggeri, "Historical Analysis of Cosmopolitan, 1886–1993" (paper presented to Med. 531, Media and Culture, St. Louis, MO, October 6, 1993).

3. Jenny Diski, "The Shadow Within," *Sight and Sound* 10 (February 1992): 12.

4. Ibid., 13.

5. Russel B. Nye, "Notes on a Rationale for Popular Culture," in *A Popular Culture Reader,* ed. Jack Nachbar, Deborah Weiser, and John L. Wright (Bowling Green, OH: Bowling Green University Popular Press, 1978), 22.

6. Ibid., 20.

7. Helmut Gernsheim with Alison Gernsheim, *The History of Photography* (New York: McGraw-Hill, 1969), 243.

8. David Considine and Gail Haley, *Visual Messages: Integrating Imagery into Instruction* (Englewood, CO: Teacher Idea Press, 1992), 3.

9. Nye, "Popular Culture," 22–23.

10. Michael MacCambridge, "Were the Rappers Right?" *St. Louis Post-Dispatch,* May 21, 1992, E1.

11. George Gerbner, "Women and Minorities on Television: A Study in Casting and Fate" (report to the Screen Actors Guild and the American Federation of Radio and Television Artists, Philadelphia, June 1993).

12. Eve Simson, "Stereotyping of Women on Television," *USA Today,* September 1978, 15.

13. Alan O'Connor, "Culture and Communication," in *Questioning the Media: A Critical Introduction,* ed. John Downing, Ali Mohammadi, and Annabelle Sreberny-Mohammadi (Newbury Park, CA: Sage Publications, 1990), 37.

14. George Gerbner and Nancy Signorielli, "Violence Profile 1967 Through 1988–89; Enduring Patterns," Report issued at University of Pennsylvania, January 20, 1990; 1–38.

15. Richard Rosenfeld and Scott Decker, "Where Public Health and Law Enforcement Meet: Monitoring and Preventing Youth Violence," *American Journal of Police,* forthcoming.

16. Naomi Wolf, *The Beauty Myth* (New York: William Morrow, 1991), 156–57.

17. Ibid., 136.

18. Ibid., 133.

19. Ibid.

20. Ibid., 167.

21. James Carey, *Communication as Culture* (Boston: Unwin Hyman, 1989), 65–67.

22. Malcolm W. Browne, "Television Blocks the View," *New York Times,* January 27, 1981, C2.

23. William B. Helmreich, *The Things They Say Behind Your Back: Stereotypes & the Myths Behind Them* (New Brunswick, NJ: Transaction, 1983), 44.

24. Carol Stocker, "Published on the First Try," *Boston Globe,* February 11, 1983, Living Section, 15–16.

25. "Women, Minorities on TV Shown in Bad Light, Report Says," *St. Louis Post-Dispatch,* June 16, 1993, 21A.

26. Linda Holtzman, *Content Analysis Tally Sheet* (St. Louis: Webster University, 1993).

27. Richard Harter Fogle, ed., *The Romantic Movement in American Fiction* (New York: Odyssey Press, 1966), 3.

28. Walt Whitman, *Leaves of Grass* (New York: Viking Press, 1959), 26.

29. Richard Weiss, *The American Myth of Success: From Horatio Alger to Norman Vincent Peale* (Urbana, IL: University of Illinois Press, 1988).

30. Reverend Aaron Wanner, *Road to Success; a Book for Boys and Young Men* (Reading, PA: Daniel Miller, 1888), 12.

31. Milton Rokeach, *Beliefs, Attitudes, and Values: A Theory of Organization and Change* (San Francisco: Jossey-Bass, 1968), 113.

32. Malcolm O. Sillars, *Messages, Meanings, and Culture* (New York: Harper-Collins, 1991).

33. "The Media Decade," *Vanity Fair,* December 1989, 180.

34. Ibid.

35. Ibid., 184.

36. Ben Bagdikian, *The Media Monopoly,* 4th ed. (Boston: Beacon Press, 1992), 21–22.

37. Ibid., 3–4.

38. Ben Bagdikian, "The Lords of the Global Village," *The Nation,* June 12, 1989, 807.

39. Harold L. Nelson, Dwight L. Teeter, Jr., and Don R. Le Duc, *Law of Mass Communications,* 6th ed. (Westbury, NY: The Foundation Press, 1989).

40. Ibid.

41. Michael Kahn, Attorney, Gallop, Johnson, and Neuman, interview by author, October 20, 1993.

42. Jim Willis and Diane B. Willis, *New Directions in Media Management* (Boston: Allyn and Bacon, 1993), 198–99.

CHAPTER 4

FRAMEWORK

- Introduction
- Plot
- Genre
- Logical conclusion

INTRODUCTION

The title of a media presentation often encapsulates the essential meaning of the total presentation. Due to the competitive nature of the media industry, titles (e.g., newspaper headlines, advertisements, political slogans, song and movie titles) must also provoke interest in the presentation. Some titles suggest thematic concerns addressed in the presentation; others titillate with promises of sex and violence. Even titles for film sequels (e.g., *Lethal Weapon III*) announce that the audience should expect more of the same formulaic characters, action, and plot. Consequently, the title is an excellent place to begin analyzing the content of media messages.

The beginning of a media presentation is often a microcosm of what to expect in the course of the program or article. The introduction acquaints the audience with the primary characters, plot outline, and a foreshadowing of events. The opening of a film, television, or radio program serves as a review of the entire presentation.

For example, the initial scene in *Rocky* begins in the midst of a boxing match between two club fighters. The fight is being held in a church recreation hall. A picture of Christ is suspended over the ring, underscoring that this is not merely a physical conflict but a spiritual struggle as well, requiring faith, courage, and conviction.

Rocky is an awkward boxer whose fate appears certain: He will lose. As the fight progresses, however, Rocky's determination, heart, and spirit enable him to transcend his physical limitations. This introductory bout, like the film itself, ends in triumph. The remainder of the film is essentially an elaboration of its first five minutes.

PLOT

"Let me tell you about the movie I just saw."

A *plot* is a series of actions planned by the artist to build upon one another, with an introduction, body, and conclusion. The foundation of plot is conflict. Characters are initially confronted with a dilemma, which is resolved by the end of the story. Some narratives contain secondary stories, called *subplots*. Subplots often may initially appear to be unrelated to the main theme. However, the subplots may tie together at the conclusion, underscoring the themes of the primary plot.

Explicit Content

Explicit content consists of events and activities in the plot that are displayed through visible action:

A man bops another fellow over the head with a brickbat, takes his money, and flees. Later in the program he is caught and carted off to jail.

The viewer constructs meaning by selecting the essential pieces of explicit information in the story. In this example, five distinct actions are described: the clubbing, theft, flight, apprehension, and incarceration.

In his study of children and television, W. Andrew Collins found that children's comprehension of explicit story material was surprisingly limited:

- Second graders recalled an average of only 66 percent of the scenes that adults had judged as essential to the plot.
- Fifth graders recalled 84 percent of the scenes that adults had judged as essential to the plot.
- Eighth grades recalled 92 percent of the scenes that adults had judged as essential to the plot.[1]

As a result, children often have difficulty remembering explicit details and identifying important scenes. Collins observes:

Young children fail to comprehend observed actions and events in an adultlike way because they arrive at different interpretations of the various actors' plans or intentions. . . . Thus, it is possible that second and third graders take away not only a less complete understanding of the program than fifth and eighth graders do, they may also be perceiving the content of the program somewhat *differently* because they retain (and work off of) a different set of cues.[2]

Significantly, the standard against which the children's performance is measured consists of a sample of adults. However, there is no guarantee that these adults have successfully identified all of the essential scenes. Although adults are generally more knowledgeable than children, they are not necessarily informed or interested in all topics. And as mentioned earlier, adults are frequently distracted by competing activities and are unable to devote their full attention to a media presentation.

Beyond this, reaching the age of 21 does not necessarily guarantee intellectual or emotional maturity. Some adults have an impaired ability to identify essential content. For instance, Charles Manson claimed that popular media instructed him to lead his "family" on a series of mass murders. Manson selected certain portions of the Bible and the Beatles as "essential content," devising a warped but quite intricate rationale to justify his heinous crimes.

And as mentioned previously in the discussion on reception theory, other factors also contribute to how individuals process media content, including:

Background
  • How much does the audience already know about the subject?
Interest level
  • How interested is the audience in the subject? How attentive is the audience?
Predisposition
  • What is the attitude of the audience toward the subject (positive or negative) going into the conversation?
Priorities
  • What issues are of particular concern to the audience? Why?
Demographic profile
  • National origin
  • Gender
  • Race
  • Ethnic origin
  • Age
  • Education
  • Income
Psychological profile
  • Self-concept
  • Primary relationships
  • Significant life experiences
  • Ways of relating to others

- Ways of dealing with emotions
- Personal aspirations

Communications environment
- What is the size of the audience?
- What are they doing while they are receiving the information?

Stage of development
- Chronological
- Cognitive
- Emotional

Identifying explicit content is essential to the analysis of media messages. The most effective way to identify the explicit content is to take notes during the presentation. Record relevant scenes and significant bits of dialogue. Making vague generalizations will not suffice. You must refer to specific detail from the narrative to support your position.

While print offers a text on which to reflect, this note-taking process is particularly tricky when viewing film or television. You are writing in darkness, recording what just occurred while new events are unfolding. However, as you become more comfortable with this process, you will be prepared to present a clear, defensible analysis of media programming.

Affective Response

We often experience a range of emotions while reading a novel or watching a film. But because the narrative is geared toward the climax, the feelings that we experience in the process often fade from memory. Media communicators often strive to elicit an emotional reaction from the audience for dramatic purposes or as a means of influencing the audience. "*Show,* don't *tell*" is an adage that can be applied to media presentations. That is, rather than simply talking about a subject, it is always more effective to arrange for the audience to experience emotions that enrich their understanding of the content.

A striking example can be found in the films produced by the Disney Studios. The true Disney experience—and a key to its success—is that the films put children in touch with their emotions and allow them to experience these feelings in an intense way. Walt Disney observed:

What is the difference between our product and the other? . . . Giving it "heart." Others haven't understood the public. We developed a psychological approach to everything we do here. We seem to know when to "tap the heart." Others have hit the intellect. We can hit them in an emotional way. Those who appeal to the intellect only appeal to a very limited group.[3]

To illustrate, *101 Dalmations* (1961) touches a range of very personal feelings in young audiences. First, children watch the formation of a family, as two dalmations (Pongo and Perdita) meet, fall in love, and raise 15 puppies. The next few scenes are filled with warmth and affection, featuring the antics of the puppies. At this point, a villainess (Cruella Deville) appears. The young audience reacts with sadness, grief, and anger, as the puppies are kidnapped and imprisoned in an old mansion. There they wait to be slaughtered, their fur to be converted to a coat for Cruella. By the conclusion of the film, the children achieve an emotional catharsis, as the puppies are rescued and order is restored. These feelings of relief and happiness complete the emotional cycle.

The effective media communicator anticipates how the audience should react at each point of the presentation and then strives to elicit that particular response. For instance, Hollywood director George Cukor was not known for his technical expertise. Instead, he surrounded himself with the best available cast and crew and, stationing himself by the camera, acted as his *own* audience while the action unfolded. If he was moved by the scene, he was satisfied. If not, he would gather his experts around him to discuss strategies that would produce the intended response.

In some cases, the media communicator attempts to evoke the same emotions in the audience that are being experienced by the characters in the presentation. For instance, in the 1956 version of *Invasion of the Body Snatchers* (see discussion, Chapter 3), director Don Siegel begins with the town doctor (a prototypical 1950s authority figure) paying a house call on a family. A boy runs to the car, screaming, "My mother's not really my mother!" The camera cuts to an emotionless zombie, who calls to her "son" to come to the house. This revelation is particularly chilling to children who (according to proponents of psychoanalytic attachment theory) often suffer from fear of separation from their parents.[4] The young audience projects these primal feelings back on the screen, making the film that much more terrifying.

The media communicator also may manipulate the feelings of the audience in order to convey messages. For example, advertisements that display animals or babies are intended to evoke a warm response, which the media communicator hopes will be transferred to the product.

One useful way to approach the analysis of media presentations is to think along with the media communicator. How does he or she want you to be feeling at particular points in the plot? Sad? Happy? Scared? Insecure? Envious?

The next step involves investigating why the media communicator is attempting to elicit that intended emotional response from the audience. Affective response can influence the audience's attitude toward people and issues. For example, political figures routinely arrange for "photo opportunities" with children, elderly people, and their own family members in hopes that we will feel positively toward them and, as a result, support them and their policies. Media communicators such as advertisers and politicians also use affective response to move the audience to action (voting or purchasing).

Finally, paying attention to your affective responses can serve as a barometer of your own personal belief system. A good illustration can be found in Charlotte Brontë's novel *Jane Eyre*. Jane is a governess who goes to work in the household of a gentleman named Rochester. The two fall in love and plan to marry. However, as the wedding day approaches, Jane becomes aware of strange and disturbing noises in the attic. It is clear that whatever is in the attic is some dreaded secret that, if uncovered, might jeopardize their future together.

Should Jane clear up this mystery before she weds Rochester, or should she marry Rochester and then make a trip to the attic? Is marriage an institution of refuge, where people blindly seek comfort regardless of consequence? Should people marry for security or love (or both)? What is the role of trust in relationships? Your emotional response can serve as the basis for critical self-analysis.

Implicit Content

Let's reexamine the scintillating scene that I presented in the earlier section on explicit content:

A man bops another fellow over the head with a brickbat, takes his money, and flees. Later in the program he is caught and carted off to jail.

What remains unclear are questions related to the connections *between* events. Why did the first man hit the second fellow? Why does he run? Why is he punished at the end of the story?

Implicit content refers to those elements of plot that remain under the surface:

- What are the motives behind characters' decisions and actions? *Motivation* applies to those reasons that compel the characters to behave in the ways that they do.
- What is the connection between events that occur early in the narrative and those events that appear later in the plot? Are the *consequences* for characters' actions made clear?

W. Andrew Collins's study revealed that children had even greater difficulty identifying implicit than explicit content:

- Second graders had an overall score of fewer than half (47 percent) of the items that adults had agreed upon. Interestingly, the girls outperformed the boys, "who appear to be performing at about chance level (between 30% and 40%) on this level of inference."[5]

- Fifth graders recalled 67 percent of the items that adults had agreed upon.
- Eighth graders recalled 77 percent of the items that adults had agreed upon.[6]

These results suggest that young children are developmentally incapable of recognizing the connection between events. Thus, despite the best intentions of the media communicator to attach a moral to programs, children may be receiving a message about a world without consequence. And once again, the standard of measurement in the study is the highly subjective comprehension level of adults. Some adults may also be unclear about the cause-effect relationship of events depicted in the media.

To further complicate the issue, many media programs present a world seemingly free of consequence. Dirty Harry, Rambo, and Oliver North routinely violate laws in the name of a higher moral good. High-speed car chases, destruction of property, and assault would not go unpunished in real life but are somehow justifiable for heroes in entertainment programs conveyed by the media.

Character Development

By the end of a narrative, characters often have changed dramatically. They may have discovered a new outlook on life, engaged in self-discovery, or developed new skills that made them successes (or failures) at the conclusion of the story. This character development gives an artist the opportunity to make thematic statements. For example, *Dead Again* (1991), a wonderfully constructed film by Kenneth Branagh, is a Hitchcockian tale focusing on the metaphysical connections that exist between the major characters. A murder committed in 1948 has come back to haunt the heroine of the film, an amnesia victim. Until the conclusion of the film, the audience does not know either who she is or who she was in a previous life. In addition, the audience is left to discover the past identity of her current lover. Had he been her husband, who was convicted of murdering her? The mysteries surrounding the characters' identities, motives, and feelings are revealed to the audience by the conclusion of the film.

The protagonists in *Dead Again* change through the course of the film. This growth and self-discovery enable them to overcome the fears and lack of faith that had prevented them from finding happiness in their prior existence.

Dead Again deals with issues related to reincarnation, the role of the past on the present, and the power and scope of love: Can it transcend death? What happens to the characters is, then, a comment on the thematic questions raised earlier in the movie.

MEDIA LITERACY TIPS
CHARACTER DEVELOPMENT
A useful method for detecting media messages is to examine the ways in which characters have been affected by the events in the story: √ Have the major characters changed as a result of the events in the story? How? Why?   √ What have the characters learned as a result of their experience?

GENRE

You have all seen dozens of situation comedies on television. But what exactly *is* a situation comedy? What are the elements that are common to all of these programs? These shared characteristics make up the *genre* of situation comedies.

The word genre itself simply means "order." A genre is a standardized format that is distinctive and easily identifiable. Examples include horror films, romances, sci-fi, situation comedies, westerns, and the evening news. A genre is not confined to one medium. For instance, at one time or another, westerns have appeared in print, on radio, television, and film.

Genres are characterized by *formula*—that is, patterns in *function, premise, structure,* and *plot.* Individual programs generally conform to the formula of the genre. As John Cawelti observes, "Individual works are ephemeral, but the formula lingers on, evolving and changing with time, yet still basically recognizable."[7]

Even works that challenge the parameters of the genre are highly conscious of the formula. As an example, *Shane* (1953) is a western film that plays off of the genre's formula for dramatic effect. The protagonist (Alan Ladd) is not the conventional gunslinger but instead is a diminutive, introspective man who longs to hang up his gun. This variation on the formula enables director George Stevens to comment about the encroachment of civilization on the Old West.

In discussing the concept of genre, it might be useful to focus on the formula of the TV situation comedy (or sitcom).

Formulaic Function

A genre shares a common manifest objective. For instance, the primary function of the situation comedy is to entertain or amuse the audience. In addition, a genre may contain shared latent functions. The sitcom is a morality play that offers instruction to the audience. Garry Marshall (producer of "Happy Days," "Laverne and Shirley," and "Mork and Mindy") observes, "We tried to be useful. We did shows about mental health, about diabetes, about death, blindness, and epilepsy. Tolerance. That's what we tried to teach. Be nice to each other."[8]

A genre may also serve a therapeutic function. Genres touch a range of primal feelings within the individual. For instance, the horror genre arouses feelings of fear. Comedies permit the audience to laugh. Action films tap feelings of anger. Tragedies make us cry. In this era in which people (particularly males) are not encouraged to confront their emotions, media presentations put people in touch with their feelings. Consequently, genres provide a very healthy release for audiences.

Formulaic Premise

How would you describe a typical sitcom?

A *formulaic premise* refers to an identifiable situation that characterizes a genre. For example, Lawrence E. Mintz describes the sitcom premise in the following manner: "a half-hour series focused on episodes involving recurring characters within the same premise. (That is, each week we encounter the same people in essentially the same setting.)"[9]

The sitcom typically revolves around family, marriage, and friendship. This makes sense, since sitcoms are generally watched by middle-class families. As its name suggests, the comedy is generated through everyday situations rather than stand-up monologues. The stories feature the characters coping with everyday life (e.g., Al Bundy faces the agony of buying a used car. Jerry Seinfeld adopts a dog.). These everyday situations, taken to the extreme, form the basis of the program's humor and enable the characters (and, by extension, the audience) to put life's minor irritations and problems into perspective. The underlying message is that life is a maze, filled with traps. However, these situations are always relatively minor and can be resolved within a 30-minute episode.

Formulaic Structure

A genre generally fits within an identifiable, unvarying *structure,* or organizational pattern. In many genres (including the sitcom), the standard formula is order/chaos/order. The initial order of the story is disrupted almost immediately. The chaotic stage consumes the majority of the program and is the source of much of its humor. The status quo is finally restored in the conclusion. A latent message is that problems are all solvable, and justice always prevails. Characters who have violated the moral code of sitcoms (by lying or trying to be something they're not) suffer the consequences. Misunderstandings are cleared up, and characters who are at odds are reconciled.

The structure of many media presentations can confuse the audience with regard to media messages. The chaos stage is often the most memorable aspect of the plot, far more exciting and engrossing than the moralistic resolution. To illustrate, the 1931 gangster film *Public Enemy* included an obligatory prologue and epilogue proclaiming that crime does not pay. At the conclusion of the film, Tom Powers (played by James Cagney) lay fatally wounded in the street, humiliated and friendless. Powers's fall was portrayed as just retribution for his disregard of the laws that govern society and heaven.

However, the preponderance of the movie was a Horatio Alger–style American success story. The Cagney character rose from poverty to a position of wealth and power, due to his enterprise, perseverance, and "moxie." Cagney's energetic and mesmerizing performance as he rose to power overshadowed the conclusion of the film. Thus, the glamour of the "chaos" stage of the film sent a message that undermined the expressed intention of the producer.

Variations can occur within the basic structure of a genre. Television programs such as "Hill Street Blues" borrowed from its "poor relative," the soap opera, so that some subplots remained unresolved from week to week. However, this innovation is a conscious response to the traditional structure. The expected resolution on the part of the audience enabled producer Steven Bochco to make a statement about the realities of contemporary urban life.

Formulaic Plot

Only a finite number of general *plots,* or stories, appear within a given genre. For example, episodes of "Cheers" generally fall into the following plot categories:

- An outsider intrudes on the family of "Cheers."
- Events create internal problems between members of the "Cheers" family.
- A member of the "Cheers" family lies or deceives others and suffers the consequences.
- A misunderstanding disrupts the "Cheers" community.
- Events affect a character, who finds comfort and support from the "Cheers" family.
- Romance affects a character and, consequently, the entire "Cheers" community.
- Characters are involved in games of sexual conquest.

While these general plots appear with regularity, the embellishments, detail, and small nuances within these plots keep each episode fresh and interesting.

Misunderstandings occur with regularity in the world of the sitcom.

Communication is clearly valued in the world of the sitcom, as a means of both preventing and resolving problems.

Deception serves as another formulaic plot device. Sitcom characters do not murder each other. Instead, they tell "white lies" or engage in some minor transgression. Deception never pays in the world of the sitcom; the characters always get caught. Another latent message of sitcoms involves the value of truthfulness. Only by admitting one's errors can one find restitution and forgiveness.

Plot complications also arise due to excess hubris, or pride. Characters who possess too much pride and ambition disrupt their world and alienate the members of their community. These characters are not evil; evil does not exist in the world of the sitcom. They are simply misguided, due to an inflated sense of self. As a result, they make errors in judgment. At the conclusion, the character's hubris is exposed to the audience and other characters alike. A latent message in sitcoms is related to identity. Know yourself and be satisfied with who you are. Ultimately, serenity and personal happiness are more important than achievement and material gain.

The subject matter for specific episodes is often determined by the interests and constraints of popular culture. For instance, "The Days and Nights of Molly Dodd" focused on sensitive topics ranging from interracial relationships to unwed motherhood. However, in order to preserve its ratings, a program must be careful not to offend its target audience. And above all, a program must present these issues in an entertaining fashion.

Convention

Genres rely on *conventions* to furnish cues about people, events, and situations. A convention is a practice or object that appears so often that it has become standard. Some basic categories of conventions include the following:

- A *plot convention* is a part of a story that can appear within a number of genres. For instance, the "buddy" plot convention has become a staple of Hollywood films, including westerns *(Butch Cassidy and the Sundance Kid)*, comedies *(Midnight Run)*, and action/adventure movies *(Thelma and Louise)*. This storyline is also common to TV sitcoms ("The Odd Couple," "Happy Days"). The recurrence of this storyline reflects the public's keen interest in relationships and the bonding that takes place in stressful situations. Other examples of plot convention include: the wedding at the conclusion of a narrative; the boy meets girl scenario; and the love/hate relationship between a couple.

- *Conventional setting* refers to a standard background against which the action takes place. The conventional setting for a sitcom is the home or workplace. Most of the activity centers around the interior, with only brief exterior shots used to establish the setting. A limited number of sets are employed in any sitcom. Indeed, the set (e.g., Archie Bunker's living room) achieves some significance within the context of the program. For instance, Archie's chair represented Archie's somewhat tenuous position as absolute head of the Bunker household. A running gag in the program consisted of other characters sitting in Archie's chair—much to his consternation.

- *Stock characters* are characters who appear so frequently that they have become recognizable types. When we watch a western, for instance, we are already acquainted with the hero's sidekick; we have met the old coot a thousand times before. As a result, the audience can become involved in the story immediately. Stock characters frequently reflect cultural stereotypes. The familiarity of these characters indicates the degree to which this stereotype is accepted in our culture. Indeed, much of the humor of these characters is derived from the exaggerated mannerisms and appearance of these stereotypes. Other examples of stock characters include the honest friend, the talkative old woman, the suave gambler, the simple country boy, the blundering drunkard, the super sleuth, the eccentric scientist, and the folksy TV weatherman.

  Sitcom characters must be generally friendly and likable. Carl Reiner observes, "Warm is an important word. You laugh easier when funny things are happening to nice people." [10] It is permissible for characters to be eccentric and annoying, however, so long as they are not malicious. The latent message is that people are basically good. The principal characters recognize the essential goodness beneath a character's imperfect exterior and accept that person because he or she is a part of their community—at home or at work.

- *Conventional trappings* include props and costumes that are common to a genre. These trappings furnish the audience with clues about the action. For instance, the white coats and surgical masks worn by the cast of "M*A*S*H" signals that these characters are doctors. At the same time, the tents and jeeps inform the audience that they are in the military.

  Occasionally the setting and trappings of a genre change over time. For instance, the western appears to have disappeared as a popular TV genre. However, it can be argued that the police show has emerged as an updated version of the western. The urban landscape has replaced the frontier, and the car has supplanted the horse. However, the function, characters, and essential premise remain the same. The lawman still fights crime, even though the outlaws are rustling drugs instead of cattle.

Shifts in Genre. Changes in the genre often signal shifts in the culture. To illustrate, the situation comedy of the 1950s reflected the cultural life of the period. After the disruption of World War II, the United States was preoccupied with a return to normalcy. Consequently, the biggest challenge facing the 1950s sitcom characters was change. For example, in "Leave It to Beaver," disruptive elements like puberty and girlfriends threatened the sanctity of the Cleaver household. However, each episode concluded with the comforting return to normalcy. Many 1950s sitcoms featured a zany character who was surrounded by a rational supporting cast. For instance, much of the humor in "I Love Lucy" stemmed from Lucy's efforts to fit into a normal world.

The setting for "I Love Lucy" was the home. Lucy's world consisted of her husband and child and her neighbors, Fred and Ethel Mertz. One of the formulaic plots consisted of Lucy's efforts to break into show business. Ricky Ricardo refused to allow his wife to realize her ambition and, within the context of the show, with good reason. Lucy was deluded; she had no talent and was incapable of functioning on her own. But in order to realize her dream, Lucy would willfully disobey her husband. Ricky would inevitably get wind of this deceit and "teach her a lesson." The message was clear: Lucy's place was in the home.

By the 1970s, the sitcom had shifted, reflecting changes in society. Central figures such as Mary Tyler Moore, Alex Rieger ("Taxi"), and Barney Miller were rational characters surrounded by a zany cast. The supporting characters provided the humor in these series. The central figure provided stability in what had become an absurd and chaotic world.

By the 1970s, sitcoms like "All in the Family" began to deal with topics of cultural interest, such as racism and homosexuality. Messages with respect to women also began to change. Independent women like Mary Tyler Moore were depicted succeeding on their own. Change was now accepted as inevitable. The chief concern became how to maintain a sense of balance in the face of change.

These programs redefined the traditional values of the 1950s sitcoms to help us to cope with cultural changes. The family at home had been supplanted by the "family" at work, reflecting the breakup of the family and emergence of the workplace as the center of activity. The crew at "WKRP in Cincinnati" may have bickered among themselves, but they rallied when a member of their community needed support.

LOGICAL CONCLUSION

In *The French Lieutenant's Woman*, novelist John Fowles agonizes over the appropriate ending to his book. Fowles compares the process of writing a novel to giving birth:

You may think novelists always have fixed plans to which they work, so that the future predicted by Chapter One is always inexorably the actuality of Chapter Thirteen. . . . [But] *we wish to create worlds as real as, but other than the world that is. Or was. This is why we cannot plan. We know a world is an organism, not a machine. We also know that a genuinely created world must be independent of its creator. . . . It is not only that [the character] has begun to gain an autonomy; I must respect it, and disrespect all my quasi-divine plans for him, if I wish him to be real.[11]

An author creates the characters, setting, and worldview of the novel but then must let go, allowing the characters to fulfill their destinies. Although this process can be agonizing for the author/parent, Fowles declares, "I let the fight proceed and take no more than a recording part in it." [12] The conclusion must be a logical extension of the initial premise, characters, and worldview, free of further intrusion by the artist.

In light of Fowles's observations, it is striking that the conclusions to popular media presentations so frequently violate this principle of logical progression. Conclusions are often false, confused, or simply illogical when considered within the flow of the program. For instance, how often have you left a movie theater feeling dissatisfied with the ending of the film?

One explanation can be found in the study of popular culture. In order to attract and maintain an audience, media presentations focus on complex issues, reflecting cultural interests, concerns, and preoccupations. Unfortunately, these complicated issues must be resolved within strict time constraints (e.g., 30 minutes for a sitcom). These conditions often lead to conclusions that offer simplistic answers to complex problems.

Illogical conclusions also respond to the audience's desire for a happy ending. In his study of fairy tales, Bruno Bettelheim observes:

The dominant culture wishes to pretend . . . that the dark side of man does not exist, and professes a belief in an optimistic meliorism. . . . The message that fairy tales get across . . . [is] that a struggle against severe difficulties in life is unavoidable, is an intrinsic part of human existence—but that if one does not shy away, but steadfastly meets unexpected and often unjust hardships, one masters all obstacles and at the end emerges victorious. [13]

Mindful of this demand for a satisfying resolution, media communicators present simplistic solutions to complex problems. Tide Detergent will make you a better mother. Ultra Brite toothpaste is the key to romantic fulfillment.

The central message of a media presentation may be undermined by an artificial conclusion. For example, *Swing Kids* (1993) is a film that focuses on a segment of German adolescents in the 1930s who found solace in American swing music as an expression of freedom and rebellion in the face of the Nazi buildup in their country. The film examines the difficult choices facing these teenagers and the seductive nature of the Aryan propaganda machine. At the conclusion of the film, the young hero is carted off to a work camp, after standing up for his principles and defying the Nazis. As the truck pulls away, his younger brother stands in the street, vowing to continue resisting the Nazis. The epilogue then reminds the audience that others (like the little brother) continued the fight and that the Nazis eventually lost the war. This upbeat "spin" at the end of the film trivializes the thematic integrity of the film; the message is that the tragic experience of this boy (or of all German youths who were faced with these choices) was, after all, not terribly important.

Audiences accustomed to the swift and immediate resolution of enter-tainment programming are ill-prepared to contend with media coverage of news events. For example, when the Iran hostage crisis began in 1979, television coverage was continuous. However, as the situation became pro-longed, without apparent end in sight, the public (and consequently the networks) began to lose interest in the crisis.

An effective strategy for identifying latent messages involves envisioning a conclusion that is consistent with the logical flow of a presentation. A good example can be found in "The Honeymooners," a highly successful 1950s TV sitcom. Ralph Kramden, played by Jackie Gleason, is a big, blustery bus driver. When the comedic elements have been stripped away, Ralph is a terribly unhappy and selfish person, plagued with hubris and a deluded sense of self. When he doesn't get his way, Ralph "playfully" threatens his wife Alice and pal Ed Norton ("Pow—to the moon!"). Each week Ralph becomes embroiled in a harebrained scheme, so that he can get what "he deserves." In order to execute his plan, however, Ralph con-tinually deceives Alice, lying to her or pilfering the household money.

Toward the end of each episode, the folly of Ralph's excessive ego is exposed. Ralph parades in front of Alice, looking repentant and trying to find the words to ask for forgiveness. After some hesitation, Alice always relents. The program inevitably concludes with an embrace of reconcilia-tion, with Ralph declaring, "Baby, you're the greatest."

This sudden shift in logic presents clear manifest messages concerning the importance of forgiveness and support in marriage. However, the la-tent messages contained in the logical progression (which occupies the ma-jority of time and attention of the program) remain the major and legiti-mate thrust of the story. What would be the logical conclusion for "The Honeymooners"? Possible scenarios include:

- Alice forgives Ralph again.
- Alice leaves Ralph.
- Ralph goes into therapy.
- Ralph and Alice see a marriage counselor.

Suggesting an ending consistent with the logical flow of "The Honeymoon-ers" reveals latent messages regarding marriage and human relationships. A key to identifying media messages is, then: Given the initial premise, characters, and worldview, how *should* the presentation logically end?

Preferred Conclusion

Finally, how would you have *preferred* for the story to end? Your re-sponse reveals a great deal about your personal belief system. Should one

In "The Honeymooners," Ralph Kramden (Jackie Gleason) bullies his buddy Ed Norton (Art Carney), much to the displeasure of wife Alice (Audrey Meadows). The happy ending at the conclusion of each episode offers a simplistic conclusion that is not consistent with the logical flow of the program. Photograph supplied by Globe Photos, Inc.

minimize problems to keep a marriage going? Is this Ralph's problem solely, or does Alice share in the responsibility? What is Ralph's attitude toward women? Why is Ralph so driven to make "the big score"? Any preferred conclusion to "The Honeymooners" reveals your personal attitudes toward marriage, sex roles, and definitions of success in American culture.

SUMMARY

Framework refers to various structural elements of a production: introduction, plot, genre, and logical conclusion.

Keys to Interpreting Media Messages: Framework

Applying the following questions related to *framework* can provide insight into media messages:

A. Introduction
   1. What does the title of the presentation signify?
   2. What events constitute the introduction of the media presentation?
   3. Does the introduction foreshadow events and themes in the body of the production?
B. Plot
   1. *Explicit content*
      a) What are the significant events in the story?
      b) What is the primary story or plot?
      c) What are the subplots, if any?
   2. *Affective response*
      a) How does the media communicator want you to be feeling at particular points in the plot?
         (1) Why does the media communicator want you to be feeling this way?
         (2) Is the media communicator successful in eliciting this intended emotional response?
      b) Do your affective responses provide insight into media messages? Explain.
      c) Do your affective responses provide insight into your personal belief system? Explain.
   3. *Implicit content*
      a) What is the relationship between the significant events in the story?
      b) What are the characters' motivations for their actions?
      c) Are the consequences to specific behaviors defined?
   4. *Character development*
      a) Have the major characters changed as a result of the events in the story? How? Why?
      b) What have the characters learned as a result of their experience?
C. Genre
   1. Does the presentation belong to any recognizable genre?

2. Is there a predictable formula for the genre?
    a) Formulaic function
    b) Formulaic plot
    c) Stock characters
    d) Formulaic structure
    e) Conventions
        (1) Storyline
        (2) Setting
        (3) Trappings
3. What does this genre suggest about:
    a) Cultural attitudes and values?
    b) Cultural preoccupations?
    c) Cultural myths?
    d) Worldview?
4. Can you trace the evolution of this genre?
    a) Have there been shifts in the genre over time?
    b) What do these shifts in genre reveal about changes in the culture?
D. Logical conclusion
    1. Does the conclusion of the presentation follow logically from the established premise, characters, and worldview?
    2. If not, how *should* the presentation have ended, given the established premise, characters, and worldview?
    3. How would you have *preferred* for the story to end? Why?

NOTES

1. W. Andrew Collins, "Children's Comprehension of Television Content," in *Children Communicating,* ed. Ellen Wartella (Beverly Hills, CA: Sage Publications, 1979), 27.

2. Ibid., 28.

3. Bob Thomas, *Walt Disney: An American Original* (New York: Simon and Schuster, 1976), 278.

4. *Encyclopedia of Psychology,* s.v. "Bonding and Attachment," by R. W. Zaslow.

5. Collins, "Comprehension of Television Content," 29.

6. Ibid.

7. John Cawelti, "Myth, Symbol, and Formula," *Journal of Popular Culture* 8 (Summer 1974): 15.

8. Lawrence E. Mintz, "Situation Comedy," in *TV Genres,* ed. Brian G. Rose (Westport, CT: Greenwood Press, 1985), 119.

9. Ibid., 115.

10. Ibid., 117.

11. John Fowles, *The French Lieutenant's Woman* (Boston: Little, Brown, 1969), 105–6.

12. Ibid., 417.

13. Bruno Bettelheim, *The Uses of Enchantment: The Meaning and Importance of Fairy Tales* (New York: Vintage Books, 1976), 7.

CHAPTER 5

PRODUCTION VALUES

- Editing
- Color
- Lighting
- Shape
- Scale
- Relative position

- Movement
- Point of view
- Angle
- Connotation
- Performance
- Sound

Production values refer to the style and quality of a media presentation. Production values are roughly analogous to grammar in print in that these elements influence:

- The way in which the audience receives the information.
- The emphasis, or interpretation, placed on the information by the media communicator.
- The reaction of the audience to the information.

The clever mass communicator employs production values to involve the audience in the media experience. For example, in *Paradise Lost* John Milton uses a literary technique to give the reader a personal sense of Satan's descent into hell. Read the following passage aloud:

> Him the Almighty Power
> Hurl'd headlong flaming from th' Ethereal Sky
> With hideous ruin and combustion down
> To bottomless perdition, there to dwell

In Adamantine Chains and penal Fire,
Who durst defy th' Omnipotent to Arms,
Nine times the Space that measures Day and Night
To mortal men, he with his horrid crew
Lay vanquisht, rowling in the fiery Gulf
Confounded though immortal.[1]

By the time that you have finished reading this exhaustive run-on sentence, you are out of breath and have vicariously experienced Satan's fall from grace.

These stylistic elements produce an affective response that often escapes our conscious attention. Referring to visual language, Rudolph Arnheim observes, "In fact, these purely visual qualities of appearance are the most powerful of all. It is they that reach us most directly and deeply."[2] Consequently, production values often create a mood that reinforces manifest messages or themes. For example, manipulation of lighting, music, and screen space in horror films arouse intense feelings of terror in the audience. These stylistic elements also can convey independent messages (e.g., the glamour associated with screen violence).

EDITING

Editing refers to the selection and arrangement of information. Editing decisions send messages regarding the significance of content. For instance, Walter Cronkite's famous signature "And that's the way it is" suggests that the only events of the day worth considering were covered on the "CBS Evening News." However, a limited number of people in the newsroom have made editorial decisions, which then influences our national perception of what we need to know.

Editing decisions are often made for pragmatic reasons. For instance, it is not uncommon for newspaper articles to be edited to make room for additional advertising. A fundamental rule of media is: "Don't fall in love with your work." The filmmaker who becomes too attached to a project may find it painful to cut the movie to a length that audiences will willingly sit through and the studio will release.

Editing decisions often fall into the following categories.

Inclusion and Omission

Given the time and space limitations, critical decisions involve both what to include and what to omit from a media presentation. These decisions have been reached before the presentation reaches the public, so that the audience is not in a position to make a critical judgment about the selection process. The only way to become aware of this *preproduction editing process* is to survey different presentations and compare coverage.

Examine a variety of newspapers or compare the nightly news with unedited C-SPAN coverage of events. What has been included? What has been omitted?

Arrangement

But Cronkite not only promised to present all of the news; he also pledged to give us the news in order of *importance*. The arrangement of information makes a statement concerning the relative value of content. What appears first is, obviously, most essential. What appears last is of lesser importance.

Temporal and Spatial Manipulation

Media communicators are able to manipulate time and space as a means of establishing relationships between people, locations, and events. For instance, in *The Pawnbroker* (1965), director Sidney Lumet employed a series of flashbacks to reinforce the theme of the effect of the past on the present. The protagonist, Sol Nazerman, is a Jew whose life has been shattered by the World War II holocaust. Nazerman has survived by denying all feelings and shutting out the past. However, as the film progresses, Sol is increasingly unable to control the memory of his tragic experience. The flashbacks become more frequent and extended, so that eventually Sol is trapped entirely in the past. Nazerman must finally come to terms with the experience he has tried so hard to deny.

Younger audiences may find it difficult to comprehend the spatial and temporal inferences depicted on screen through editing. For instance, a formulaic establishment shot in television consists of a wide shot of a building. The camera zooms in, dissolving into an interior scene. The audience is expected to recognize the chronological ordering of events as well as the relationship between the external/internal space. However, Daniel Anderson found that four-year-olds found it particularly difficult to draw temporal inferences and that inferences of space were "of intermediate difficulty": "[Children's] failure to comprehend cinematic transitions cumulatively gives them a fragmented comprehension of lengthy televised narratives. With age and viewing experience, however, the child more rapidly and automatically makes the bridging inferences necessary to achieve connected comprehension."[3]

COLOR

Color is a visual element that has a powerful effect on audiences. Wallace Baldinger declares, "[Color] affects our waking moments, consciously or unconsciously, and also, when we are dreaming, our sleeping moments. It influences—sometimes to a frightening extent—our moods and states of

Sol Nazerman, the protagonist in *The Pawnbroker*. Stills from *The Pawnbroker* courtesy of REPUBLIC PIC-TURES CORPORATION

In *The Pawnbroker* (1965), director Sidney Lumet employs editing as a dramatic device to link Sol Nazerman (Rod Steiger) with his past life as a victim of the holocaust. By juxtaposing images on screen, the filmmaker is able to reinforce the theme of the effect of the past on the present. Stills from *The Pawnbroker* courtesy of REPUBLIC PICTURES CORPORATION

mind, soothing or amusing us, stimulating or revolting us, driving us even to madness."[4]

"I am feeling blue," "He is green with envy," and "This news is red hot" are examples of how colors are associated with, and inspire, particular emotions. In general, the affective nature of colors is as follows:

- Warm colors, like red, orange, and yellow, tend to make us feel happy, secure, positive, and intensely involved.
- Cool colors, like blue or violet, make us feel calm.
- Dead colors, like gray or black, make us feel sad, alone, or uncomfortable.

To illustrate, a group of preschool children from Reggio Emilia, Italy, were asked to describe four pictures of a tiger. These pictures were identical, with one exception: Each version was reproduced in a different color. The children described these pictures in very different terms, revealing the influence of color on perception:

- *Yellow tone.* "It's an enchanted and hot forest, full of sun like an enormous fire. The tiger is also on fire and ferocious."
- *Blue tone.* "It seems to be a dream. The tiger seems to be a fantasy. It's like a forest at the bottom of the sea. Or else a land far away in the clouds."
- *Green tone.* "It's like being immersed in a sea of tall grass. It's the most normal because it's green. It's a quiet forest. It makes me feel [sleepy]. You can almost smell the scent of mint."
- *Gray tone.* "It's frightening, scary, because it's dark like the night. There isn't even a ray of sun. It's a magical forest with strange noises. It's like being in a place that doesn't exist, like a ghost town."[5]

To complicate matters, all primary colors contain degrees of saturation, or shades, that touch different emotions. For instance, although blue is generally thought of as a cool color, a light blue is warm and enveloping.

The *context* in which colors appear can also determine its meaning. For instance, green is often associated with nature and health. However, in *The Wizard of Oz* (1939) the green complexion of the Wicked Witch of the West looks unnatural and evil.

Color contrast may also evoke particular moods. Warm colors and pleasing color contrasts generate a positive response in the audience. However, two contrasting colors (i.e., red and purple) are visually disturbing, producing a tension that is sensed by the audience.

Interior designers take the affective properties of color into consideration when they decorate business offices, hospitals, and schools. For instance, restaurants make generous use of the color orange, which has been found to stimulate the appetite.[6] Faber Birren describes the ideal color scheme for schools:

Carefully planned experiments by psychologists have well proven that modern principles of color applied to schools will improve in a striking way the scholastic performance of school students. . . . A well designed environment not only facilitates learning new subject matter, but reduces behavioral problems. . . .

It is good standard practice to use white for all ceilings, both for consistent appearance and to reflect an abundance of shadow-free illumination. . . . Libraries, rest rooms for teachers, school offices . . . could well be in the subdued tones of Pale Gold, Fern Green, Colonial Green, Smoky Blue.

Cafeterias should be in Peach, Coral, Rose, Pumpkin, Flamingo. All of which are cheerful and appetizing.

The gymnasiums, shops, manual training, and domestic arts rooms probably are best in luminous tones of Soft Yellow, Peach, Beige. Locker rooms and dressing rooms in Coral will reflect a flattering light.[7]

Cultural context may also play a role in the meaning of color. For instance, Herbert Zettl observes that pink and purple commonly are identified as feminine colors in Western culture: "If the essential quality of the product is softness (such as hand lotion or tissue paper), we expect the color of the product to express this quality. Desaturated pastel colors are the most appropriate to express softness. Strong spices, on the other hand, are best expressed by strong, highly saturated colors."[8]

Media communicators often select color schemes to reinforce messages. An example of thematic use of color occurs in *The Wizard of Oz*. The beginning of the film is shot in black and white, reflecting Dorothy's rather mundane existence in Kansas. After her home has been uprooted by a tornado, she opens the door to discover that she has landed in Oz. And what a world! At this point, the film is transformed into color. Oz is portrayed as a warm, enchanting place, thanks in large measure to the pastel color scheme. The set is dominated by delicate shades of gold, blue, and green.

This dramatic effect is in marked contrast to a subsequent scene in which Dorothy and her friends enter the forest on their way to meet the Wizard of Oz. The scene is dominated by dark colors, including the sky and costume of the Wicked Witch of the West. This color scheme contributes to the creation of a dark, foreboding world.

LIGHTING

Lighting can also affect the mood of a presentation. A brightly lit photograph evokes feelings of security and happiness. In contrast, a dark picture filled with shadow creates a mysterious atmosphere and arouses fear and apprehension. Dim lighting also can trigger a sense of powerlessness and loss of control, as the viewer must struggle to grasp a clear visual understanding of the environment.

Lighting can also be used for dramatic emphasis (see Figure 5.1). Those

Figure 5.1
Standard Lighting Techniques

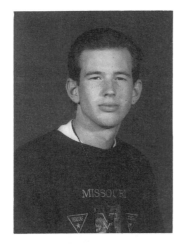

Key light: principal light source—directional spot

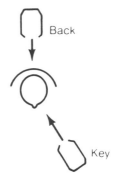

Back light: rims top and separates object from background—directional spot

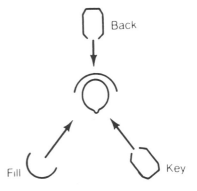

Fill light: slows shadow falloff—flood or soft (spread) spot

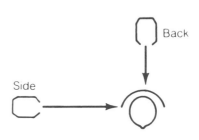

Side light: spotlight coming from the side (usually opposite key) directional

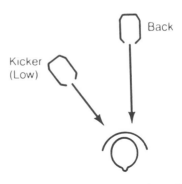

Kicker light: directional spot from back, off to one side, usually from below

Source: Herbert Zettl, *Sight, Sound, and Motion: Applied Media Aesthetics,* 2nd ed. © 1990 by Wadsworth, Inc. Reprinted by permission of the publisher. Photographs by Brandy Johnson

aspects of a page or screen that are "in the light" attract attention and are considered to be of prime importance. Flat lighting exposes everything equally and, as a result, makes the world of the photo appear dull and monotonous. Different gradations of light are more lively and create an interesting and exciting world.

The *source* of light is another device for dramatic effect and thematic expression. Rudolf Arnheim describes a painting by Rembrandt:

[The] light, again hidden, brightens the body of Christ, which is being taken down from the cross. The ceremony is performed in a dark world. But as the light falls from below, it heightens the limp body and imparts the majesty of life to the image of death. Thus the light source within the picture tells the story of the New Testament—that is, the story of the divine light transferred to the earth and ennobling it by its presence.[9]

In a two-dimensional form such as photography, film, or television, lighting can cast shadows that are as substantial as any of the "real" objects being depicted. Consequently, shadows can dramatize relationships between people or objects by literally connecting them. Shadow can also be employed as a narrative device. For instance, Alfred Hitchcock's *Dial M for Murder* (1954) is a thriller in which Tony (Ray Milland) devises an elaborate scheme to murder his wife Margot (Grace Kelly). However, Margo resists this attempt on her life and kills the intruder in self-defense. Tony then frames Margo so that it appears that Margo had killed the man in an act of premeditated murder. However, with the arrival of Inspector Hubbard (John Williams), Tony's plan begins to unravel. As Tony shows the inspector around the apartment, he opens the door to the kitchen, which has bars across the windows (out of sight of the camera). The light through the window casts a shadow of bars across the doorway, foreshadowing Tony's eventual incarceration.

Lighting has its own distinct code of meaning. David Goen has identified qualities suggested by bright lighting:

- Innocence
- Purity
- Religious faith
- Delicacy
- Delight
- Joy and goodwill
- Life
- Discovery

Goen presents some other messages associated with dim lighting:

- Death
- Evil
- Lack of communication
- Pollution
- A problem of religious faith
- Foreshadowing trouble
- Force and strength
- Something hidden[10]

The *quality* of light—hard or soft—comments on the objects depicted in the picture. Lighting can either flatter characters or produce a glare that accentuates their flaws, depending on the intention of the communicator. Goen explains:

Soft light creates minimal contrast: It seems to wrap around an object, enveloping and bathing it, obscuring defects and minimizing surface detail. It is light that doesn't seem to come from any particular direction. Soft light can reveal the subtleties of gradation of tone, that is, the transition of light to dark tones.

Hard light creates high contrast: Light that produces sharply defined outlines brings out any texture in the subject and can seem harsh and brutal. . . . High contrast lighting shows a much more limited range of tones. Your shadow under a direct light, such as a bare light bulb or the midday sun, is much more consistent in tone and is a fairly uniform darkness.[11]

In *Blade Runner* (1982), director Ridley Scott employs hard lighting to create a pessimistic world of the future. Due to man's abuses of the environment, the climate is dark and gloomy, and it is continually raining. From an aerial view, flames leap up at the camera from some unknown fuel source. It looks like hell. There is no natural source of light in the film, reflecting man's unnatural condition. The street is illuminated by hideous neon signs, accentuating the imperfections in the faces of the people who inhabit this world. A sense of hopelessness permeates the film, much of it due to the use of lighting.

SHAPE

The primary unit of visual communication is the dot. The dot is a reference point that attracts the eye of the viewer and delineates space on the page by defining the space around the dot. The dot is also the beginning of a more complex visual plan; a series of dots, when linked together, form a *line*.

A line suggests a sense of direction. For instance, in Western culture, a diagonal line running from the left-hand bottom corner to the right-hand top has an ascending quality, suggesting positive feelings of progress and enlightenment. Conversely, a diagonal from left-hand top to right-hand bottom has a descending quality, producing a sense of pessimism, forecasting danger, falling, and failure.

A line may also suggest messages based upon its "quality"—that is, the amount of pressure that the artist applies to the paper. A delicate line can suggest caution, refinement, or hesitancy. A bold line connotes conviction or passion.

A *shape* is created when a line comes back to itself and is distinct from any other shape or space. Each of the three basic shapes has its own distinctive character.

The Circle

The circle possesses a mystical quality. This shape has direction and is complete; as a result, it is associated with endlessness and wholeness. The circle represents the endless, cyclical conception of time (e.g., the zodiac and clock faces). In many cultures, the circle is a symbol of the sun and, as a result, stands for warmth and life.

However, while the circle joins people and things together, it also separates, setting objects apart (e.g., a "social circle"). In that respect, the circle represented protection in ancient civilizations. Stonehenge and Avebury are examples of ancient use of the circle to mark the boundary of a sacred area. Similarly, a Babylonian rite involved laying a circle of flour around a person's sickbed to keep demons away.

The circle was also used by magicians in medieval Europe as a way to delineate sacred space:

The circle is not only intended to keep something out but also to keep something in—the magical energy which the magicians will summon up from within themselves in the course of the ceremony. . . . If it were not for the circle the energy would flow off in all directions and be dissipated. The circle keeps it inside a small area and so concentrates it. The same motive lies behind the circle of people who link their hands at a seance.[12]

According to Eva C. Hangen, the circle image has a universal significance that can be traced through a variety of cultural artifacts:

- Circle of fire: monastic chastity, magic, inviolability
- Wedding ring: continuing devotion and love
- Four circles linked to a fifth, larger one: the words of wisdom
- In Mexico, two serpents entwined into a ring: time without end
- In China, a circle separating two serpents: the two Principles claiming the universe.[13]

The circle also has a friendly, nonthreatening quality. The roundness of cartoon characters like the Troll Dolls, the Seven Dwarfs, or the Pillsbury Dough Boy gives them a lovable quality, while villains like the Big Bad Wolf are often angular.

The Square

In contrast to the circle, the square is very much of this world. A square is precise, consisting of horizontal and vertical direction. College students asked to describe the square came up with the following properties:

• Fair	• Honest
• Precise	• Dull
• Dependable	• Ordinary
• Solid	• Boring
• Stable	• Lacking imagination
• Straight	

The Triangle

A triangle consists of radical angles. It is associated with motion, conflict, tension, abandonment, and power. The tension between the angles endows this shape with a mysterious power. The ancient Egyptians claimed that the triangular structure of the pyramids preserved the bodies and spirits of the kings buried within their walls: "The true pyramid was merely a representation in stone of the sun's rays shining to earth through a gap in the clouds, and by its possession the king could transport himself at will to the celestial kingdom of the sun god." [14]

Similarly, a modern legend claims that the Bermuda Triangle is the locus of some "sinister force field." [15] Since 1854, approximately 50 ships have been lost without trace in this area of water, formed by the southern tip of Florida, Puerto Rico, and Bermuda.

Hangen has identified the following meanings ascribed to triangles:

- In general symbolism: equality, democratic thinking, perfection
- In Christian symbolism: the Trinity
- When pictured with divergent rays: eternity, the rays indicative of glory and brightness
- In art and architecture, in designs with apex pointing upward: heaven
- In flower arrangement: triangular form lying on long side—repose; standing on the acute angle—stateliness and power; standing in an inclined position—dynamic force [16]

SCALE

Scale refers to the relative size between objects. Scale is a very basic means of conveying messages: The larger an object appears, the more important it seems. For instance, in response to the competition of television during the 1950s, film studios released a series of epic films, including *The Ten Commandments, Sparticus, Ben Hur,* and *Around the World in Eighty Days.* These movies took advantage of the medium's capacity for size to display grand landscapes. And by extension, film could present epic themes as well.

The relative size of objects on screen is also a device for thematic exploration. For example, in *King Kong* (1933), size is a metaphor for the complex relationship between humankind and nature. The scene that introduces King Kong juxtaposes the giant ape with the diminutive expedition party. Where Kong (or nature) is powerful, man is frail, weak, and ineffectual. Fay Wray is particularly vulnerable, a victim of her own feminine nature (as defined by 1930s American culture).

After King Kong has been captured, Fay Wray relaxes in her Manhattan apartment with her boyfriend. Within the sanctity of these walls, which are scaled to the dimensions of its human occupants, Fay is reassured by her boyfriend, "You're safe now, dear." But alas, Kong has escaped. At this moment the huge ape's face appears at her window, reducing the "normal" bedroom to dollhouse proportions. The ape's huge arm sweeps into the room, brushing off the feeble defenses of the boyfriend and snatching the heroine. Civilization is again exposed as a rather thin facade. Nature (including man's nature) looms large in all of us, despite our pretenses of control and civilization.

King Kong eventually seeks refuge atop the Empire State Building. Significantly, the initial shot shows a *tiny* Kong clinging to the mammoth structure. The audience discovers that relative size reflects relative position; that is, that Kong (and by extension, nature) ultimately has become a victim of civilization. Man has succeeded in denying his own nature, including the instinct, passion, and devotion that characterize King Kong. The ape gently lays Fay on a ledge before plunging to his death. Fay is left only with some vague, ambiguous emotions and her cultivated, uninspiring boyfriend.

RELATIVE POSITION

Where a character or object appears on the screen (or page) sends distinct messages to the audience. Objects appearing toward the front attract immediate attention, whereas things in the background are generally considered of secondary importance (see Figure 5.2). Zettl observes that people tend to pay more attention to objects situated on the *right* side of the screen:

In practice, this means that if you have a choice, you should place the more important event on the right side of the screen. In an interview show, for example, if you consider the guest more important than the host, place the guest on screen-right rather than the host. Most prominent hosts, however, do not want to be upstaged, and so they occupy the more conspicuous screen-right position.[17]

Human beings tend to look for balance, that is, an equal distribution around the center. Because of this natural predisposition to order, or

In *King Kong* (1933), relative size serves a metaphor for the complex relationship between man and nature. In this scene, King Kong overwhelms the powerless Fay Wray. © 1933 RKO Pictures, Inc. All Rights Reserved.

King Kong pays a housecall. Civilization is exposed as a feeble refuge against the forces of nature. © 1933 RKO Pictures, Inc. All Rights Reserved.

King Kong climbs the Empire State Building. Tiny Kong has ultimately become the victim of civilization. © 1933 RKO Pictures, Inc. All Rights Reserved.

Figure 5.2
Relative Position of a Character or an Object

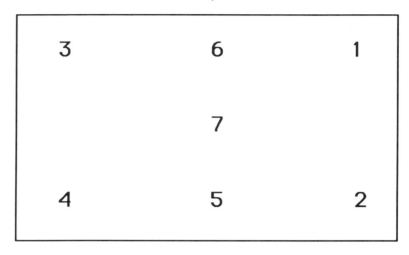

gestalt, the audience tends to feel unsettled if all the activity is placed on one corner of the screen. The media communicator can take advantage of the audience's natural desire for order to convey a particular message.

For instance, in the film *Camille* (1937), starring Greta Garbo and Robert Taylor, the two lovers are positioned so that their faces are equidistant from the center of the screen during the pivotal love scene. This use of space establishes a sense of romantic harmony and anticipates the climax of the love scene, when the lovers' lips meet in the exact center of the screen.

However, *imbalance* can also be an effective stylistic device, producing a sense of tension that the communicator can use to his or her advantage. Art educator Albert Henry Munsell observed, "[A]ny long duration of unbalance, either mental, physical or spiritual is an aggravated form of disease. . . . Yet short periods of unbalance are very stimulating in the effort which they produce to regain balance."[18]

In addition, the space *outside* of the screen is frequently employed in suspense and horror films. Because this space is beyond the visual control of the viewer, it represents the unknown and can be used to surprise or shock the audience. In Hitchcock's *Psycho* (1960), the tension in the famous shower scene stems from the attack from the other side of the shower curtain, beyond the sight of both Janet Leigh and the audience. *Aliens* (1986), directed by James Cameron, takes this principle a step further. In this film, the source of terror is hidden *within* the characters, waiting to emerge at the opportune moment.

The media communicator can employ relative position to comment on the relationship between objects and events. For instance, juxtaposing two apparently unrelated shots, a filmmaker can establish relationships be-

In *Camille* (1937), Marguerite (Greta Garbo) and Armand (Robert Taylor) are deep in reverie. The two lovers are positioned so that their faces are equidistant from the center of the screen. This use of space establishes a sense of romantic harmony and anticipates the climax of the love scene, when the lovers' lips meet in the exact center of the screen. © 1936 Turner Entertainment Co. All Rights Reserved.

tween people and events or create an entirely new meaning. To illustrate, in *Psycho,* Hitchcock juxtaposes shots of Norman Bates with the stuffed birds that he kept in his study. This positioning suggests that Norman was both predator and victim of his past.

MOVEMENT

As mentioned earlier, the principle of movement reduces the distance between illusion and reality and, in the process, also narrows the distinction between *media* and reality. Because movement appears so lifelike, people tend to assume that the events depicted are true and believe the messages that are conveyed on screen.

For instance, in 1895, during the infancy of film, the Lumiere brothers produced a film entitled *Arrival of a Train.* As the title suggests, this celebration of movement consisted of a train pulling into a station at an angle 45 degrees from a stationary camera. Reportedly, some members of the audience fled from the theater, terrified.

Motion includes not only direction but also *rhythm*—that is, the rate or pace at which movement occurs. A slow camera movement or the use of slow motion can be very restful and reassuring. This rhythm, which is commonly employed in sporting events and newscasts, also furnishes the viewer with the opportunity to study detail in a shot. The viewer has the opportunity to understand both what happened and how it occurred.

Many media communicators are sensitive to the psychological principles of movement. In Western cultures, left-to-right movements are more restful and natural than right-to-left movements, due in part to the way that members of these cultures are trained to read. As a result, Hollywood filmmakers employ left-to-right movements to establish a positive and harmonious atmosphere and right-to-left movements to intensify feelings of tension and disharmony.[19]

The media communicator must also respect the natural logic of movement. A car moving from left to right across the screen must continue this directional flow, or *vector,* unless the director deliberately shows the car changing directions. Otherwise, the audience feels disoriented and may disengage from the narrative.

The direction of movement has distinct dramatic properties:

- Movement directed toward the audience can either be friendly (e.g., an invitation or sign of intimacy), aggressive, or menacing.

- Movement directed away from the audience can signal either abandonment, retreat, avoidance, or resolution.

- Movement directed upward often is a positive sign (something going to heaven or, perhaps, outer space).

- Movement directed downward often is a negative sign (e.g., crashes or fights) or signaling defeat.

Arrival of a Train (1895), a documentary, was shot during the infancy of film at the turn of the century by the Lumiere brothers. Audiences found the movement of the film to be disturbingly lifelike. Photo courtesy of the Museum of Modern Art

David Puttnam's film *The Mission* (1987) illustrates the use of motion as a dramatic device. In an early scene, a young missionary (Jeremy Irons) struggles to scale a steep mountain in order to reach a South American Indian tribe. His climb is contrasted with the falling action of a majestic waterfall. Water cascades from the cliffs above, showering the young missionary as he ascends the mountain. This juxtaposition of movement reinforces thematic concerns that are examined throughout the film: While it is difficult for man to control his nature and ascend to heaven, it is all too easy to fall from grace.

POINT OF VIEW

Point of view refers to the source of information—who tells the story. Point of view has an impact on:

- How a story is told.
- What information is conveyed.
- The audience's orientation and sympathies.

Point of View in Print

Writers have a range of perspectives that they can employ. The *first-person point of view* presents the action as interpreted by one character. For instance, Melville's *Moby Dick* begins, "Call me Ishmael." The reader's understanding is colored by the predispositions and values of the first-person narrator.

The *second-person point of view* makes the reader the primary participant in the story. This perspective makes use of the pronoun "you."

The *third-person point of view* describes the activities and internal processes of one character. The third-person point of view commonly employs the pronouns "he" or "she." The author is privy to the thoughts and activities of this character but retains some critical distance and is therefore not accountable for the behavior of the character.

The *omniscient,* or all-knowing, *point of view* enables the author to enter the heads of any and all of the characters so that the reader has a comprehensive exposure to the people and events depicted in the work. This point of view is used frequently in journalism, which creates the appearance of objectivity in news coverage.

While writers generally try to maintain a consistent perspective, they may occasionally adopt a *panoramic point of view,* in which the perspective is constantly shifting. For instance, *Moby Dick* shifts to an omniscient narrator during the climactic whale-hunting scene. Although Ishmael is stationed in a different boat, the audience somehow overhears Captain Ahab's dialogue. Journalists may also adopt this panoramic point of view by incorporating their own (first-person) perspective into an "objective" third-person account through production techniques such as connotative words and images, space, and editing decisions.

Point of View in Film and Television

Filmmakers can create a literal first-person point of view by employing a *subjective camera technique*. For instance, in *The Lady in the Lake* (1947), the camera assumes the perspective of the protagonist, Philip Marlow (Robert Montgomery), so the audience sees the world through the eyes of the main character. The only time that Marlow actually appears in front of the camera occurs when his reflection briefly appears in a mirror. This first-person perspective was effective—for a brief period. However, without a focal character to watch, the film proved to be disorienting. For example, the fight scene degenerated into a burlesque, in which the camera spun around (as "Marlow" was hit). The effect was to make the audience dizzy.

Film and television also can approximate the first-person perspective through use of the *extreme close-up (XCU)* camera shot. This shot studies a character's reaction to events and people. Skilled actors such as Marlon Brando or William Hurt have the ability to subtly reveal their thoughts and emotions through a lifted eyebrow or a quick grimace.

Obviously, the second-person ("you") perspective is nearly impossible to achieve in television and film unless you actually appear on screen. However, TV and filmmakers will simulate the second-person perspective by selecting performers to represent you. For instance, the "man in the street" approach in advertising casts normal, everyday people who are supposed to reflect your concerns and interests. Audience participation programs such as game shows and some talk shows (e.g., Oprah Winfrey and Phil Donahue) enable "average" people *like* you to express their concerns. And some programs even encourage direct audience involvement by calling an 800 number.

The *medium shot (MS)* is analogous to the third-person perspective in print. This shot is more detached than the CU (close-up) yet furnishes detail related to the activity of a character. This shot often includes several actors interacting in the shot. Close-ups are used to record conversations (e.g., shooting over the shoulder from one participant to the other), but, as Zettl notes, this is consistent with a third-person perspective:

Are we now using the camera subjectively, with the viewer alternately associating with the person not seen on the screen? Not really. Even if the person on the screen (A) speaks directly to the camera, we know from the context that person A's target is not us, the viewers, but person B. . . . We are not in any way involved in the exchange . . . and are, therefore, not enticed to participate in the event or to assume person B's role.[20]

In *The Lady in the Lake* (1947), a battered Philip Marlow (Robert Montgomery) checks his wounds in the mirror with Audrey Totter (Adrienna Fronsett). In this experiment in subjective camera technique, the camera assumes the perspective of Marlow. This fleeting image in the mirror provides the only opportunity in the film for the audience to see Marlow. © 1946 Turner Entertainment Co. All Rights Reserved.

The simplest way to determine third-person perspective when several actors are on screen is to ask: Whose story is this? Another tipoff is: In screen romances, who is facing the camera when the couple embraces? The main character is receiving the attention from the other character. And the audience is vicariously in the position of the subordinate character.

Film and television use several different devices to simulate the omniscient perspective employed in print. The *extreme long shot (XLS)* takes in a wide expanse of visual information and often establishes the setting at the beginning of a scene. This shot provides broad context for the subsequent action. The viewer can see a great deal within the frame and thus has some latitude in terms of what to watch. In addition, the *omniscient camera* moves freely in time and space, enabling the director to focus on characters in different settings (unbeknown to the other characters). To illustrate, in the TV series "Columbo," only the omniscient camera (and by extension, the audience) has made the connections and knows "who done it"; the members of the cast are totally unenlightened. The narrative then becomes a matter of watching Columbo discover what the audience already knows.

Filmmakers also use the narrative strategy of *parallel action* to create the illusion that events on screen are occurring simultaneously. This can be accomplished by the editing technique of *cross-cutting* in which footage from different locations is juxtaposed to give the impression of events occurring at the same moment.

The omniscient point of view in television news contributes to the impression that the information contained in the broadcasts is unimpeachable. Technical innovations (e.g., satellite transmission and videotape) enable the television news industry to transmit reports instantaneously from around the globe. This omniscient perspective sends the message that the broadcast journalist is all-knowing as well.

ANGLE

Angle refers to the level at which the camera is shooting in relation to the subject. The choice of angle can affect the audience's attitude toward the subject. For instance, in the film *Annie* (1982), the camera height is stationed at the eye level of the children (rather than looking down at them from an "adult" perspective). This camera angle compels the audience to take the children seriously and treat them with respect.

A person filmed from a high angle looks small, weak, frightened, or vulnerable. In contrast, a person filmed from a low angle appears larger, more important, and powerful. Joseph V. Mascelli observes, "In the right dramatic context the angle can create a feeling of subjective fear in the audience especially if used in conjunction with a wide angle lens."[21]

A classic example in film is Leni Riefenstahl's *Triumph of the Will*

(1935), a documentary about Adolf Hitler's first party convention at Nuremberg. The camera was continually tilted upward at Hitler to create a sense of divine presence and inspire awe in the audience. The film successfully deified Hitler, to the degree that the Allies banned the film for several years after the end of the war.

CONNOTATION

Connotative Words

Connotation refers to the meaning associated with a word beyond its dictionary definition. The meaning of a connotative word is universally understood and agreed upon. The more that an audience brings to a message, the easier it is for the communicator to inform, persuade, entertain, and so on.

For instance, the word *house* simply describes a structure. However, *home* suggests a much richer meaning—a family gathered around the hearth, children playing video games, and the smells of dinner wafting in from the kitchen.

Journalists, advertisers, political consultants, and people involved in entertainment programming understand the power of language and therefore select words that have the greatest impact on the audience. Consequently, connotative terms can provide insight into the media communicator's attitude and intentions toward the subject.

Labels are connotative words or phrases that describe a person or group. Labels such as *oil-rich, archconservative, liberal,* and *special interests* possess connotative meanings that transcend their *denotative* (or dictionary) definition. Labels often appear with such frequency in the media that they no longer simply describe but in fact define the group. In the process, adjectives (e.g., *liberal*) are transformed into nouns (*a liberal*).

The appearance of labels in the media can disclose cultural values and attitudes. For instance, columnist Clarence Page observes that the label *warlord* became commonly associated with clan leader Mohammed Aidid in Somalia. He cites a Somalian refugee who observes, "A warlord is a clan leader you don't like."[22] Page adds:

In international news parlance, "strongman" and "warlord" are like "terrorist" and "freedom fighter," essentially the same creature, but on different sides of the political acceptability line. As my Somalian friend might say, a "terrorist" is a "freedom fighter" whose cause you don't like.

In some countries you call such a person a "leader" and you try to negotiate with him. But . . . we are going to show Aidid who is boss. He's in trouble now. We're already calling him names, like "warlord."[23]

This dramatic image of Adolf Hitler is taken from *Triumph of the Will* (1935), Leni Riefenstahl's documentary about Hitler's first party convention at Nuremberg. Riefenstahl's use of camera angle made Hitler appear powerful and imposing on screen. Photo courtesy of the Museum of Modern Art

In addition, the media can establish a new layer of connotative meaning to a term by consistently using a word within a particular context. For example, *cult* once was a neutral term that referred to ritual devotion to a god or saint. However, after repeatedly being used in connection with several well-publicized incidents (most recently the Branch Davidian massacre), *cult* has assumed a negative connotation, suggesting a group's involvement in sinister activities. James T. Richardson, religion professor at the University of Nevada at Reno, declares, "The indiscriminate use of the word 'cult' by the media helped to demonize [Branch Davidian leader David] Koresch and his followers and the demonization continues as other groups are characterized with that term."[24]

Media communicators may also employ *euphemisms* in an attempt to manipulate public response to media messages. Euphemisms are words that possess an innocuous connotation; these neutral terms are substituted for language that could offend the audience. To illustrate, politicians use euphemisms to avoid using the inflammatory word *tax*. The Reagan administration never raised taxes; instead, they collected increased "revenue enhancement." Similarly, President Bill Clinton used the term "contribution" to soften the impact of his call for higher taxes when he announced his economic package to the nation on February 17, 1993.

Connotative Image

Connotative images also possess universal associative properties. For example, Eva C. Hangen describes the characteristics generally associated with water:

- Invigorating qualities of the spirit; sanctifying power
- Refreshment
- Cleansing; purification
- Rebirth; regeneration[25]

Some images derive their meaning through context. For instance, fire can symbolize both protection and destruction. The precise connotative meaning becomes clear through the context of the presentation. Other connotative images have a cultural significance. For instance, the American flag is associated with the democratic traditions, principles, and history of the United States.

Astute media communicators use connotative images to their advantage. For example, on New Year's Day of 1988, President Ronald Reagan addressed the Soviet Union by televised satellite transmission. Stationed behind Reagan was the Nobel Peace Prize won by Theodore Roosevelt. This prop reinforced Reagan's message of freedom to the Soviet people.[26]

Image from Ronald Reagan's New Year's Greeting to the Soviet People, 1988. President Reagan's message of freedom to the people of the Soviet Union was underscored by the placement of a Nobel Peace Prize behind him on the mantle. Photo courtesy of Ronald Reagan Library

PERFORMANCE

A strong performance can transform a mediocre film, TV, or radio script into an electrifying experience. Audiences go to the movies to see their favorite actors, regardless of the film's subject matter. A Clint Eastwood fan doesn't care whether the actor plays a police sergeant, cowboy, or marine drill instructor. A fundamental media message is who the actor is and how he or she is uniquely able to move the audience.

Nonverbal Performance Skills

Nonverbal performance skills constitute a subtle yet powerful performance element. Communications scholars estimate that nonverbal communication comprises 65 percent of all communication between people.[27] Mahima Ranjan Kundu defines nonverbal communication skills as "all the gestures, expressions, postures, etc. that are used in the process of communication."[28] The clear and persuasive nature of nonverbal communication is epitomized in the performance of silent film stars like Charlie Chaplin, whose walk, gestures, and facial expressions were a central part of his familiar endearing persona—the Little Tramp.

Tripp Frohlichstein is a media relations consultant who has identified a series of nonverbal performance elements to be considered when making a media presentation:

- *Eye contact.* Good eye contact is important in convincing the viewer of your credibility. Wandering eyes may represent deceit, confusion, or lack of sincerity. When on television, maintain eye contact with the reporter asking the questions. If you are on a talk show, talk primarily to the host and do not look at the camera. If someone else is talking, look at them to show your interest. Even with a print reporter or a radio host, maintain solid eye contact. Some reporters assume that shifty eyes signal shifty thoughts.

- *Gestures.* Use gestures when appropriate and natural. Since we think in pictures, gestures can help augment points being addressed. . . . Do not use broad sweeping gestures for TV because the camera sees only a limited area. (When standing, keep your hands at your side except when gesturing.)

- *Open face.* Keep your eyebrows up and smile when appropriate. This helps you better convey your pride, as well as intensity. When the eyebrows are flat, so are your voice and feelings. When your eyebrows are down, so is the interview and you may be perceived as angry or negative.

- *Nodding.* Don't nod in agreement if the interviewer is reciting a litany of your company's negatives. You may simply be saying, "I'm listening," but this could be perceived by the audience as agreeing [with those negatives].

- *Glasses.* Avoid shiny metal or chrome frames which will catch and reflect the light. Thin tortoise shell frames are best. Neutral shades that blend with your hair and skin tone are recommended. Make sure they fit correctly so you are not always pushing them up on your nose.

Silent film star Charlie Chaplin developed his distinctive film persona, the Little Tramp, through nonverbal performance skills, such as costume, mannerisms, gestures, and walk. Photo courtesy of the Museum of Modern Art

● *Mannerisms.*

Do	Don't
—Sit up straight	—Fold your arms
—Lean forward	—Make fists
—Keep your hands folded in your lap or on the arm of your chair when not talking	—Dig fingers into arms of chair
	—Pick cuticles
	—Tap fingers
—Keep your head perpendicular to your shoulders to add to your authority	—Fiddle with pencils
	—Jiggle legs
—Pay attention to the person who is talking (mentally and visually)	—Slouch
	—Swivel back and forth on a swivel chair
—Keep an open face and smile when appropriate	—Smoke
—Sit with legs together or crossed at the knee	

In addition to the above rules, women have several additional guidelines to observe:

Do	Don't
—May sit with legs crossed at the ankles	—Cross your legs at all if your skirt is short
	—Coyly tilt your head
	—Have purse visible
	—Play with earrings or hair

Costume and *makeup* are other important ingredients in performance. Frolichstein includes the following tips for men:

—Blues, tans and grays are best

—Blue or pastel shirts

—Appear in outfit that explains your profession (doctors, construction, business-men, etc.)

—Polished shoes

—Don't wear black, brown, yellow-reds, red-oranges or loud, clashing colors (causes bleeding and blurring on home screen)

—Don't wear sunglasses outside or photogray glasses inside (makes you look like a criminal)

—Accept make-up if offered

In addition to the rules cited above, women should observe the following guidelines:

—Wear closed-toe shoes

—Avoid sexy or frilly outfits

—Avoid clunky or glittering jewelry (distracting)

—Red, grays, and blues are acceptable colors for women

—Women shouldn't wear too much lipstick. The same color as tongue looks natural. Women should get a pancake make-up as close to skin tone as possible, cheating toward a slightly darker shade if you can't get an exact match. Test it on the back of your hand. . . . Put on exposed areas, including back of hands.[29]

These nonverbal performance elements are not limited to media entertainment. Dr. Brian Mullen conducted a study to determine whether there is a link between newscasters' facial expressions and viewers' voting behavior. Mullen monitored the nonverbal performances of the network anchormen (with the sound off) during the week prior to the 1984 presidential election. He then rated the anchors' facial expressions as they referred to presidential candidates Ronald Reagan and Walter Mondale.

Mullen next surveyed a cross section of Americans to determine their choice of candidate and the television newscaster they watched most. Mullen discovered the following: (1) Peter Jennings of ABC consistently appeared more positive when referring to Ronald Reagan; and (2) the voters who regularly watched Jennings were more likely than others to vote for Reagan. Mullen hastened to qualify the results of his study. The methodology was admittedly subjective (after all, what *is* a positive expression?). And it remains unclear whether Jennings actually influenced his audience or merely attracted viewers already predisposed to support Reagan.

However, Mullen concluded that the results "are consistent with a link between newscasters' facial expressions and viewers' voting behaviors."[30] The study suggests that performance influences the public, even in the "objective" world of broadcast journalism. Jennings was undoubtedly unaware that he exhibited positive behaviors when he spoke of Reagan; however, the message was clear to the public. Audiences look to media figures for approval and disapproval on a wide variety of topics. Consequently, media communicators should be aware that even subtle nuances can have a powerful influence on the public.

Verbal Performance Skills

Media communicators must also develop their *verbal performance skills*. When used effectively, a performer's voice quality and delivery reinforce the manifest message. Frohlichstein points out the following aspects of effective verbal performance:

- *Volume.* "Do not use loudness to make a point—you'll lose warmth. Too soft a voice makes you hard to hear and the listener loses the message. . . . Also, low volume lacks emotional commitment."

- *Tone.* Tone refers to the quality or character of sound. A deep tone suggests authority, power, and confidence. Frolichstein observes, "Exercise your voice before doing interviews. Use varying pitch and modulation."
- *Clarity.* People must understand the words you are saying. "Nuance" can become "new ants."
- *Speed.* "Too fast and listeners can't follow you. Too slow and you become ponderous and boring."
- *Pacing.* "Vary it to keep listener interest."
- *Feelings.* "Vital that your voice reflect your interest and concern with the topic." [31]

But beyond all of the technical reasons behind an actor's success, there is also an intangible quality to performance. Marilyn Monroe enjoyed a special relationship with the camera. The camera seemed almost to look inside Marilyn Monroe, to reveal her vulnerable side to the audience. Marilyn Monroe did indeed look larger than life on the silver screen, which is one reason why Monroe has retained her following long after her death.

SOUND

Sound sends very subtle messages, by either enhancing or altering moods. Sound occurs in three different forms in media productions: dialogue, music, and background sound.

Dialogue

Dialogue is a primary vehicle for media messages. However, it is not always easy to follow dialogue when it is performed on radio, film, and television. Dialogue is written material that is intended to *sound* like conversation. A script may contain a great deal of information and complex layers of meaning. This material is presented very rapidly, like speech, so that the audience member easily can confuse the message being delivered.

A good example of dialogue can be found in Ted Tally's screenplay of Thomas Harris's novel *The Silence of the Lambs* (1991). Consider the first encounter between FBI candidate Clarice Starling and the sophisticated, nefarious Dr. Hannibal "The Cannibal" Lecter:

DR. LECTER:
    You're so ambitious, aren't you . . . ? You know what you look like to me, with your good bag and your cheap shoes? You look like a rube. A well-scrubbed, hustling rube with a little taste. . . . Good nutrition has given you

some length of bone, but you're not more than one generation from poor white trash, are you—Agent Starling . . . ? That accent you've tried so desperately to shed—pure West Virginia. What is your father, dear? Is he a coal miner? Does he stink of the lamp?

His every word strikes her like a small, precise dart.

DR. LECTER (cont.):
And oh, how quickly the boys found you! All those tedious, sticky fumblings, in the back seats of cars, while you could only dream of getting out. Getting anywhere, yes? Getting all the way to the F . . . B . . . I.

CLARICE (shaken):
You see a lot, Dr. Lecter. But are you strong enough to point that high-powered perception at yourself? How about it . . . ? Look at yourself and write down the truth. (She slams the tray back at him.) Or maybe you're afraid to.

DR. LECTER:
You're a tough one, aren't you?

CLARICE:
Reasonably so. Yes.

DR. LECTER:
And you'd hate to think you were common. My, wouldn't that sting! Well you're far from common, Clarice Starling. All you have is the fear of it. (pause) Now please excuse me. Good day.[32]

A great deal has occurred in this very brief bit of dialogue. Although Clarice is conducting the interview, it is clear that Dr. Lecter is very much in control. Clarice (and the audience) learns that Dr. Lecter is far from a common criminal. He is extraordinarily charming, intelligent, and perceptive—dangerous qualities when combined with Lecter's vicious nature.

We also learn about Clarice in this sequence. Dr. Lecter has zeroed in on her background and motivation for pursuing a career in the FBI. She (with good reason) feels violated, as Lecter coldheartedly exposes her fears and insecurities. However, Clarice fights back, showing Lecter (and us as well) that she is indeed tough enough to withstand the trials awaiting her in the remainder of the film.

During this scene, a strange, complex relationship forms between Starling and Dr. Lecter. Clarice is fascinated by Lecter's certainty about the world, his powers of perception, and even the evil that drives him. Lecter has been testing the novice FBI agent. However, Clarice has successfully withstood his attempt to intimidate her and destroy her resolve. By the end of the conversation, Lecter acknowledges that Clarice is "far from common." This admission, however, does not prevent him from continuing to play games with Agent Starling, a challenge that she recognizes and accepts.

Music

Music has a powerful influence on individuals. It can enhance our moods or distract us from our immediate concerns. Indeed, some companies install Muzak in their offices to improve productivity in the office.

In film and television, music is more than merely background for the visuals. Music can work in conjunction with the visuals, to "punctuate" or emphasize the major points of the presentation. Music elicits an affective response in the audience, arousing feelings of excitement, tension, drama, or romance in the audience that can be used to reinforce media messages.

Music can also be employed as a narrative device. Often a tune, rhythm, or chord will recur throughout a program to provide thematic continuity or foreshadow an upcoming event. The theme from *Jaws,* for instance, always signaled the approach of the killer shark well before he attacked.

Music can prepare the audience for a narrative shift, signaling a transition between scenes. At the same time, music can be used to provide narrative continuity. For instance, in *The Graduate* (1967), a song ("April Come She Will" by Simon and Garfunkel) plays over a series of seemingly unconnected visuals of Ben Braddock lounging by the pool, lying in his bed, and having an affair with Mrs. Robinson. As the song suggests, the young man is drifting, unsure about his future and even more unsure about how to take control of his life.

In addition, music can function as a convention, sending subtle messages to the audience. For instance, theme music for the evening news often simulates the rhythm of teletypes. In this case, the musical score helps to establish the seriousness and legitimacy of the news operation.

Background Sound

Natural sound consists of the noises that normally occur within a given setting (e.g., crowd noise at a baseball game). Frequently, natural sound is added to the audio tracks of media presentations to add a feeling of verisimilitude. A beach scene would be noticeably artificial if we did not hear the waves hitting the shore or the squeal of seagulls. Without this background noise, the message would be one of *omission*—that what we are watching, in fact, is a movie and not real life.

Sound effects consist of sounds that are added to broadcast presentations for dramatic emphasis. For instance, radio serials from the 1940s made generous use of sound effects to advance the plot. Doors closing, horses galloping, and spurs jingling also made the dramas seem more real. Sound effects are also used in film and television. Much of the dramatic thrust of martial arts movies is created during the postproduction process, when the action is "sweetened" by appropriate sound effects, created by such techniques as thumping rugs and tearing sheets.

The synthesizer has emerged as an important technological innovation that produces a range of sound effects—from the most mundane to the eerie and supernatural.

SUMMARY

Mindful of the principle of economy, the skillful media communicator uses style not merely as ornamentation but as a means of reinforcing messages. Production values subtly affect how the audience responds to media content.

Media communicators often make conscious decisions with regard to production values such as color, lighting, and angle. However, at other times they may make an intuitive choice—because it "feels right." In this case, media communicators instinctively select the color scheme or camera angle that best fits the intended mood of the presentation. Consequently, even if communicators do not articulate the reasons behind their selections, they nevertheless are making decisions based on the affective properties of production values.

A sensitivity to production elements is therefore a useful way to approach the interpretation of media messages.

Keys to Interpreting Media Messages: Production Values

Production values can be broken down into the following elements as a means of providing insight into media messages:

A. Editing
B. Color
C. Lighting
D. Shape
E. Scale
F. Relative position
G. Movement
H. Point of view
 I. Angle
J. Connotation
   1. *Words*
   2. *Image*
K. Performance
L. Sound
   1. *Music*
   2. *Dialogue*
   3. *Background sound*

NOTES

1. John Milton, *Paradise Lost, Paradise Regained, and Samson Agonistes* (Garden City, NY: Doubleday, 1969), 20.

2. Rudolf Arnheim, *Art and Visual Perception* (Berkeley: University of California Press, 1974), 97.

3. Daniel R. Anderson, "Online Cognitive Processing of Television," in *Psychological Processes and Advertising Effects,* ed. Linda F. Alwitt and Andrew A. Mitchell (Hillsdale, NJ: Lawrence Erlbaum Associates, 1985), 191.

4. Wallace Baldinger, *The Visual Arts* (Fort Worth, TX: Holt, Rinehart and Winston, 1960), 15.

5. George Forman, "Viewer's Guide to 'The Hundred Languages of Children' " (University of Massachusetts at Amherst, 1991, mimeographed).

6. NBC Radio, June 19, 1992.

7. Faber Birren, *Light, Color, and Environment* (New York: Van Nostrand Reinhold, 1982), 81–82.

8. Herbert Zettl, *Sight, Sound, and Motion: Applied Media Aesthetics* (Belmont, CA: Wadsworth, 1990), 77.

9. Arnheim, *Visual Perception,* 324.

10. David Goen, "Attaining Visual Literacy: How Pictures Function as Signs and Symbols" (master's thesis, Webster University, 1991), 54–55.

11. Ibid., 51–52.

12. Richard Cavendish, ed., *Man, Myth, and Magic* (Wichita, KS: McCormick-Armstrong, 1962), s.v. *circle.*

13. Eva C. Hangen, *Symbols: Our Universal Language* (Wichita, KS: McCormick-Armstrong, 1962), 72.

14. Cavendish, *Man, Myth, and Magic,* s.v. *pyramid.*

15. Ibid.

16. Hangen, *Symbols,* 255–56.

17. Zettl, *Sight, Sound, and Motion,* 112.

18. Albert Henry Munsell, *A Grammar of Color* (New York: Van Nostrand Reinhold, 1969), 14.

19. Richard L. Stromgren and Martin F. Norden, *Movies: A Language in Light* (Englewood Cliffs, NJ: Prentice-Hall, 1984), 49.

20. Zettl, *Sight, Sound, and Motion,* 225.

21. Joseph V. Mascelli, *The Five C's of Cinematography* (Hollywood, CA: Cine/Graphic, 1965), 115.

22. Clarence Page, "What's A 'Warlord'? Any Leader We Dislike," *St. Louis Post-Dispatch,* August 24, 1993, B7.

23. Ibid.

24. Kathryn Rogers, "Scholars Call 'Cult' a Dangerous Term," *St. Louis Post-Dispatch,* May 2, 1993, B1.

25. Hangen, *Symbols,* 266–67.

26. Joel Brinkley, "Reagan's Greetings, in Soviet Exchange, Have a Barbed Edge," *New York Times,* January 2, 1988, A1, A6.

27. Mahima Ranjan Kundu, "Visual Literacy: Teaching Non-Verbal Communication Through Television," *Educational Technology* 16 (August 1976): 31.

28. Ibid.

29. Tripp Frohlichstein, *Media Training Handbook* (St. Louis: MediaMasters, 1991), 31–37.

30. Ruth Moss, "Candidate Camera," *Psychology Today*, December 1986, 20.

31. Frohlichstein, *Media Training Handbook*, 31.

32. *The Silence of the Lambs*. Screenplay by Ted Tally based on the novel by Thomas Harris. 4th Draft. October 6, 1989.

Keys to Interpreting Media Messages

These pages may be used as a reference for media literacy analysis.

I. Process (Chapter 2)
   A. Function
      1. What is the purpose behind the production?
      2. Does the media communicator want you to act in a particular way as a result of receiving the information?
   B. Comparative media
      1. What are the medium's distinctive characteristics?
      2. In what ways does the choice of medium affect:
         a) The content of the message?
         b) The presentation of information?
         c) The role/choice/effectiveness of the media communicator?
         d) The ways in which the audience receives the information?
   C. Media communicator
      1. Who is responsible for creating the media production?
      2. What are the demographic characteristics of the media communicator(s)?
      3. How do these characteristics affect the content and outlook of the media production?
   D. Audience
      1. For whom is the media presentation produced?
      2. Is there more than one intended audience?
      3. What values, experiences, and perspectives are shared by the audience?
      4. How do the experiences and perspectives of the *individual* audience member affect his or her interpretation of the presentation?
      5. How does the choice of audience influence the *strategy, style*, and *content* of the media presentation?
      6. Do the strategy, style, and content provide insight into the intended audience(s)?

II. Context (Chapter 3)
   A. Historical context
      1. In what ways has the media presentation been influenced by the events of the day?
         a) When was this media production first presented?
         b) What prior events led to the climate in which this media presentation was produced?
         c) How did people react to the production when it was first presented? Why?
            (1) How do people react to the production today?
            (2) How do you account for any differences in reaction?
         d) In what ways does an understanding of the historical context provide insight into the media messages contained in the presentation?
      2. What does the media production tell us about the period in which it was produced?

3. What can be learned about shifts in cultural attitudes and concerns by tracing the evolution of a particular medium, genre, or presentation?

B. Cultural context

1. *Media and popular culture:* In what ways does the media presentation reflect, reinforce, inculcate, or shape cultural:

   a) Attitudes
   b) Values
   c) Behaviors
   d) Preoccupations
   e) Myths

2. *Worldview:* What kind of world is depicted in the media presentation?

   a) What culture or cultures populate this world?
      (1) What kinds of people populate this world?
      (2) What is the ideology of this culture?
   b) What do we know about the people who populate this world?
      (1) Are characters presented in a stereotypical manner?
      (2) What does this tell us about the cultural stereotype of this group?
   c) Does this world present an optimistic or pessimistic view of life?
      (1) Are the characters in the presentation happy?
      (2) Do the characters have a *chance* to be happy?
   d) Are people in control of their own destinies?
      (1) Is there a supernatural presence in this world?
      (2) Are the characters under the influence of other people?
   e) What does it mean to be a success in this world?
      (1) How does a person succeed in this world?
      (2) What kinds of behavior are rewarded in this world?
   f) What is the *hierarchy of values* that appears in this world?
      (1) What embedded values can be found in the production?
      (2) What values are embodied in the characters?
      (3) What values prevail through the resolution?

C. Structure

1. What are the ownership patterns within the media industry? How do these ownership patterns affect media content?

   a) What are the ownership patterns within the media industry?
   b) What are the ownership patterns within the particular media system you are examining (e.g., television, film, radio)?
   c) Who owns the production company that has produced the presentation you are examining (e.g., television station, newspaper, film company)?

2. How is the media industry regulated? How does government regulation affect media messages?

3. What is the internal structure of the media organization responsible for producing the media presentation? How does this internal structure influence content?

   a) What are the resources of the production company?

b) What is the organizational framework of the production company?

c) What is the process of decision making in the production company?

III. Framework (Chapter 4)

  A. Introduction

    1. What does the title of the presentation signify?

    2. What events constitute the introduction of the media presentation?

    3. Does the introduction foreshadow events and themes in the body of the production?

  B. Plot

    1. *Explicit content*

      a) What are the significant events in the story?

      b) What is the primary story or plot?

      c) What are the subplots, if any?

    2. *Affective response*

      a) How does the media communicator want you to be feeling at particular points in the plot?

        (1) Why does the media communicator want you to be feeling this way?

        (2) Is the media communicator successful in eliciting this intended emotional response?

      b) Do your affective responses provide insight into media messages? Explain.

      c) Do your affective responses provide insight into your personal belief system? Explain.

    3. *Implicit content*

      a) What is the relationship between the significant events in the story?

      b) What are the characters' motivations for their actions?

      c) Are the consequences to specific behaviors defined?

    4. *Character development*

      a) Have the major characters changed as a result of the events in the story? How? Why?

      b) What have the characters learned as a result of their experience?

  C. Genre

    1. Does the presentation belong to any recognizable genre?

    2. Is there a predictable formula for the genre?

      a) Formulaic function

      b) Formulaic plot

      c) Stock characters

      d) Formulaic structure

      e) Conventions

        (1) Storyline

        (2) Setting

        (3) Trappings

3. What does this genre suggest about:
    a) Cultural attitudes and values?
    b) Cultural preoccupations?
    c) Cultural myths?
    d) Worldview?
4. Can you trace the evolution of this genre?
    a) Have there been shifts in the genre over time?
    b) What do these shifts in genre reveal about changes in the culture?
 D. Logical conclusion
    1. Does the conclusion of the presentation follow logically from the established premise, characters, and worldview?
    2. If not, how *should* the presentation have ended, given the established premise, characters, and worldview?
    3. How would you have *preferred* for the story to end? Why?
IV. Production Values (Chapter 5)
  A. Editing
  B. Color
  C. Lighting
  D. Shape
  E. Scale
  F. Relative position
  G. Movement
  H. Point of view
  I. Angle
  J. Connotation
    1. *Words*
    2. *Image*
  K. Performance
  L. Sound
    1. *Music*
    2. *Dialogue*
    3. *Background sound*

- What are the *manifest* media messages in the program?
- What *latent* messages were you able to identify?

PART II

MEDIA FORMATS

CHAPTER 6

PRINT JOURNALISM

PROCESS

Function

American newspapers serve a variety of manifest functions:

Information. American newspapers are essential to the public's ability to make informed decisions. The Society of Professional Journalists' Code of Ethics states:

The public's right to know of events of public importance and interest is the overriding mission of the mass media. The purpose of distributing news and enlightened opinion is to serve the general welfare.

Journalists who use their professional status as representatives of the public for selfish or other unworthy motives violate a high trust.[1]

Newspapers also provide vital information about the reader's local community. Weather forecasts, television listings, and calendars of events help the individual function on an everyday basis. Birth announcements, weddings, and obituaries keep the reader informed about significant rites of passage.

Persuasion. The press puts events in perspective, serves as a forum for debate, and presents a point of view for the consideration of its readers. Journalists take this charge seriously. To illustrate, the *St. Louis Post-Dispatch* carries an editorial platform authored by Joseph Pulitzer in 1907 that clearly defines this function:

I know that my retirement will make no difference in its cardinal principles, that it will always fight for progress and reform, never tolerate injustice or corruption, always fight demagogues of all parties, never belong to any party, always oppose privileged classes and public plunderers, never lack sympathy with the poor, always remain devoted to the public welfare, never be satisfied with merely printing news, always be drastically independent, never be afraid to attack wrong, whether by predatory plutocracy or predatory poverty.[2]

Ideally, this persuasive function is confined to the editorial section of the paper. However, as we will discuss in this chapter, journalists can subtly influence public opinion throughout the paper through such production elements as word choice, editing decisions, and story placement.

Disclosure. The American press has played a critical role in detecting injustices and abuses within the system. Watergate is a prime example; investigative reporters Bob Woodward and Carl Bernstein of the *Washington Post* uncovered a story leading to criminal convictions, a presidential resignation, and legislative reforms.

Entertainment. In an effort to attract the largest possible audience, newspapers contain an increasing amount of *soft news* at the expense of *hard news* coverage. Hard news stories deal with topical events and issues that have an impact on the lives of the readers. The principal function of hard news is to inform. This information provides readers with a vital connection to the nation and the world.

Soft news is not necessarily timely, has minimal societal consequence, and is primarily designed to entertain. For instance, the "Lifestyle" section contains soft features, ranging from advice columns to horoscopes. However, soft news can be found in the news section of the paper as well. Further, newspapers are now pressured to present news as entertainment, which affects both the presentation and content of the paper.

In addition, newspapers fulfill several latent functions as well.

Agenda setting. Even if newspapers don't tell us what to think, they do tell us what to think about. To illustrate, newspapers may take different editorial positions on issues such as national health care or legalized abortion. However, there is no doubt that media coverage brings these issues to the attention of the public as matters of importance.

Profit. As a market-driven industry, American newspapers are geared to produce a profit. These market considerations have an impact on the amount of news coverage contained in American newspapers. Advertising typically accounts for about 60 percent of newspaper space.[3] (See Figure 6.1.) Another 16 percent of space is devoted to public relations (PR)–oriented content, including public relations releases, story memos, or suggestions that come from corporations. Newspapers also routinely cover *staged events* (e.g., speeches and ribbon-cutting ceremonies that primarily serve the interests of the organizations sponsoring the events). Martin A. Lee and Norman Soloman explain:

Figure 6.1
Distribution of Newspaper Space

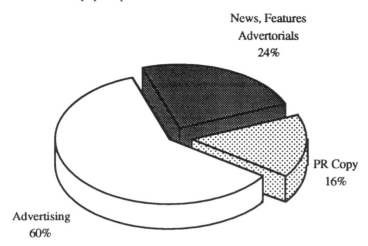

News, Features
Advertorials
24%

PR Copy
16%

Advertising
60%

PR copy from real estate agents, developers and industrial firms typically masquerades as authentic news stories. It's not unusual for articles about fashion, for example, to be lifted straight from press releases by designers and fashion shows. Food editors rely heavily on food company blurbs for recipes and stories. Sections on home improvement, travel, and entertainment are likewise filled with PR-related fluff.[4]

Even more disturbing, economic pressures may have a bearing on the *nature* of news coverage as well. Lee and Soloman argue that advertisers, who account for 75 percent of newspapers' revenue, can exercise an enormous influence on news content:

The *New York Times* news department, which prides itself on independent journalism, has submitted to pressure from advertisers. The automobile industry is a major advertiser in the *Times,* and consequently *Times* coverage of auto safety and pollution has been skewed. According to a *Times* staffer, the paper of record ran stories "more or less put together by the advertisers" as the industry lobbied for looser safety standards in the 1970s. *Times* publisher and CEO Arthur Sulzberger admitted that he leaned on his editors to present the auto industry's position because it "would affect advertising."[5]

Even *editorial content* is affected by the profit function. (Editorial content refers to news content: everything in the newspaper that is not paid space.) Companies often purchase *advertorials* in newspapers—that is, ads that appear in the form of editorial content. Very little effort is made to distinguish these advertorials from other stories featured in the newspaper. The advertorial either conceals the disclaimer "advertisement" within the presentation or simply includes the name of the product in small print.

To illustrate, 'Teen Magazine sends out a flier to potential clients promoting its advertorial service:

'TEEN's advertorial services are top-notch! Last year we produced 150 advertorial pages . . . that's more advertorial pages than any other national magazine. 'TEEN has its own advertorial staff: three editors whose only responsibility is the creation and production of advertorial pages. We work with both client and agency from preliminary layouts through the day of the shoot to the final selection of film, copy, and color corrections.

Why Advertorials Will Work For You

- 'TEEN advertorials are designed to look like our editorial pages. Our editors know the looks our reader's like and the advertorial pages are presented in that style.

- The advertorials can take your (advertising) campaign one step further by providing additional information that is not provided in your advertisement. Additionally, they dramatically increase the frequency of your advertising message.

- The advertorials receive extremely high notation. In the May issue, the Malibu U advertorial received the second highest starch notation of any advertisement in the magazine. 85% noted and 82% associated.[6]

As an example, an "article" in the November 1993 'Teen Magazine entitled "Having a Bad Hair Day?" reports that the residue from ordinary shampoos can be the culprit behind those "Frustrating Bad Hair Days." This article concludes, "But what seems like an endless cycle doesn't have to be. One shampoo clears out 70% of residue the very first time you use it and keeps on working to get rid of all of it! Neutrogena."[7]

The product name "Neutrogena" appears inconspicuously on the bottom right-hand portion of the page, indicating that the article is, in fact, an advertisement.

Lee and Soloman declare that multinational companies often place advertorials in the guise of editorials in order "to promote [their] politics and benevolent image—and to attack anything that sullies this image."[8] For instance, an advertorial appeared in the July 26, 1993, Time Magazine defending Mobil Oil's large profit margin: "Obviously, we don't hold on to all of that, what with our employees and shareholders and the vendors we do business with deserving their share of the wealth. So, the money moves around in what some call the 'ripple effect.' "[9] The editorial's use of the indefinite pronoun we makes it clear that the voice behind the advertorial is not Time Magazine but rather the Mobil Corporation. The company logo appears at the bottom of the page, from which the audience must infer that this is an advertisement.

Audience

The newspaper audience is relatively anonymous since the reader is physically removed from the writer. However, research provides a clear portrait of the regular newspaper reader. Although newspapers are readily available, the audience is selective; as was mentioned earlier, reading presupposes a certain level of education. Clearly, the newspaper has emerged as an elite medium. The typical audience member is older, well educated, and of relatively high income.[10] This demographic pattern cuts across racial and gender lines. Older, well-educated, and affluent African Americans read newspapers even more faithfully than their white counterparts. And working women are more likely to read newspapers than women who do not work outside of the home.[11]

People tend to read the newspaper for the following reasons:

- Immediacy and thoroughness
- Local awareness and utility
- Habit
- Entertainment
- Social extension or gossip.[12]

Although almost all readers (92 percent) leaf through the entire newspaper, people generally read only about one fifth of the paper. At the same time, over 50 percent turn to a newspaper two or more times in a given 24-hour period. This would suggest that the newspaper serves as a reference at various times of the day (i.e., consulting the paper for sales or movie schedules).[13]

Habit plays a large role in newspaper consumption. Content preferences among readers remain remarkably stable over time. People read the paper according to an established order (e.g., the sports section first, then the front page). Although some sections of the paper may be of interest to a relatively small number of people, those readers maintain a fierce loyalty to that feature of the paper.

American daily newspaper consumption is in decline, due principally to young people's indifference to the medium. Young people often regard newspapers as:

- An "old people's habit . . . something you see old people do while waiting for a bus."
- Speaking for the status quo and against societal change
- Being cold and impersonal
- As a middle-aged medium (produced by older adults for an older audience).[14]

However, role modeling can be a factor in determining newspaper consumption patterns among young people. College students are far more likely to read the paper if their parents routinely read newspapers. In fact, students are likely to read the paper at the same time of day and in the same location as their parents.[15] This would suggest that one way for parents to encourage their offspring to read the newspaper is simply to read the paper themselves.

CONTEXT

Historical Context

One way to identify issues of current interest and importance is by conducting a *content analysis* of newspaper coverage. As discussed in Chapter 3, content analysis employs quantitative techniques to look for patterns, messages, symbols, language, art forms, and potential biases in print and electronic media.

To illustrate, a content analysis of the July 28, 1991, edition of the *Chicago Tribune* reveals that, based on the percentage of stories that appear in the paper, several issues dominated the news:

- The economy—11 percent
- The Mideast—8 3/4 percent
- Serial killers—8 3/4 percent
- Education—4 percent
- Drugs—4 percent

Cultural Context

Content analysis can also be used to identify areas of cultural interest and concern. To illustrate, the same content analysis of the *Tribune* identifies the following general story categories:

Trends. By reading the *Tribune*, readers learn about the latest directions in which the culture is moving and, if they choose, keep up with these new developments. One story deals with a new children's squirtgun, the Super Soaker: "What may be the hottest—and coolest—toy in the U.S." New fashion developments are also spotlighted, including the world of male cosmetics.

Health. American's fixation with health is also reflected through a succession of articles on the subject throughout the newspaper. A series entitled "Amazing Discoveries" summarizes developments in health-related areas, including caffeine withdrawal, obesity, breast cancer (in men), and stress disorder (in returning servicemen). Other articles pertain to the unveiling of a Woman's Health Campaign by the American Medical Association and a study suggesting that panic attacks may be genetic.

Stages of life. The newspaper often contains articles that deal with various stages of life, including adolescence, career changes, and retirement.

Relationships. Relationships are also frequently discussed and examined. For instance, a column entitled "Tales from the Front" responds to the question, "What are the best parts of marriage?" These comments tell us a good deal about cultural attitudes toward marriage:

- *Marriage as possession.* "Another person actually belongs to you. I tell my husband he's my property, he belongs to me. He tells me I'm his."

- *Marriage as convenience.* "You don't have to try so hard." "You don't need to do anything to feel connected."

- *Marriage as comfort.* "I have someone to throw a leg over mine in bed at night when my legs are aching."

- *Marriage as security.* "When talk shows have a segment about 'The Man Shortage,' I no longer nod my head and say, 'So true, so true.' "

- *Marriage as history.* "Waiting for grandchildren together."

Cultural preoccupations. In the wake of the discovery and arrest of serial killer Jeffrey Dahmer, the Sunday *Tribune* published six related articles, indicating the degree of public outrage, shock, and fascination with the topic.

Celebrities. Celebrity profiles are also prominent, including features on Robin Givens, Carol Alt, Ice T, and Kathleen Turner. The emphasis on these media figures is a barometer of the public's fascination with famous people.

Subcultures. Content analysis can also provide perspective on the various subcultures that are reflected in newspaper coverage:

Local culture. A number of stories deal with aspects of local culture, such as bargain hunting in the city and a human interest feature on amateur gardeners. In addition, a calendar of events publicizes lectures, exhibits, festivals, and exhibits in the Chicago area.

Elite culture. Articles appear in the paper that appeal to elite interests and tastes, including a story on the American Conservatory and a book review focusing on a biography of Carl Sandberg. In addition, a local gossip column spotlights prominent Chicago activities and citizens.

African Americans. This edition of the *Chicago Tribune* contains the following articles:
- "Black Filmmakers Outside Hollywood"
- "N.Y. Schools to Teach More Minority History"
- "Tomorrow's Minority Doctors Are at ITT Today"
- "Youths Get More Than Just Jobs" (detailing a summer work program for urban youth)

- "Urban Children Find Refuge in the South"
- "Minorities Isolated from Job Hot Spots"

Women. "Womanews," the section traditionally devoted to the interests of women, reflects the cultural changes that have occurred over the years. Stories include:
- Involvement of young women in the National Women's Political Caucus.
- Fit after 50: A physical therapist outlines an exercise program.
- Health article; pregnant women.
- A book review of a biography on Georgia O'Keeffe, which discusses her unconventional life.
- Article entitled "Preventing Date Rape: Knowledge Is Power."
- Article about the premiere of *Daughters of the Dust,* directed by black female Julie Dash. The film focuses on "women at pivotal moments in their lives."
- "The New Face of Japanese Politics" about a female Japanese politician, Takako Doi.
- A story about a female rabbi in Israel.

Worldview. The world of American journalism is very small indeed. A limited amount of attention is devoted to international news, for several reasons. Space constraints require that editors select foreign news carefully; it is impossible to provide complete international coverage without omitting news of national and local interest.

In addition, the reader does not have the time to devote to full international coverage. Each country has a complex story to tell on a daily basis. For instance, if a paper provided comprehensive coverage of events in Holland, we would be reading a section nearly as large as a Dutch newspaper. If you multiply this by the 248 nations, dependent areas, and other entities in the world, it would take the American reader a week to digest one day's worth of international news.

Limited resources further restrict foreign news coverage. Newspapers have reduced their overhead by consolidating their foreign bureaus. Correspondents now are responsible for a large region and, as a result, lack the familiarity with a single country—and the contacts—that are so important to insightful reporting. In addition, vast regions—in Africa and South America, for instance—lack the technical capability to enable reporters to relay information to the United States. And some countries, like China, have limited Western reporters' access to information for political reasons.

Ethnocentrism may also contribute to the lack of international coverage in American newspapers. The majority of U.S. territory is not in close physical proximity with other countries and, consequently, not directly affected by events taking place on foreign shores. As a result, many Americans remain uninformed and disinterested in other cultures.

This lack of international coverage reinforces the latent message that America is the only country that matters. In fact, Herbert Gans observes that most of the international news that does appear in U.S. newspapers consists of *American* activities in other cultures:

- Implementation of U.S. foreign policy
- Stopovers by U.S. officials
- American entertainers on tour
- International events that affect Americans and American policy.[16]

What, then, accounts for the attention given to certain countries in our newspapers? Only a few, select countries appear with any consistency in the American press. Some countries, like Iraq, become the center of national attention through a political crisis or natural disaster. However, Philip Gaunt observes that certain countries and regions receive sustained coverage, based on political, commercial, and ethnic linkage with the United States:

Political Interests
  Soviet Union
  Central America
  Southeast Asia
  China

Commercial Ties
  Taiwan
  Japan

Ethnic Identification
  Britain
  Germany
  Italy
  Ireland
  Israel

And, to a lesser degree:

  Poland
  Greece
  Lithuania
  Sweden[17]

STRUCTURE

Ownership Patterns

According to Ben Bagdikian, 14 companies currently own half or more of the daily newspaper business in America.[18] Before this huge conglomerate takeover, the small-time owners depended on newspapers as their sole source of income. At the same time, these publishers chose the newspaper profession because of a commitment to the field of journalism. Today, however, vital decisions often are driven by economic considerations. Many newspapers have initiated a series of cost-cutting measures: reducing staff, closing foreign bureaus, relying on wire service copy (Associated Press [AP] or United Press International [UPI]), and hiring younger, inexperienced journalists at lower wages. These factors contribute to a homogeneity of news content.

Bagdikian argues that because the media are a major industry in the United States, the corporate worldview has become predominant in media-carried content:

No sacred cow has been so protected and has left more generous residues in the news than the American corporation. . . . [At the same time,] large classes of people are ignored in the news, are reported as exotic fads, or appear only at their worst—minorities, blue-collar workers, the lower middle class, the poor. They become publicized mainly when they are in spectacular accidents, go on strike, or are arrested. . . . But since World War I hardly a mainstream American news medium has failed to grant its most favored treatment to corporate life.[19]

As part of the corporate community, newspaper owners may be susceptible to conflicts of interest:

The *Los Angeles Times* is owned by Times Mirror Company, which also owns other newspapers, cable systems, book publishing houses, agricultural land, urban real estate, commercial printing plants, and other nonjournalistic operations. The *Times* over the years has been a persistent advocate for state and federal subsidy of agricultural water, most of which is used for agricultural land. In 1980, the *Times,* as it had for all such water projects over the decades, pressed for a new, $2 billion, tax-paid canal system. A Times-Mirror subsidiary would be a beneficiary, particularly a planned real estate and recreational project. Other papers, the *New York Times* and the *Bakersfield Californian,* reported the project and its dependence on the controversial canal, but the *Los Angeles Times* did not, saying it was not newsworthy.[20]

On occasion, owners have intervened in editorial decisions when the issues affected corporate interests:

When Walter Annenberg, a dominant magazine publisher, owned the *Philadelphia Inquirer* he routinely banished from the news the names of people he disliked, including people normally reported. He used his newspaper to attack a candidate for governor who opposed action that would benefit the stockholders of the Pennsylvania Railroad, but Annenberg never informed the readers that he was the largest single stockholder in the railroad.[21]

Newspapers' dependence on advertising revenue can also have an impact on content. Ronald K. L. Collins cites instances in which reporters have been called off stories involving advertisers: "In a confidential survey of 42 real-estate editors by the Washington Journalism Review, nearly half said publishers and senior editors had prohibited critical coverage of the industry for fear of offending advertisers." [22]

Collins also notes a trend of *self-censorship* in the press, in which editors either suppress or rewrite a story without being asked, for fear of offending advertisers. For instance, in February 1988 *Newsweek* featured a cover story entitled "What You Should Know About Heart Attacks" but failed to mention the role that smoking plays in heart failure. The back cover of the magazine consisted of a Malibu cigarette ad. Collins notes, "A *Time* Magazine spokesperson explained the curious way the major news-weeklies cover health issues this way: '*Time,* as does *Newsweek,* has a lot of cigarette advertising. Do you carry material that's insulting to your advertiser?' " [23]

Newspapers may also assign reporters to cover "advertiser-friendly" stories. Collins cites a 1991 incident in which the Woodbridge, New Jersey, *News Tribune* removed an award-winning reporter from the environmental beat, leaving the beat open. At the same time, the paper promoted the renovation of a local mall by creating a regular column called "Gone Shopping." A post-Christmas column began, "Just because Santa paid a visit yesterday, littering your living room with tinsel, shredded gift wrap and cardboard shirt boxes, don't you dare entertain the silly notion that your Christmas shopping is finished!" [24]

Finally, the distinction between editorial content and advertising may be blurred. In addition to the advertorials mentioned above, news and features in reality may be thinly disguised promotions:

Omni magazine raised eyebrows in November 1990 when it carried a two-page advertising spread that was partly visible through a window cutout on the cover. The hole revealed a silver hologram of a cellular phone—courtesy of Motorola, which bought the cover space to tout "the future of global communications." The magazine's president defended the cover as a celebration of modern science, but the editor didn't buy it. After reportedly offering to forego three months' salary in exchange for not putting the ad on the cover, he resigned, as did the managing editor. [25]

A number of other recent economic and organizational developments have made an impact on news content:

One-newspaper cities. In 1920, there were 2,722 urban communities and 2,400 daily papers in the United States. [26] By 1992, the number of cities had greatly increased; the number of dailies had decreased to under 1,700. [27] Tripp Frohlichstein, a media relations consultant and former news executive, observes, "This lack of competition reduces the quality of newspaper coverage."[28]

In cities with more than one newspaper, the papers frequently offered opposing political viewpoints, as expressed on the editorial page. However, the trend toward one-paper cities means that readers are no longer exposed to a range of political perspectives. In response, some papers feature both liberal and conservative perspectives on their op-ed page. But unfortunately, this approach often means that *neither* side has much of a forum for opinion.

Newspaper chains. In 1993, almost 75 percent of U.S. daily papers were part of *newspaper chains.*[29] A newspaper chain refers to a large company that owns a series of newspapers in different locations throughout the country. Bagdikian found that this ownership pattern can have an impact on the content of newspapers. Newspapers that made the transition from an independent company to part of a conglomerate saw an increase in advertising, accompanied by a decrease in news content. In addition, editorial policies either reflected the ideology of corporate ownership or "became bland to avoid controversy."[30] Bagdikian also cites studies that found that chains tend to hire less-qualified journalists to curb expenses.[31]

The emergence of the "national daily." The emergence of the national daily *(USA Today)* has also had a significant impact on media messages. To illustrate, consider the October 10, 1991, front page of *USA Today* (see Figure 6.2). In order to appeal to a wide audience, *USA Today*'s stories are noticeably shorter than most of its journalistic counterparts. The lead story (the Supreme Court nomination hearings of Clarence Thomas) is 9½ column inches, as opposed to 51 column inches devoted to the Thomas story in that day's edition of the *New York Times*.

News capsules on the left-hand portion *USA Today*'s front page promise "A Quick Read on the News" for people in a hurry. Sports stories are presented as news ("Blue Jays Tie AL Series"), although full playoff coverage is promised in Section C. Two public opinion stories also appear on the front page of *USA Today* (health insurance and attitudes about drinking and driving). These stories merely *reflect* public sentiment, as opposed to introducing fresh information on these topics.

In addition, national dailies are often reluctant to espouse a partisan editorial philosophy for fear of alienating any segment of the general public. For instance, *USA Today* refrains from endorsing presidential candidates, since "electing a president is your choice, not ours" (October 23, 1992). Instead, they present bland opinions designed to offend as few people as possible. For instance, the April 7, 1991, lead editorial took the following position: "If baseball is to remain a family affair, owners must strike out escalating costs."

In an era typified by media narrowcasting, it is ironic that the newspaper chain and national daily have reversed this trend through a broadcasting

Figure 6.2
Impact of a National Daily on Media Messages

approach—that is, presenting generic, inoffensive content intended to appeal to as many people as possible.

Internal Organization

The internal structure of newspapers also has an impact on the selection and presentation of information. The newspaper editor conducts daily meetings in which department editors plan the contents of the day's newspaper. In the course of these meetings, decisions are reached concerning *what* appears in the paper, *where* it appears, and *how much* coverage a story should receive. These preproduction decisions help set the agenda of what should be considered newsworthy without the knowledge or consent of the public. As Tripp Frohlichstein observes, "News is whatever the editor says it is." [32]

In response, each year *Project Censored* identifies the top ten underreported news stories of the year. A panel of distinguished media professionals and scholars collaborates to "seek, identify, and publicize stories on important issues that have been overlooked or under-reported by the news media." 1992's top underreported stories included:

A story by Russell Mokhiber revealing that public corruption, environmental degradation, financial fraud, procurement fraud, and occupational homicide are on the rise, while the press continues to focus on the more dramatic aspects of street crime and violence.

Election year issues:

- George Bush's Team 100, major financial contributors who were rewarded with ambassadorships and federal advisory committee appointments. Federal regulatory issues that adversely affected members of Team 100 were toned down.
- The issue of homelessness and its neglect by all three presidential candidates.
- Covert operations run from a clandestine airfield in Mena, Arkansas, during Bill Clinton's administration including guns, drugs, and other activities related to the Iran/Contra affair.
- Iraqgate and the silent death of the Watergate Law.
- "We are winning the war on drugs" was a lie. [33]

Conversely, Dr. Carl Jensen of Sonoma State University has identified what he calls the top ten "Junk Food News" of 1992, stories receiving much more coverage than they deserved. These stories included:

- Dan Quayle Misspells Potato
- Madonna's "Sex"
- Woody Allen vs. Mia Farrow

- Gennifer Flowers
- The Barbara/Hillary Cookie Bake-off.[34]

The *frequency* with which a story appears is another key editorial decision. Sustained coverage keeps the public apprised about issues that editors consider important. These stories remain in the public's consciousness and assume a level of importance. On the other hand, sporadic coverage signals that these issues are insignificant.

A third management decision involves *depth of coverage.* Brief mention of a subject suggests that the issue is of minimal importance, whereas in-depth stories send the message that the public should treat the subject seriously.

Homogeneity in the Newsroom. The composition of the newsroom staff is another organizational factor that can affect the treatment of stories. The typical newsroom is predominantly young, male, and white. This lack of diversity is reflected in a homogeneity of news coverage. Tim McGuire, managing editor of the Minneapolis *Star Tribune,* observes, "It's time we stop and listen to minority voices that have an understanding and perspective white editors and reporters don't have."[35] At a fall 1991 Poynter Institute conference entitled Redefining the News: Reaching New Audiences Through Diversity, professionals and scholars made four recommendations geared to infuse a diversity of viewpoints in the newspaper:

- *Develop story ideas within the community*
- *Cultivate sources from a variety of backgrounds and perspectives*
- *Redesign news beats*
- *Reshape newsroom culture*

The composition of the newsroom is changing (see Figures 6.3 and 6.4). However, Seymour Topping, director of editorial development for the New York Times Co. Regional Newspapers, maintains, "We must forge ahead even more strongly to reach the . . . goals of accurately representing the diversity in American society."[36]

FRAMEWORK

Introduction

The Headline. Readers receive their initial impressions about a story through the headline. However, headlines are rarely written by the reporter who wrote the story. Instead, this task is delegated to a copywriter who may not understand the intent, or even the main point, of the story.

A primary function of a headline is to *inform* the reader about the prin-

Figure 6.3
Gender of Journalists (percent)

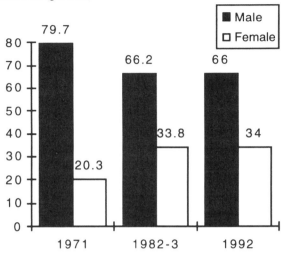

Source: David Weaver and G. Cleveland Wilhoit, *The American Journalist* (update) (Arlington, VA: The Freedom Forum, 1992), 4.

cipal thrust of the story. At the same time, however, the headline must *attract attention* by being provocative, if not sensational. Unfortunately, these competing functions can work at cross-purposes, distorting the essential meaning.

Figure 6.4
Minority Journalists (percent)

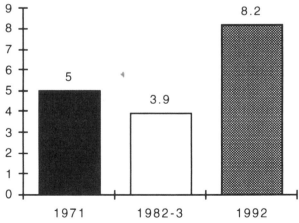

Source: David Weaver and G. Cleveland Wilhoit, *The American Journalist* (update) (Arlington, VA: The Freedom Forum, 1992), 5.

For instance, consider the following headline for a story about a science student who won a prize at a science fair for a project that studied the effects of radiation on the regeneration of planaria (flatworms): "Student Worms Way to Honors Division."[37] The attempt here was to be cute. However, students who "worm their way" into something are considered unscrupulous, sneaky, and undeserving. This headline distorted the meaning of the story and, in the process, belittled the accomplishments of the science student.

The Introductory Paragraph. In print journalism, the most essential information is positioned in the first paragraph of the story. This *pyramid style* of American journalism dates back to the nineteenth century with the invention of the telegraph. Concerned that the telegraph lines would go down at any moment, editors insisted that reporters send the most important information across the wires first. Background information and details were then included later in the story. The pyramid structure also enables editors to make room for late-breaking stories or additional advertisements at the last minute by cutting the least essential information from the end of the story. Readers should therefore expect to find the answers to the following questions in the first paragraph: *who, what, when, how,* and *why*.

The body of the story should elaborate on the information presented in the lead paragraph. However, as Lee and Soloman note, the first paragraph is sometimes an incomplete or even inaccurate summary of the body of the story:

In November 1987, *New York Times* reporter Lindsey Gurson puffed the popularity of the Nicaraguan Contras in a 50-paragraph article that featured a front page above-the-fold photo of a contra soldier holding an adoring child. Buried near the end of the piece was a passing reference to a just-released Americas Watch report stating that "the Contras systematically engage in violent abuses . . . so prevalent that these may be said to be their principal means of waging war." Then why weren't contra abuses, which included the murder of hundreds of innocent children, a bigger focus of Gurson's article?[38]

Consequently, it is important to determine whether the lead paragraph indeed encapsulates the major thrust of the article.

Plot

Implicit Content. Newspaper accounts often focus on explicit content (events) but ignore the implicit content (causes, connections, and consequences) *behind* the incidents. The factors contributing to an event (e.g., the situation in Bosnia) are often complex and therefore difficult to include in a brief newspaper article. In addition, a news event may only represent an installment in a far larger story, which is still in the process of unfolding. And sometimes the consequences of events aren't readily apparent. For instance, it will be many years before the ramifications of the Chernobyl nuclear plant meltdown tragedy become clear.

MEDIA LITERACY TIPS

IMPLICIT CONTENT

In light of the complexity of events, it is particularly critical to give some thought to implicit content when reading articles. When you are reading a story, ask:

√ Why did this event occur?

√ What are the possible connections between events?

√ What are the possible consequences of these events?

PRODUCTION VALUES

Editing

Production Decisions. When writing a story, a journalist assembles an abundance of information that must be condensed into a coherent and concise article. The reporter makes a series of decisions that can convey subtle messages, including:

What information to include (and omit) in a story. A reporter is faced with difficult decisions about what information to include in a story. It is appropriate to ask:

- What information is missing from the story that would be of value?
- What is the reporter's justification for including the information contained in the story?

The order of presentation. Information presented first generally is considered to be the most important.

How much emphasis to devote to certain pieces of information. Reporters may furnish detailed explanation on specific aspects of a story they deem to be important.

Whose perspective should be presented. In order to maintain a balance, reporters should include all sides to a story—although this isn't always the case.

Whose perspective should be presented first. Even when all sides are presented, the viewpoint presented first is often considered to be the most legitimate, established point of view.

The use of quotes. In the course of a five-minute interview, a subject furnishes far more information than can be used in an average newspaper article. A reporter can misuse quotes in a number of ways:

- Include only those statements that support a particular point of view
- Take quotes out of context to magnify or distort its meaning
- Juxtapose separate statements together to form an entirely new meaning
- Use editorial license

Including grammatical or syntactical errors can make a person appear unprepared, uneducated, or foolish. On the other hand, cleaning up a quote can make a subject appear more knowledgeable and authoritative.

Postproduction Editing Decisions. After an article has been completed by a reporter, a copy editor revises the material. The text is corrected for stylistic errors, including grammatical and syntactical mistakes, and improper word choice. The story may be rearranged to improve the flow of information. Finally, portions of a story can be omitted to eliminate redundancies.

Although the copy editor tries not to tamper with the content of a story, he or she may not understand the rationale for including a particular phrase or specific quote in an article. Further, the copy editor may be pressed to condense an article when a timely story is added at the last moment or if advertisers want more space—even if the content is affected.

Scale

The size of a story sends a signal about its importance. Consider the page layout shown in Figure 6.5. The dominant 70-point headline ("Charges Grip Senate") calls attention to the hoopla surrounding the confirmation hearings of Judge Clarence Thomas. On the same page, an 18-point headline announced President George Bush's veto of legislation to extend benefits to the unemployed. Even the subheading on the Thomas story (28 points) is larger than the main headline of the veto story. The latent message is that the veto story does not deserve much public attention.

Relative Position

The arrangement of newspaper space influences the significance we attach to a story. On a practical level, most of us start to read a section of a paper at the beginning. As a result, an article placed on page five is not as likely to be read as a story appearing on page two. *Chicago Tribune* managing editor Dick Siccone points out that many factors enter into decisions about story placement, including available space, the local interest of the story, and other local priorities. However, Siccone acknowledges that story placement does send messages regarding the relative importance of news items: "One of the most important things a paper does is give read-

Figure 6.5
Story Size Signals Its Importance

ers guidance about what is the most meaningful. The stories which are most desirable for readers appear in consecutive order . . . page one, page two, page three. [Placement] signals to readers exactly what they most need to read." [39]

Story placement may vary from newspaper to newspaper. To illustrate, the October 23, 1991, *New York Times* carried a front page story detailing definitive findings by the scientific community regarding ozone damage in the atmosphere. On the same day, the *St. Louis Post-Dispatch* buried the article on page A15—the second to last page of the section. As a result, St. Louis area readers received a very different message about the significance of the ozone story than the *Times* readers.

The arrangement of stories *within* a single page also affects the audience's perception of news content. Stories on the top half of the page are accorded greater importance by the reader than stories appearing near the bottom. How much of a story appears in the front section before the *jump* to a back page also affects how people react to it. (A "jump" refers to the continuation of a story to another page.) According to Edmund C. Arnold, only 30 percent of readers follow the story past its jump line.[40]

Readers often regard the composition of a newspaper page as a collection of separate stories. However, editors often consider the relationship *between* the stories when laying out the stories. As Siccone observes, "Some days you make statements, some days you don't." [41] By activating our gestalt and seeing the page as a whole, we can draw connections between events and identify cultural preoccupations and concerns.

For instance, consider the page of the *St. Louis Post-Dispatch* shown in Figure 6.6. The articles portray a liberal world in retreat, as basic institutions (labor) and principles (abortion) are being threatened. The larger photo, placed directly under the bold headline, depicts an innocent infant whose future has been "set back" by the results of the labor strike. William F. Woo's column calls on the press to assume an interpretive role, helping the community understand how policy decisions are affecting our neighbors. This theme is further reflected by a *sidebar* (related) story focusing on the impact of the labor setback on the Osborn family. The picture graphically shows how a tradition—three generations of workers—has been disrupted in the aftermath of the labor strike.

Point of View

The Illusion of Objectivity in the Press. The American press adheres to the principles of accuracy and objectivity. The Society of Professional Journalists' Code of Ethics declares,

Good faith with the public is the foundation of all worthy journalism.
1. Truth is our ultimate goal.

Figure 6.6
Messages Conveyed through Relative Position of Stories

Reprinted with permission of the St. Louis Post-Dispatch and Pulitzer Publishing Company, copyright 1992.

2. Objectivity in reporting the news is another goal which serves as the mark of an experienced professional. It is a standard of performance toward which we strive. We honor those who achieve it.[42]

This code assumes that an absolute truth exists and that journalists are in a position to present an accurate depiction of this ideal, without distortion or personal bias. However, we live in a complex, subjective world in which the truth may be difficult to identify.

As Walter Lippmann observed, news can only be expected to approach truth in cases of quantifiable information, such as the temperature, sports scores, and election results.[43] But even in these cases, information can be far from absolute. For instance, weather reports are only exact in regard to the specific place where the temperature is being measured. A number of variables—green space versus highly constructed areas, wind patterns, and amount of sunshine—can account for a fluctuation of several degrees in temperature within a 30-mile radius.

Readers often confuse the statement of fact with truth. For instance, consider the following headline: "Reagan Calls Summit 'Momentous.'"[44] While it is a *fact* that Reagan made this observation, it may or may not be *true* that the summit was successful.

Since there is no universal agreement on truth, faithfulness to this ideal becomes an impossibility. As a result, the press is frequently the target of criticism for biased reporting from both the Left and the Right, depending on each group's *own* versions of the truth. Ted J. Smith observes:

Critics on the left . . . attack journalists for being insufficiently critical of mainstream policies, leaders, and institutions, for excluding minority views, and for unreflective repetition of the assumptions and values of capitalist economics and bourgeois democracy. Supported by numerous academic studies, there can be little doubt about the basic validity of this claim.

Among conservatives, belief in the liberal bias of the media is almost an article of faith. . . . Conservatives base their case on the claims that journalists, especially in the prestigious national media, are liberal in their political views, and that those views are reflected in coverage.[45]

Some scholars find this notion of objectivity in the press to be not only unrealistic but *undesirable*. Ben Bagdikian maintains that the basis of solid journalism is values: "Objectivity contradicts the essentially subjective nature of journalism. Every basic step in the journalistic process involves a value-laden decision."[46]

Mark Hertsgaard argues that American journalists have become trapped by the modern ethic of objectivity, forcing the press to forego its responsibility as opinion leader: "How could the public be expected to develop an opinion on a given issue unless that issue was posed for their consideration? In the American system, that was the responsibility of the press. Yet the modern ethic of objectivity precluded such journalism."[47]

Bagdikian declares that journalists have been limited to reporting the official lines of authority as news that "leaves unreported large areas of genuine relevance that authorities choose not to talk about."[48] As a result, the press can only report information if a specific event has occurred or if someone else has brought it up, such as impeachment. Hertsgaard declares, "In accordance with their avoidance of partisanship, many journalists seemed to regard strenuous challenging of the government as an improper violation of the rules of objectivity. Honest adversarial journalism they equated with, and often dismissed as, 'advocacy' journalism."[49]

New Journalism, a genre of reporting that emerged in the mid-1960s, was based on the premise that objectivity places an impossible burden on both reporter and the audience. Authors like Tom Wolfe, Norman Mailer, and Hunter S. Thompson felt that the most honest approach was simply to admit their biases up front. By taking the declared biases of the New Journalists into account, readers were in a better position to put information into perspective and come to their own conclusions.

The defining issue in American journalism, then, may not be objectivity but rather *fairness:* Do journalists strive to include alternative perspectives as clearly and accurately as possible?

Bias Techniques. Point of view can be introduced subtly into reporting through several journalistic techniques:

Presentation of opinion as fact. Reporters sometimes present opinion disguised as fact in news stories. For example: "President George Bush's administration, *in a largely symbolic move* [emphasis mine] announced Monday that the United States would forswear production of plutonium and highly enriched uranium for nuclear weapons."[50]

Vague authority. Reporters may cite undocumented and generalized groups to impose a particular point of view. Examples include:

- A *Chicago Tribune* article covering the trial of two men accused of beating Reginald Denny during the 1992 Los Angeles Riots: "The juror's 11th-hour replacement was just the latest of a series of bizarre twists that have fueled charges *among many African-Americans* [emphasis mine] that the judicial system has a double standard for blacks."[51]

- A *New York Times* report on the Clinton Health Care proposal: "But at the same time, *critics* [emphasis mine] are asking whether Mr. Clinton's proposed new layers of State and Federal oversight will simply replace one set of costly bureaucratic headaches with another."[52]

- A *Chicago Tribune* story on the American peacekeeping mission in Haiti: "As Haiti awaited the arrival of about 500 U.S. troops on Monday, *local government officials* urged that the peacekeeping mission go forward, while *some U.S.*

lawmakers worried that the troops could come under fire as has happened in Somalia [emphasis mine]." [53]

One-person cross section. This technique consists of using one person as a metaphor for a larger group—which may not be the case. Consider this story about the grassroots popularity of H. Ross Perot:

Bob Hayden, 38, became the California coordinator for Perot by happenstance: He was the first volunteer in the state to fax Perot a letter. Hayden's real job is specializing in earthquake preparedness.
   But neither he nor anyone else could predict the rumblings that have disrupted the 1992 political landscape and left his town the epicenter of a movement. [54]

The designated spokesperson. Sometimes the press arbitrarily appoints a spokesperson to represent a particular cause or point of view. They may be leaders of an organization or an "expert" (e.g., university professor). But whether these people actually enjoy the support of a broad constituency is open to question.

The slanted sample. Sampling the public for their response to issues and events is a very common journalistic approach. However, this sample may be chosen in an arbitrary fashion and therefore is not representative of the public at large. For instance, an AP postelection story carried the headline "What Americans Want from New Administration." The 20-person sample consisted of 18 men and 2 women. The 18 men commented on national defense, health care, aid to cities, the economy, and the deficit. The comments of the 2 women were confined to traditional "women's issues" such as family leave, lower-income working women, and day care. [55]

The "not available" ploy. Investigative pieces often include the statement that the subject was unavailable for comment, which implies that the subject was uncooperative, ducking the reporter, and had something to hide. This statement often neglects to clarify the circumstances:

- Whether the person was in town
- When the person was contacted (i.e., day or evening)
- Where a person was contacted (i.e., at home or at work)
- How often the reporter attempted to reach the person
- The time frame in which the reporter attempted to contact the subject (e.g., over a three-day period)

The passive catchphrase. Sentences can be written in either the active or passive voice. In the active voice, the subject is explicitly responsible for the action (e.g., Bob threw the ball). In the passive voice, the subject is the *receiver* of the action (e.g., The ball was thrown to Bob). Warriner's *Hand-*

book of English mentions that this construction is particularly useful in the following situations:

- *Expressing an action in which the actor is unknown.* To illustrate, in the sentence "The door had been closed before we arrived," it is unclear who closed the door.

- *Expressing an action in which it is desirable not to disclose the actor.* For example, the statement "A mistake has been made" deflects responsibility for the action, since it is unstated who made the mistake.[56]

Use of the passive voice also creates the impression that an opinion is common knowledge. Some examples of passive catchphrases that have appeared in the newspapers include:

- A *Time* Magazine story reporting on the bombing of the World Trade Center: "Yet even before the answers were in as to who had planted the bomb, a new question—whether a season of terrorism might begin in the U.S.—*had been raised* [emphasis mine]."[57] This story conveniently leaves out *who* has raised the question.

- A *New York Times* news article on Somalia: "President Clinton's envoy to Somalia, Robert B. Oakley, arrived in Mogadishu today and met with members of the clan led by Mohammed Farah Aidid, *the faction leader blamed for the killings of American and other United Nations peacekeepers* [emphasis mine]."[58] Blamed by whom?

- Another *New York Times* news report on the American mission in Somalia: "The Red Cross is also working to get proper medical treatment for the helicopter pilot, *who is said to have a bullet wound in his leg* [emphasis mine]."[59] Once again, where is this information coming from?

Selective quotes. As mentioned earlier, reporters can color a story by choosing *when* to use quotes, *whose* quotes to include, and *which parts* of the person's interview to extract into a quote.

Biased interviewing strategies. A reporter can slant a story through the type of questions he or she poses to subjects while conducting research for the story:

- *Compliance as assertion.* Reporters may come prepared with a point of view (and a quote) ready to include in an article and is only asking for the *consent* of the subject. In this case, reporters may phrase a question, "Would you agree that . . . ?" "Would you say that . . . ?" or "So what you are saying is . . ."

- *Leading or loaded questions.* Tripp Frohlichstein of MediaMasters observes that reporters can present questions that are loaded with negative allegations or a false premise. An example would be, "Are you concerned that higher rates as proposed by the electric company might force many people to give up their service?" Any response to a question phrased like this (even a denial) legitimizes the position of the reporter.

- *Hypothetical question.* Questions beginning with phrases such as "What would happen if . . . ?" puts the subject in a speculative position that is then interpreted by readers as fact. In addition, hypothetical questions frequently catch the interviewee off guard, so that he or she may offer an opinion that is not properly thought out.

- *Either/or choices.* Reporters may offer only a limited range of responses to their interviewees. Like students taking a multiple-choice exam, subjects may then feel compelled to select the best answer among the choices offered, even though it may not actually be the "best" answer. However, Frohlichstein reminds the public, "There are five different responses to an 'either/or' question. If the choices are 'a' or 'b,' you can respond with

  1) 'a'
  2) 'b'
  3) both 'a' and 'b'
  4) Neither 'a' or 'b'
  5) 'c' (an alternative not given by the reporter)." [60]

Intention and Objectivity. An important consideration in a discussion of objectivity concerns the issue of intention. Are reporters always surreptitiously trying to sway readers to their point of view? Certainly, there are times in which a careful analysis of content reveals the embedded values of the journalist. However, the journalistic process inevitably calls for choices that may signal a particular point of view. For instance, in reporting a story, one side must always be mentioned first, which then makes a statement about relative importance.

Ultimately, however, the question of intention is irrelevant. Journalists must recognize that decisions they make in writing and editing the news convey messages that influence the reader. As a result, journalists must be more conscious of the ramifications of the choices they make.

For their part, readers must understand that objectivity is in many cases an unobtainable ideal.

In becoming media literate, the public can develop a critical awareness of point of view in stories that will enable them to come to an independent analysis of journalistic content.

Sources. Reporters often rely on a network of sources as they research stories. In some cases, sources have access to information that would otherwise be unavailable. Journalists also rely on experts to assimilate and interpret complex information since industry pressures demand that reporters cover a wide range of topics within a limited time span.

However, the use of sources potentially can undermine the integrity of news coverage. *New York Times* columnist Tom Wicker declares that a source can punish reporters in a number of ways, including "lost access, complaints to editors and publishers, social penalties, leaks to competitors, [and] a variety of responses no one wants." [61] As a result, the sources are often treated with special consideration by reporters. Wendell Rawls, Jr., assistant managing editor of the *Atlanta Journal and Constitution,* admits, "Yes, there are times when I feel uncomfortable reporting facts that I imagine will cause a source some pain. I deal with it by calling up the source and telling him what I'm going to do. I don't let the source get ambushed." [62]

It is important to identify the sources who appear in the paper in order to put their contributions into perspective.

Identifying the *demographic profile* of sources can provide perspective into an expert's opinion. For instance, if all of the sources are white males over 50 years of age who earn over $200,000 per year, the reader may be exposed to a homogeneity of opinion. Factors that should be considered in identifying sources include name, range of expertise, gender, age, education, and income.

The media often rely on a limited number of sources who share similar backgrounds. A White House correspondent is quoted by Stephen Hess as explaining, "We're in small quarters with access to only a small number of official people, getting the same information. So we write similar stories and move on the same issues." [63]

Identifying the *affiliation* of a source can also be revealing. For instance, an article may refer to a source as a member of the Heritage Foundation, "a conservative thinktank." But what does this mean? Who funds this organization? And what is its mission?

It is also valuable to consider the source's *level of expertise.* Anyone who appears in the newspaper as a source is instantly accorded the status of expert. But is this person truly qualified to speak authoritatively on the subject?

Why has a source decided to come forward in the newspaper? Understanding *motive* is critical to putting a source's contributions into perspective. Administration officials routinely "leak" information as a way of testing public response before policy decisions are reached. Eager for information, journalists are duped into serving the interests of the source, and the public is manipulated as a result. Readers should consider the following questions:

- Why is the source volunteering this information?
- What is the anticipated outcome of this contribution?
- Does this information reflect a personal or professional bias on the part of the source?

It is also important to consider the *reporter's* motive for consulting a source. *Los Angeles Times* staffer David Shaw charges that reporters sometimes speak through sources by selecting experts who will corroborate their point of view: "Reporters often call a source because they want a quotation to illustrate a particular point, and they are sure to get exactly what they want if they call a source whose attitudes they already know." [64]

Finally, it is critical to assess the nature of the *contribution* provided by the source. Experts are expected to provide informed analysis, clarification, or background on a particular subject. Instead, sources may offer opinions on a wide range of topics outside their realm of expertise.

Anonymous Sources. Identifying sources is often complicated by the issue of anonymity. The use of unnamed sources gives reporters wider access to information while enabling potential sources to supply information without fear of recrimination. To illustrate, during the Watergate investigation, *Washington Post* reporters Bob Woodward and Carl Bernstein depended on a confidential source within the Nixon administration (code-named "Deepthroat") to obtain vital inside information that otherwise would not have been available.

Twenty-five states have passed shield laws, permitting reporters to maintain the confidentiality of sources. However, in states without shield laws, reporters can be jailed for defying court orders to reveal the names of sources.

The most common use of anonymous sources occurs when the source remains confidential, but the reporter is free to publish the information. However, sources can go "off the record" in other ways as well:

- Sources may provide *deep background*—that is, providing the context that puts a story into a broader perspective and guides the reporter into a particular direction. In this context, the source is never directly acknowledged in the story.
- Both the source and the information remain confidential. However, the reporter is free to seek corroboration elsewhere.

Anonymity protects the source while serving the public's right to know. However, as Lee and Soloman note, this practice also prevents the reader from determining the credibility of sources:

If the unnamed source is a whistleblower speaking accurately and truthfully about his or her boss or agency, the information can be considered a "leak," and in all likelihood the reporter will be serving the public interest. If, on the other hand, the unnamed source is the voice of a government agency and there's no legitimate reason for the source to be unnamed, the information can be considered a "plant," and in all likelihood the reporter will be serving the interest of the agency, not the public. [65]

Disclosure Versus Privacy. At times the point of view of the press is disturbingly intimate—particularly with regard to coverage of public figures. People can be subjected to media scrutiny as "public figures" if they have met the following criteria:

√ Voluntarily stepped into the spotlight
√ Assumed an important role in the resolution of important public issues
√ Had an impact on a public issue
√ Become a public figure through means other than simply media attention[66]

However, unscrupulous journalists can abuse this journalistic license to intrude into the personal affairs of celebrities. For instance, in April 1992, *USA Today* learned that former tennis star Arthur Ashe had been infected with the HIV virus during heart surgery in 1988. A reporter then called Ashe to ask for confirmation before running the story. Ashe, who had kept the matter private out of concern for his family, was then forced to go public with the information. After the story was published, former tennis pro and friend Billie Jean King declared angrily, "Can't [the press] just leave him alone? Can't they leave people alone, just once?"[67]

Connotation

Word Choice. Examining language from a grammatical perspective is a useful way to analyze word choice. For instance, journalists are presented with a range of choices in the selection of *nouns.* (A noun is a word used to describe a person, place, or thing.) The choice of nouns can reflect a distinct connotative meaning. As columnist John Leo explains, " 'Actress-model' and 'onetime beauty queen' really mean 'bimbo,' whereas 'womanizer' means 'lecher.' "[68]

The *Dictionary of Cautionary Words and Phrases,* compiled by a group of professional journalists, includes the following connotative nouns:

- "Community" implies a monolithic culture in which people act, think and vote in the same way. Do not use, as in Asian, Hispanic, black or gay community. Be more specific as to what the group is: e.g. Black residents in a north side neighborhood.

- Avoid gender enders. For instance: *actress, comedienne, heroine, poetess* and *starlet.* Instead, use gender-neutral terms such as *actor, comedian, executor, hero, poet* and *star.*

- Use "leader" with caution. Be more specific: black *politician,* black *activist.* Implies person has approval of an entire group of people.

- *"Man"* may be used when both men and women are involved and a more clearly defined term is not available. Frequently the best choice is a substitute, such as "humanity," "a person" or "an individual."[69]

"Stadium Spadework," the original photo cutline, illustrates how a word can possess layers of meaning that transcend its dictionary definition. After a strong public outcry, the newspaper issued an apology for this unintentional racial slur. To be sure, mistakes like this can result from carelessness. But regardless of intention, irate readers responded to a clear message about the insensitivity of the paper to the black community. Reprinted with permission of the St. Louis Post-Dispatch, copyright 1989.

Adjectives are complements to nouns, providing additional information about a person, place, or thing (e.g., a tall person). Leo declares, "One of the richest veins in journalese is the proliferating set of terms that mean 'guilty.' These include 'scandal-plagued,' 'embattled,' [and] 'reputed.' "[70]

The *Dictionary of Cautionary Words and Phrases* supplies the following adjectives, along with their connotative meanings:

- "Articulate" can be considered offensive when referring to a minority, particularly a black person, and his or her ability to handle the English language. The usage suggests that "those people" are not considered well educated, and the like.

- "Burly" is an adjective too often associated with large black men, implying ignorance, and considered offensive in this context.

- "Gorgeous" is an adjective that describes female attributes. Use carefully. Do not use as a noun.[71]

The selection of *verbs* and *adverbs* can also influence readers' attitudes. Verbs describe action (e.g., walking, strolling, or rushing someplace). Adverbs describe *how* something is done (e.g., quickly, carelessly). To illustrate, consider the connotative properties of the following verbs and adverbs:

- "Bill Clinton *played* the press *masterfully.*"
- "Mr. Clinton *battled desperately.*"
- "Clinton *flip-flops* on issue."[72]

One way to determine the impact of connotative words is to substitute synonyms for these words and see how the meaning changes. Using the above example, "Clinton *reconsiders* issue" provides the same general description (i.e., denotation) of his action but offers a very different perspective on this activity.

Connotative Image. Photographs can provide visual support to a story. In some cases, however, photos convey independent messages. Photographs often are posed; indeed, newspapers often rely on *file photos* that may have been taken long before the event being covered. The public relations department of a company may also provide photographs if a story involves one of their employees.

Photos can also be altered. Photojournalist Howard Chapnick observes:

Over the years, I have seen many examples of journalistic distortion by pictures taken out of context, by the use of prejudicial rhetoric in captioning of photographs, and by editors making composites of two separate news photographs and publishing it as one image. There are dozens of ways to alter reality if journalistic integrity is absent.[73]

Now You See It, Now You Don't: Photographic images can be altered through computer manipulation. The Coke can was electronically removed from the original picture when it was published in the *St. Louis Post-Dispatch*. The newspaper argued that publishing the picture without the Coke can improved the appearance of the photograph. However, this raises some ethical questions about photo editors tampering with the "reality" of a situation. Photo by J. B. Forbes, reprinted by permission of the *St. Louis Post-Dispatch*, copyright 1993.

The framing of a photographic image can construct a new reality. This photo, taken at the 1992 Environmental Summit, captures an instant in which U.S. president George Bush and Cuban leader Fidel Castro seemingly are involved in a small group discussion. However, the camera simply caught a moment in which Castro passed in front of Bush. In reality, the two politicians did not acknowledge each other at the meeting. Photo courtesy of Agence France-Presse

The framing of a picture establishes arbitrary boundaries that can affect our perceptions of reality. For instance, a photographer can establish relationships that do not exist by isolating two figures in a crowd. Tabloids take this principle a step further by creating composite pictures—that is, taking two separate pictures (e.g., Bill Clinton and Elvis) and positioning them next to one another to create a new meaning.

MEDIA LITERACY TIPS

PHOTOGRAPHS

The following questions are useful in considering the role of *photographs* within the context of print journalism articles:

√ What is the function of the photo?

√ How do I feel as a result of looking at the photograph? (What is your affective response?)

√ Is this a posed or spontaneous shot? What does this reveal?

√ What is the relationship between the print article and the photograph?

√ What messages are conveyed by the photo?

Graphics. In order to cater to the skimming habits of its readership and attract readers, mainstream papers have followed the lead of *USA Today* by relying on attractive graphics. However, this format is often more flashy than informative. For instance, the front page of each section of *USA Today* includes a regular "USA Snapshots" feature, a "look at statistics that shape the nation" in handy graph form. One issue charts the distribution of sexual harassment charges filed nationally. However, a close examination of the graph (see Figure 6.7) raises more questions than it answers:

- The graph only includes four states plus the District of Columbia. Why were these areas singled out? How do other districts compare to the ones cited? What accounts for the frequency of harassment charges filed in these areas?

- What do these numbers mean? How do these statistics compare with the 1989 figures? How do they compare to other countries?

- Why does the graph exclude federal and state government harassment charges filed? How significant are *those* numbers?

- These statistics reflect the number of sexual harassment charges *filed* in 1990. How many of these charges are upheld in court? How many complaints go unfiled, and why?

- What patterns emerge in regard to the nature of the complaints?

Figure 6.7
Graphics: Truly Informative or Just Flashy?

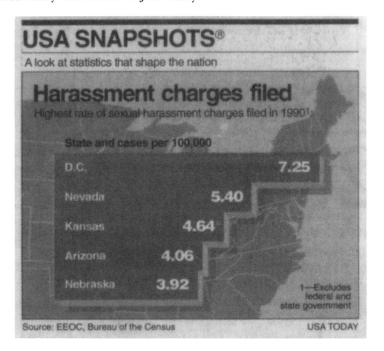

USA SNAPSHOTS®

A look at statistics that shape the nation

Harassment charges filed

Highest rate of sexual harassment charges filed in 1990[1]

State and cases per 100,000

D.C.	7.25
Nevada	5.40
Kansas	4.64
Arizona	4.06
Nebraska	3.92

1—Excludes federal and state government

Source: EEOC, Bureau of the Census   USA TODAY

CASE STUDY

Kelly Cann, a graduate student in Media Communications at Webster University, conducted the following media analysis of *USA Today*'s coverage of the mass suicide by the Branch Davidian cult in Waco, Texas, using selected keys to interpreting media messages (see Figure 6.8):

Page 4A of the April 20, 1993 edition of *USA Today* provides a good example of how placement of stories, editing techniques, and biases create messages. Four articles are arranged on this page. The top right article depicts the reaction of the Branch Davidians' kin to the Waco fire. The facts were presented in the following order: kin express dismay over loss of family members; many of these kin had already accepted a violent outcome and knew the cult members were prepared to die; relatives are divided on who is responsible for the tragedy (some blame the FBI, others blame Koresh). The order in which these facts are presented builds to the question of who is responsible and leaves the impression that this tragedy may have been avoided. Selecting other facts, such as concentrating on the sorrow the kin felt, would have changed the focus entirely.

The message underlying the first article, "who is responsible?," becomes the topic of the second, which states that FBI tactics are being questioned "in some

Figure 6.8
USA Today's Coverage of the Branch Davidian Mass Suicide

SIEGE IN TEXAS

TIMELINE

A CHRONOLOGICAL LOOK AT THE 51-DAY SIEGE OUTSIDE WACO

BEFORE GUN BATTLE: Agents attempt to enter the Texas compound from the roof on Feb. 28.

KWTX-TV via AP

7-week standoff: How it happened

THE FIRST ATTACK: Sunday, Feb. 28: About 100 Bureau of Alcohol, Tobacco and Firearms agents move in on the compound of Branch Davidian leader David Koresh, suspected of illegal firearms violations. Four agents are killed and 16 others wounded in the 45-minute battle. Koresh, also known as Vernon Howell, later says he and others were wounded and his 2-year-old daughter killed.

WEEK OF MARCH 2: Koresh talks for about 25 minutes to station KRLD, saying the gun battle was "unnecessary." The broadcast is the last live public comment from Koresh. ATF spokeswoman Sharon Wheeler tells reporters the agency was "outgunned" by the cult Sunday.

Koresh, in a 58-minute taped sermon broadcast on radio and TV, says he will surrender. But no one leaves the compound. ATF announces later that Koresh said he would surrender when he received "further instruction from God." During the week, two women and 21 children leave the compound, including a young boy with a box of 12 puppies.

WEEK OF MARCH 7: Sect members hang a banner outside a window: "God Help Us We Want the Press." Koresh tells authorities in the evening that he has a headache, leaving negotiations to other cult members for the next two days. Koresh's mother, Bonnie Halderman, and attorney Dick DeGuerin, whom she hired on the sect leader's behalf, are turned away from approaching the law enforcement compound, where negotiations are taking place. Kathy Schroeder and Oliver Gyarfas leave the cult compound.

WEEK OF MARCH 14: Schroeder and Gyarfas talk with sect members inside the compound and ask them to come out peacefully and surrender.

Another banner appears from a compound window: "FBI broke negotiations, we want press." Later, similar messages are sent in Morse code, via a flashing light that appears in a window after dark.

Authorities illuminate compound with stadium-type spotlights, saying they want to protect agents from gun-toting cult members.

DeGuerin urges Koresh to surrender. Steven Schneider, Koresh's top aide, and Wayne Martin, a Harvard-educated attorney, meet for almost an hour with an FBI negotiator and McLennan County Sheriff Jack Harwell. Schneider indicates 30 sect members are ready to leave. FBI uses loudspeakers to blare tapes of negotiations to cult members. Brad Branch and Kevin Whitecliff leave compound, first to exit in a week. Cult members collect rainwater in pots and pans.

WEEK OF MARCH 21: In biggest exodus of siege, seven sect members leave — James Lawter, Gladys Ottman, Sheila Martin, Annetta Richards, Ofelia Santoyo, Rita Riddle and Victorine Hollingsworth, who is hospitalized with heart condition. They are joined later by cult member Livingston Fagan. Authorities blast compound with chants of Tibetan monks praying. They say Koresh allows only those who would be a drain or a liability in a shootout to leave. Koresh breaks off negotiations, saying cult is celebrating a "high holy day." Louis Alaniz, a Houston man described as a "religious fanatic," and a California man who identifies himself as "Jesse Amen" sneak into compound.

WEEK OF MARCH 28: After four days of silence, Koresh talks to negotiators again. Houston attorney DeGuerin has a phone conversation with him. DeGuerin talks with Koresh on the porch of the compound, describes conversation as "very good, useful." Federal officials say those who left the compound noted the significance of Passover and that a breakthrough might occur in conjunction with the religious holiday. DeGuerin meets with sect leaders. FBI says Koresh appears closer to ending standoff but is still waiting on a sign from God. They say they will change tactics if Passover comes and goes without a surrender.

WEEK OF APRIL 4: Koresh says he will surrender after members of the cult celebrate Passover — their highest holy day — but only he knows when their version begins and ends. Branch Davidians negotiate multimillion-dollar book or movie contracts to pay legal fees. FBI is optimistic that an end to the siege may be near. Sect leaders now say there is no significance to Passover observance and no plan to surrender when it's over. FBI reports FBI says Koresh's plan to sell book and movie rights to his life story for more than $2.5 million doesn't mean the standoff may not end violently. Koresh sends out angry, four-page "letter from God," depicting a powerful and vengeful God "who will smite his enemies." FBI says Koresh now appears to be waiting for a natural disaster before surrendering.

WEEK OF APRIL 11: Agents blast louder music. Cult members appear at windows and walk out doors, apparently to gauge FBI response. Passover ends with no end to the standoff. Koresh sends out word he will surrender after writing a manuscript in which he reveals the contents of the seven seals referred to in the Bible's book of Revelation. FBI agents say they won't wait forever. Officials: Agents clear debris from the compound, using tanks to move three vehicles, including Koresh's prized black Camaro.

THE FINAL ATTACK: Monday, April 19: The Branch Davidian compound burns to the ground after FBI agents, in an armored vehicle, smash the buildings and pump in tear gas to force cult members outside. The Justice Department says cult members set the fire. Some sect members are taken into custody. The fate of Koresh and as many as 86 others is not immediately known. They are believed to have perished.

OUT OF COMPOUND: A child holds a drink after being freed in March.

Jeff Mitchell, Reuters

Kin: 'This is just bloody unreal'

Tragic end no surprise for some

By Andrea Stone and Deeda Moss
USA TODAY

The long and fretful sleep of Bruce and Lisa Gent ended abruptly Tuesday morning when the phone rang in their Melbourne, Australia, home.

The long-awaited news from Waco couldn't be worse.

"I just lost my whole family. Two kids and two grandkids," said Bruce Gent. "This is just bloody unreal."

But the fiery end to the 51-day standoff at the Branch Davidian compound — aired as it happened — was all too real. The inferno is believed to have left as many as 86 people dead, including 17 children. Only nine cult members are believed to have survived.

The Gents' daughter Nicole, 24, and her two young children by cult leader David Koresh were not among the known survivors. Nicole's twin brother, Peter, died in the Feb. 28 shootout.

"They were all prepared to die for" Koresh, Lisa Gent says of her children.

Many family members of those inside the compound had long resigned themselves to the violent outcome.

Others, like Gladys Williams of Tottenham, England, stayed glued to the TV, watching for clues to the fate of her sister and brother-in-law.

But Kiri Jewell, 12, whose mother Sherri may have died in the blaze, was "very calm, very controlled" Monday, said her aunt Lisa Jewell-Swaine.

"This is what (cult members) told her was going to happen," Jewell-Swaine said.

"It was inevitable," said Kirt's father David, who last February sued to remove his daughter from the compound.

"There was no chance for a peaceful resolution."

Relatives and friends were divided on who was responsible for the fiery ending.

Federal agents say cult members set the deadly blaze.

"No, no way," said Jean Holub, Koresh's grandmother. "He wouldn't do that to those children."

Cult member Karen Doyle, 21, accused federal agents of starting the fire, but said she was not concerned about her father and sister inside.

"God will take care of them," she said. "They're fine. I'm not worried about them."

June Craddock took a more practical approach. "I don't blame the FBI," she said before leaving her son Graham, 31, survived.

"They have been very patient after what happened."

ROADBLOCK: Federal officials and Texas public safety officers try for a look at the burning Branch Davidian compound Monday as they enforce a roadblock several miles from the compound. As many as 86 people, including 17 children, are thought to have died during the cult's final stand.

By Steven D. Reece, Waco Tribune-Herald via AP

What could they do? Those people would have probably remained in there for two years. They had enough food."

Federal agents "screwed up again," said Karen Buda. Her father-in-law, Don Bunds, is a Branch Davidian leader not involved in the standoff, but who worked with the FBI during the negotiations.

"Last week they were saying 'we'll wait this out as long as it takes.' This morning they come in punching holes in the place. They made the people mad."

"I am scared to death," said Koresh's mother, Bonnie Halderman. "Where's our civil rights? It's just terrible. The way they handled this whole thing has been wrong."

But other relatives were angry at Koresh, whom they blame for their misfortune.

"He wasn't a normal man," said Oliver Gyarfas, whose granddaughter, Aisha Gyarfas, is believed among the dead. "I never trusted him. The people inside were brainwashed."

Contributing: Jim Greenhill

FBI tactics questioned in some quarters

By Dennis Cauchon, Bruce Frankel and Robert Davis
USA TODAY

The FBI came in for some second-guessing Monday for its decision to initiate an attack against the Branch Davidians.

Frank Bolz, a hostage negotiator, said law enforcement should have relied on time and not forced a resolution.

"A little stimulation is OK, but you do it and then wait," said Bolz, who said he developed the negotiation strategy while the FBI used in Waco.

Jerry Mungadze, a cult expert who had supplied a report on the Branch Davidians to the FBI, was even harsher. "I would have said: 'This is the worst thing you could do. If you want everybody to die, go ahead and do this.'"

The FBI's assertiveness pushed David Koresh over the edge, Mungadze said. "The God inside his head was going to (say) destroy everybody."

But ex-U.S. Marshals Service operations director Howard Safir said even the best planning can't always prevent people from killing themselves.

He said he couldn't second-guess the FBI's timing.

"There may have been an event that was about to take place that compelled them to act," he said. "I'm less concerned

SPECTER: Says congressional hearings should be held

act," he said, "like a suicide or harming the children."

Some compared the FBI effort to the attempt in 1985 to remove the MOVE cult from a Philadelphia row house. The police dropped a bomb on MOVE's house, triggering a fire that killed 11, including five children, and left 250 homeless.

"This is MOVE all over again. Why did they go in there?" said Notre Dame law professor G. Robert Blakey.

Blakey questioned why law enforcement officials lost their patience. "If you waited 45 days, why not wait another 45," he said. "I'm less concerned

AFRICA: Police 'should have left them people alone.'

about adults than the children.

The potential loss of life was too great to say that the cost of encirclement was too high."

Ramona Johnson Africa, the only adult to survive the attack on MOVE, said it was unwise to attack the compound.

"They should have left them people (alone)," she said.

Africa said people should doubt the official version.

"While I or my family did not expect the situation to end like this, we certainly are not surprised," she added.

Louis William Brown, chairman of the Philadelphia commission that investigated the MOVE bombing, downplayed

STOKES: We're damned if we do and damned if we don't.

the comparisons. "There are more differences than similarities between Waco and MOVE," he said.

He said the FBI tried to negotiate a settlement over-weeks, even allowing lawyers into the compound. In the MOVE incident, police bombed immediately in a residential neighborhood.

Also, Brown noted, the cult members appear to have started the fire in Waco; in Philadelphia, the police did.

Law enforcement defenders insist that outsiders can't judge the best approach.

"We're damned if we do and damned if we don't," com-

plained Dewey Stokes, president of the Fraternal Order of Police. "If we negotiate, people say we're wasting money. If we act, they say we should've negotiated."

Stokes said people should defer to the experts on the scene.

He said he fears people will shift the blame from Koresh to law enforcement: "We would not have been there if he hadn't broken a law that you, the people, wanted us to enforce."

Sen. Arlen Specter, R-Pa., said hearings should be held on the Waco incident but, for now, he urged withholding judgment. "I think we will have to await the events, to cool off, both figuratively and literally, to take a look at it."

But anti-abortion activist Randall Terry blamed law enforcement's strong-arm tactics. "They finished it the way they started in raw firepower and brute force."

Minister Billy Graham took a different tack. He said he didn't have all the facts, but "I grieve for all those involved. I am especially sorry for the parents and families of those children led astray by a cultist who certainly was not following biblical teaching."

Contributing: Lee Michael Katz

White House maintains distance from FBI decision

By Richard Benedetto
USA TODAY

As the assault on the Branch Davidian compound turned from confrontation to tragedy Monday, the White House remained strategically distant from shouldering blame.

Even in its earliest phases, when the tear gas attacks began, President Clinton tried to distance himself from the decision-makers who said "Go."

"Talk to the attorney general or the FBI," he told reporters in the morning. "I knew it was going to be done, but the decision was entirely theirs. They made the tactical decision."

Later, as TV cameras showed fire raging through the cult's compound, Clinton spokesman George Stephanopoulos declined to say Clinton approved the FBI's plan.

Instead, he said Clinton "raised no objections" when briefed Sunday by Attorney General Janet Reno and the FBI about the plan.

Stephanopoulos said Clinton "did not initiate the action." And he shifted the focus to Reno and FBI Director William Sessions.

"Certainly, he (Clinton) is responsible, but the attorney general and the FBI have operational control over this," Stephanopoulos said.

Later, after it was confirmed that most cult members died, Reno said she took "full responsibility" for the decision.

"I approved the plan," she said, adding that while she discussed it with Clinton by telephone on Sunday, "I did not advise him as to the details."

She said Clinton asked if the plan was "carefully considered," and "the best way to go." "I told him it was the best way to go," Reno said.

But she said she did not, and could not, "assure" the president that there would be no major loss of life.

Reno also tersely denied she was trying to shield Clinton from the flak sure to fly: "The buck stops with me."

Later Monday, Clinton appeared to assume more responsibility for the attack, saying in a statement that "the law enforcement agencies involved in the Waco siege recommended the course of action I pursued today." Reno "recommended that we pro-

ceed with today's action given the risks of maintaining the previous policy indefinitely. I told the attorney general to do what she thought was right, and I stand by that decision."

Meanwhile, Reno and Sessions separately appeared on CNN to defend their decision.

And early today, Reno offered to resign to defuse the political heat.

"If that's what the president wants, I'm happy to do so," she said of possibly offering her resignation. She made the comment on the ABC program Nightline.

On Capitol Hill, Sen. Arlen Specter, R-Pa., a member of the Judiciary Committee, said, "At this moment ... it is impossible to evaluate the wisdom of what the FBI did," but called for hearings.

House Judiciary Committee Chairman Jack Brooks, D-Texas, also said he wants to know if "steps could have been taken to minimize the loss of life, or whether it was a mass suicide ... that could not have been prevented."

Some analysts say it's too early to tell whether Clinton will suffer political damage.

IN WASHINGTON: 'I approved the plan,' Attorney General Janet Reno said at a news briefing Monday. The buck stops with me.

By Charles Tasnadi, AP

But some say he should have been more openly supportive of his attorney general once the assault was made.

"I don't think Americans expect their president to be focused on a matter like this," Secrest said.

But Democratic pollster Alan Secrest doesn't expect the tragedy to affect Clinton's fortunes over the long haul.

quarters." The article emphasizes the FBI's judgment in using aggressive tactics to end the Waco standoff. Although "experts" speak both for and against the FBI's decision, the emphasis suggests that the FBI's impatience caused a tragedy that otherwise could have been averted. This message is reinforced through order of presentation, selection of facts, word choice reflecting the embedded values of the reporters, and the presence of the adjacent Timeline article, running from top to bottom on the left-hand side of the page, which lists the events at Waco from first to final standoff. Various clues are presented through quotes by and descriptions of the behavior of David Koresh that point to his irrationality, unpredictability, instability, and mystical orientation, which suggests that he operated by an entirely different logic than that of the average person or the FBI. Pieces of this article reinforce the message that it would have been foolish to negotiate with Koresh as if he were level-headed, honest, forthright, and played by the rules of military logic (so that when the FBI defended themselves [in the "FBI tactics . . ." article] by saying, "But he said . . ." and "We never expected him to . . .", they sound rather foolish).

The "FBI" article also described the FBI's attempts to hasten negotiations by means of harassment, supporting the previous article's suggestion that their aggressive tactics pushed Koresh over the edge, whereas patience may have produced less grim results. The article thus begins its investigation with a hostage negotiator Jerry Bolz, who states that the FBI should have relied on time and not "forced a resolution." His opinion is immediately reinforced by "cult expert" Jerry Mungadze (previously quoted on page 2A) who says, "I would have said, 'This is the worst thing you could do. If you want everybody to die, go ahead and do this!' " Jerry seems to be *USA Today*'s designated spokesperson for cult experts. A lame alternative view is presented by Howard Safir in response to these strong statements, suggesting that perhaps the FBI had a good reason for acting as they did. The journalist then turns to vague authority and writes that "some" compared the FBI's move on Waco to the MOVE cult disaster in 1985 that killed 11 and left 250 homeless. Two opinions back up this comparison, one being from a survivor of the MOVE attack, who says that the FBI should have left the cult alone. Two opposing views are then inserted, but word choice makes their opinions appear slanted and defensive. William Brown "downplayed" the comparison between MOVE and Waco, and Dewey Stokes "complained" that law enforcement officials are blamed no matter what choice they make. Such word choices help reveal the journalist's embedded values (against the FBI). Two more opinions hint that the FBI screwed up. A senator calls for a hearing on the Waco action, and an anti-abortion activist (what's the connection with abortion?) suggests that the government relies too heavily on brute force to get their way.

Now that the reader has made the connection between the Waco tragedy and the impatience of the FBI, the newspaper links the FBI's actions with President Clinton. The bottom article suggests that Clinton is ducking responsibility for the federal action at Waco and letting Attorney General Janet Reno shoulder the blame. She is presented as a scapegoat, while he is portrayed as a coward. The article opens, "As the assault on the Branch Davidian compound turned from confrontation to tragedy Monday, the White House remained *strategically distant from shouldering blame.*" The journalist's opinion seem to be embedded in the fact, since who is responsible for the tragedy is at this moment a matter of opinion.

The article describes Clinton as purposefully trying to distance himself from the Waco decision, although he gave the ultimate go-ahead to Reno. In this article, the fact that he was not presented with the details makes him look irresponsible.

Page 4A of *USA Today* uses interplay between the four articles to create a bigger, more dramatic message than each article could create alone. A kind of synergy. Embedded values are omnipresent, each article slanting a little more to pointing the finger at the federal government for being hasty and irresponsible. The flow of this message is dictated by the positioning of stories, the selection and order of facts, and incorporating opinion into the factual account.[74]

NOTES

1. *The Quill,* November–December 1991.

2. Daniel W. Pfaff, *Joseph Pulitzer II and the Post-Dispatch* (University Park, PA: Pennsylvania State University Press, 1991), 76.

3. Edmund C. Arnold, *Modern Newspaper Design* (New York: Harper & Row, 1969), 329.

4. Martin A. Lee and Norman Soloman, *Unreliable Sources: A Guide to Detecting Bias in the News Media* (Secaucus, NJ: Carol Publishing Group, 1990), 66.

5. Ibid., 64.

6. "Why Advertorials Will Work For You," *'Teen* Magazine Media Kit (Chicago: 'Teen Magazine, 1993).

7. "Having a Bad Hair Day?" *'Teen,* November 1993, 29.

8. Lee and Soloman, *Unreliable Sources,* 67–68.

9. Mobil Corporation, "When Ripples Make Waves," *Time,* July 26, 1993, 7.

10. Lee and Soloman, *Unreliable Sources,* 110.

11. Ibid., 112.

12. Gerald C. Stone, *Examining Newspapers* (Newbury Park, CA: Sage Publications, 1987), 116.

13. Leo Jeffres, *Mass Media Processes and Effects* (Prospect Heights, IL: Waveland Press, 1986), 123–24.

14. Lee and Soloman, *Unreliable Sources,* 122.

15. Stone, *Examining Newspapers,* 109.

16. Herbert Gans, *Deciding What's News* (New York: Pantheon Books, 1979), 31–37.

17. Philip Gaunt, *Choosing the News: The Profit Factor in News Selection* (New York: Greenwood Press, 1990), 127.

18. Ben Bagdikian, *The Media Monopoly,* 3d ed. (Boston: Beacon Press, 1990), 18.

19. Ibid., 47–48.

20. Ibid., 39–40.

21. Ibid., 41–42.

22. Ronald K. L. Collins, *Dictating Content: How Advertising Pressure Can Corrupt a Free Press* (Washington, D.C.: Center for the Study of Commercialism, 1992), 25.

23. Ibid., 17.

24. Ibid., 34.

25. Ibid., 36.

26. U.S. Bureau of the Census, *Historical Statistics of the United States, Colonial Times to 1970, Bicentennial Edition, Pt. 2* (Washington, D.C.: Government Printing Office, 1975), 11.

27. Editor & Publisher, *1993 Editor & Publisher International Yearbook* (New York: Editor & Publisher, 1993).

28. Tripp Frolichstein, interview by author, St. Louis, MO, July 21, 1992.

29. Editor & Publisher, *1993 Editor & Publisher International Yearbook.*

30. Bagdikian, *Media Monopoly,* 85.

31. Ibid.

32. Tripp Frohlichstein, interview by author.

33. "The 10 Best-Censored Stories of 1992," *St. Louis Journalism Review,* December 1992–January 1993, 14–15.

34. "Junk Food News of 1992," *St. Louis Journalism Review,* February 1993, 3.

35. Charles L. Klotzer, "There," *St. Louis Journalism Review,* October 1991, 2.

36. Pat Widder, "Minority's Newsroom Presence Edges Higher," *Chicago Tribune,* Business section, 3.

37. Patricia Corrigan, "Student Worms Way to Honors Division," *St. Louis Post-Dispatch,* April 10, 1991, A3.

38. Lee and Soloman, *Unreliable Sources,* 44.

39. Dick Siccone, managing editor, *Chicago Tribune,* telephone interview by author, April 28, 1992.

40. Arnold, *Newspaper Design,* 309.

41. Dick Siccone, interview by author.

42. Society of Professional Journalists, Sigma Delta Chi. Greencastle, IN, 1984.

43. Edward Jay Epstein, "Journalism and Truth," in *Mass Media Issues,* ed. George Rodman (Chicago: SRA, 1981), 90.

44. "Reagan Calls Summit 'Momentous,' " *St. Louis Post-Dispatch,* June 4, 1988, A1.

45. Ted J. Smith III, "The Watchdog's Bite," *The American Enterprise,* January–February 1990, 63–64.

46. Bagdikian, *Media Monopoly,* 63.

47. Mark Hertsgaard, *On Bended Knee* (New York: Farrar Straus Giroux, 1988), 334.

48. Bagdikian, *Media Monopoly,* 64.

49. Hertsgaard, *On Bended Knee,* 65.

50. "U.S. Won't Make More Plutonium," *St. Louis Post-Dispatch,* July 14, 1992, A1.

51. Hugh Dellios, "Denny Beating Trial Juror Is Replaced," *Chicago Tribune,* October 12, 1993, sec. 1, 5.

52. Peter Kerr, "A Cure for Paperwork, or Just New Headaches?" *New York Times,* September 25, 1993, A8.

53. Nathanial Sheppard, Jr., "U.S. Troops Arrive in a Tense Haiti," *Chicago Tribune,* October 11, 1993, A1.

54. Bill Lambrecht, "Californians Flock to Perot," *St. Louis Post-Dispatch,* May 28, 1992, A1.

55. Rick Hampton, "What Americans Want from the New Administration," *St. Louis Post-Dispatch*, November 8, 1992, 5.

56. John E. Warriner, *Handbook of English*, Book Two (New York: Harcourt, Brace, 1951), 153.

57. Richard Lacayo, "Tower Terror," *Time*, March 8, 1993, 35.

58. Stephen Engleberg, "U.S. Envoy Meets Clan Leader's Kin in Somali Capital," *New York Times*, October 11, 1993, A1.

59. Paul Watson, "U.S. Troops Continue Hunt for Missing Army Ranger," *New York Times*, October 8, 1993, A9.

60. Tripp Frohlichstein, *Media Training Handbook* (St. Louis: MediaMasters, 1991), 54–56.

61. Lee and Soloman, *Unreliable Sources*, 18.

62. Martin Gottlieb, "Dangerous Liaisons," *Columbia Journalism Review*, July–August 1989, 26.

63. Walter Karp, "Who Decides What Is News? (Hint: It's Not Journalists)," *Utne Reader*, November–December 1989, 61.

64. Lee and Soloman, *Unreliable Sources*, 17.

65. Ibid., 42.

66. William E. François, *Mass Media Law and Regulation*, 2d ed. (Columbus, OH: Drake University School of Journalism, 1978), 137–38.

67. Joan Ryan, "The Greatest Tragedy Is That Ashe Didn't Have a Choice," *Sporting News*, April 20, 1992, 4.

68. John Leo, "Reading Between the Hyphens," *U.S. News & World Report*, May 21, 1990, 23.

69. 1989 Multicultural Management Program Fellows, *Dictionary of Cautionary Words and Phrases: An Excerpt from the Newspaper Content Analysis Compiled by 1989 Multicultural Management Program Fellows* (Columbia: University of Missouri School of Journalism, 1989).

70. Leo, "Reading Between the Hyphens," 23.

71. 1989 Multicultural Management Program Fellows, *Dictionary of Cautionary Words and Phrases*.

72. Maureen Dowd, "How a Battered Clinton Has Stayed Alive," *New York Times*, March 16, 1992, A15.

73. Howard Chapnick, "Markets & Careers," *Popular Photography*, August 1982, 42.

74. Kelly Cann, "Literacy Analysis: USA TODAY" (paper delivered for MED 531, Media and Culture, St. Louis, MO, May 1993).

CHAPTER 7

ADVERTISING

OVERVIEW

The average American is immersed in advertising:

- In 1990, corporations spent $130 billion on advertising—the equivalent of $522 for every person in the United States.
- The average American consumer is exposed to 1,500 advertising messages per day.[1]
- By the age of 17, the average American will have seen 350,000 commercials.[2]

Some disagreement exists about the effectiveness of advertising messages. Studies show that nine out of ten people can't remember the product or company featured in the last commercial they watched, even if it was less than five minutes ago.[3] However, research also indicates that two thirds of all consumers buy *only* well-known brands, suggesting that advertising indeed does play a role in consumer buying decisions.[4]

Tony Schwartz makes an important distinction between *memory* and *recall* in advertising:

Researchers narrowly focus their questions on a subject's recollection of commercial content, which they consider the essence of what makes a message effective. . . . [However,] if we make a deep attachment to the product in the commercial, there is no need to depend on their remembering the name of the product. Seeing the product in the store should evoke the association attached to the product in the commercial.[5]

Thus, although people may not remember specific information about a product as expressed in an advertisement, the consumer may *recall* the product once they wander down the grocery store aisle and spy the product.

But beyond the promotion of specific brands, advertisements send cumulative messages about what kind of world we live in, media stereotypes, sexual roles, and measures of success. To illustrate, in November 1991, Surgeon General Antonia Novello criticized alcohol ads aimed at underage drinkers. Novello asked the alcohol industry to voluntarily eliminate ads that "make drinking look like the key to fun and a wonderful and carefree lifestyle." The surgeon general identified the following cumulative messages in ads related to alcohol and young people:

- It is acceptable to drink.
- Alcohol is safe.
- Alcohol builds confidence.
- Alcohol is part of a sexy, glamorous, and active lifestyle.[6]

PROCESS

Function

Advertising performs a variety of manifest functions:

- Informing the public about a product.
- Attracting the attention of the consumer to the product.
- Motivating the consumer to action.
- Stimulating markets.
- Supporting the business community.
- Establishing and maintaining a lasting relationship between the consumer and a company.

American consumers rely on advertising for services and goods. We scan the papers for bargains, entertainment information, holiday gift ideas, and trends in fashion. Public service spots warn us about dangers in society (e.g., "Say no to drugs") and encourage us to be better citizens by giving to various charities.

However, advertising serves a number of latent functions as well:

Persuasion. Advertising cannot convince consumers to purchase something that they truly don't want: If you don't like coconut, no ad will convince you that you do.[7] However, impulse displays located by the checkout counters in stores are designed to stimulate a desire for items that you do fancy but may not be thinking about at the moment. And in cases in which the customer is already shopping for a product, ads are designed to steer the consumer to their particular brand.

Nevertheless, advertisers try to convince us that we don't merely want a product but in fact *need* it. Advertisements often contain an imperative (e.g., "Buy it today!").

Shaping attitudes. Before advertisers can alter specific consumer behaviors, they are often faced with the more fundamental problem of shaping attitudes. Indeed, the agency of Campbell-Mithun-Esty sees its primary task as creating "desired attitudes" among consumers: "What attitudes must we establish or change? What habits do we want formed? Do we want that person to know something new has happened, or become aware of additional product uses, or sample our product, or change a negative attitude or misconception?"[8]

In that regard, some ad campaigns are designed to create a positive image for the company rather than sell a particular product. For example, General Dynamics, a defense contractor, sponsored a 1990 PBS series on heroic figures such as Winston Churchill, Dwight D. Eisenhower, Lyndon B. Johnson, and Pope John XXIII. The ads stressed the value of education, help for the handicapped, peace, and patriotism.

When encountering a public relations advertisement like the General Dynamics campaign, it is appropriate to ask *why* the company has chosen to solicit the goodwill of the public. In this case, the ad campaign was designed to cultivate a climate in which the government would feel more comfortable awarding contracts to General Dynamics in the wake of a series of financial scandals. Robert A. Morris, corporate vice president of General Dynamics, commented, "If you have credibility . . . it will pay off on the bottom line."[9]

Fostering consumer culture. Advertisers encourage the audience to think of themselves in terms of their consumer behavior. Advertising promotes membership in a group (e.g., "The Pepsi Generation"), based on common buying patterns. Indeed, by wearing designer labels or sweatshirts with commercials logos, consumers have been transformed into living advertisements for products.

In this regard, the mission of education in contemporary culture has been reduced to educated *consumerism.* In the past, an educated person was regarded as someone who had been exposed to the world of ideas and had developed the critical skills that enabled him or her to ask questions, analyze options, reach logical conclusions, and make decisions. Today, however, an educated consumer is measured by whether he or she has the background and ability to be a "smart shopper." Ads for Syms Department Stores refer to their salespeople as "educators"; they have taken over the teacher's role of instructing their "pupils" on matters of importance—that is, how to consume wisely.

Some ads have even equated consumerism with American democracy. A

1989 McDonald's ad features a young man lauding the choices and convenience of breakfast at the fast-food restaurant: "Is this a great country, or what?" he asks. Freedom has been translated into the freedom to *buy*.

Establishing standards of behavior and lifestyle. Advertising influences how consumers spend their time and money. For instance, each season, fashion designers present a new "look" to boost sales. Ad slogans have been incorporated into peoples' common vernacular ("You Got the Right One, Baby! Uh Huh!").

Advertising also has assumed a principal role in the delineation of taste. A marketing executive for Pepsi-Cola once offered the opinion that his competitor, Diet Coke, had made a conscious decision to keep the taste of its product indistinct. Consequently, while nobody initially liked Diet Coke, no one disliked the product either. Through clever promotion ("Just for the taste of it"), consumers learned that it was stylish to drink Diet Coke, eventually developing a taste for the soft drink.

Entertainment. Advertising was one of the first public communications formats to realize that any message, if presented in an entertaining fashion, will attract the interest of the public. A 1989 survey reveals that 16 percent of the American public devote as much attention to television commercials as compared with the attention they give the programs. And 2 percent of the public admits that they devote *more* attention to ads than the programs themselves.[10]

In some cases, advertising has merged with entertainment. For instance, the Home Shopping Network attracts large numbers of viewers who enjoy the merchandising of products. Only slightly less subtle is MTV. The entertainment content (music videos) provides exposure for recording artists and promotes sales for concerts and compact discs (CDs).

As principal message. Instead of simply supporting programming, in some cases advertising has emerged as the predominant message. Content is merely a marketing strategy to attract readers to the ads. Deborah Baldwin cites a former *Self* magazine editor: "It's not just a matter of individual advertisers influencing editorial content. The whole point of the magazine is to promote products, so the advertiser doesn't even have to ask."[11]

Comparative Media

Finding the most efficient way to reach their target audience presents a formidable challenge for advertisers. (See Figure 7.1 for a summary of comparative media.) Obviously, the most direct means of convincing a consumer is through interpersonal communication, so the customer can feel, smell, see, and taste the product. However, in order to reach a mass audience, the advertiser must rely on *indirect* experience to promote the merits of the product. For instance, in order to sell beer on television, visuals must suggest the taste and texture of the beverage. In a Miller Draft

Beer campaign, opening the bottle instantly transforms a hot climate into a frosty winter world. The intent is to suggest the cold, crisp taste of Miller through the visuals.

Every medium has its own distinctive characteristics that determine its ability to promote particular types of products to specific audiences. Jay Schulberg of the ad agency Ogilvy and Mather observes that

the mediums [sic] can do different things. TV can create awareness more quickly with a larger percentage of the population at a lower cost. To do that in print becomes prohibitively expensive; it's almost impossible. However, print can inform better.

If one has a complicated message, or where the consumer is spending a lot of money for a product, such as a VCR or a television set, people want information, and you can get a lot more into print than you can get into a 30-second spot. So where TV may create the awareness, say, for a car, people want to read about what the car has, in my view.[12]

Advertisers consider the following factors when deciding which medium to employ to promote their products:

- Which medium is best suited to convey the advertising message?
- Which medium is the target audience most likely to use?
- How can the client make the most efficient use of the advertising budget?
- Which medium can display the product most attractively and effectively?

Print. Print is a medium that can accommodate detailed information about a product. The tangible nature of print allows consumers to refer back to ads when they want specific information. As a result, people rely on newspapers more than any other medium when they are ready to buy.[13]

In addition, print ads also have the advantage of blending in with editorial content. For instance, in fashion magazines it is often difficult to distinguish between fashion articles and ads promoting a line of apparel. In addition, print ads are often associated with the publication in which it is published, so ads placed in prestigious periodicals are accorded commensurate respect.

Print ads generally are very carefully crafted. In contrast with television, an advertising team concentrates on one frame. As a result, all elements have been carefully selected to fulfill the objective of the ad in this one moment.

Radio. The lack of visual support in radio obviously makes it impossible for an ad to demonstrate the features of a product. However, radio advertisers can take advantage of the imaginative possibilities of the medium to sell their product. For instance, a radio spot for the Volkswagen Jetta asks, "How do I help you visualize the Volkswagen Jetta?" The narrator then

Figure 7.1
Comparative Media: Advertising

Newspapers

Advantages	**Disadvantages**
Geographic Market Selectivity	Lack of Permanence
Flexibility--Ease of Ad Insertion	Poor Printing Quality
Editorial Support	Limited Demographic Orientation
Broad Coverage	Wasted Circulation
Considerable Reader Interest	High Cost for National Advertisers
	Ad Can Be Buried

Magazines

Advantages	**Disadvantages**
Demographic Market Selectivity	Lack of Flexibility--Difficult to Make Last-Minute Changes
Long-Life Ad Capability	Limited Availability
Good Quality Print Production	High Cost--Especially for Color
Editorial Support	Limited Local Ad Opportunities
Reader Interest	Ad Can Be Buried
Upscale Audience/Prestige	

Radio

Advantages

Geographic and Demographic Market Selectivity

Universal Accessibility

Relatively Inexpensive

Personal Nature of Radio

Pace Determined By Advertiser

Local Appeal

Portability

Costs for Ads Have Remained Stable

Growth of the Radio Audience

Flexible Format
- Time can be bought on short notice
- Changes can be made on short notice

Disadvantages

Lack of Permanence--Perishability

Clutter

Lack of Visual Support

Limited Impact--
Background Medium

Television

Advantages

Visualization of Product

Geographic Market Selectivity

Significant Market Penetration

Can Deliver Huge Audiences

Legitimacy of Medium

Disadvantages

Perishable Ad Message Unless Repeated

Relatively Expensive

Clutter--Message May Become Lost in Group of Ads

Not Terribly Selective Medium

Limited Time for Presentation

Relatively Inflexible Format
- Ad slots often bought up well in advance of
presentation

plays a variety of classical selections to suggest gracefulness, performance, and being "at one" with the car. He concludes by inviting us to "imagine the difference between mere transportation and pure driving pleasure."

Like print ads, radio commercials can blend in with the regular programming. For instance, sports broadcasters used to drop commercials in the middle of their play-by-play, casually mentioning that this would be an appropriate moment to "pour yourself a cold one." Sports announcers are now required to include a disclaimer during the course of a broadcast that "any mention of the product is a paid commercial message."

Radio ads feature catchy jingles as well as sophisticated recording techniques and performance. In fact, former ad composer Barry Manilow was able to parlay his understanding of jingles (simple melodies and snappy lyrics) into a successful career in the popular music market.

The radio advertiser must condense as much information into the abbreviated time allotted, at the same time making sure that the information is presented clearly enough to be easily followed. The message must be simplified and the presentation concise. The radio advertiser is limited to one minute, or approximately 200 to 300 words; in contrast, the print advertiser can use as many as 1,000 words to promote the product.[14] The pace is determined by the advertiser; as a result, if the audience is inattentive, the message is irretrievably lost. But, as mentioned earlier, the radio listener is often engaged in competing activities, so he or she may be particularly susceptible to advertising messages.

Television. Television is certainly the most prestigious advertising medium. Merely by appearing on the airwaves, products (and companies) assume a measure of legitimacy. Local pitchmen often enjoy a minor celebrity status in their community, simply by appearing before the camera.

Arthur Bellaire observes that an effective television spot must combine visuals, sound, and narrative information to present the message:

The video and the corresponding audio should relate. Don't be demonstrating one sales feature while talking about another. . . . While the audio should be relevant to the video, don't waste words by describing what is obvious in the picture. Rather, see that the words interpret the picture and thereby advance the thought. Rely on the video to carry more than half the weight. Being a visual medium, television is more effective at showing than telling. Avoid static scenes. Provide for camera movement and changes of scenes.[15]

The distinctive features of television offer a number of advantages in promoting products:

Demonstration. Television is supreme in its ability to show how a product is used.

Dramatization. Advertisers find that ads are effective when they "activate" the product by showing it being used by people. Beyond simply demonstrating how a product is used, television ads present a scenario in which the product makes a significant impact on the lives of the characters.

Performance. More than other medium, television is particularly adept at presenting people who are consuming and enjoying the product. A convincing performance can make a difference in persuading its audience to purchase the product.

Affective appeal. The combination of music and pictures can touch the emotions of the viewer.

Audience

The American Marketing Association offers a rather curious definition of advertising: "A paid form of a *non-personal* presentation and promotion of ideas, goods, or service by an identified sponsor aimed at a particular target market and audience [emphasis mine]." [16]

In many respects, advertising is an *extraordinarily* personal form of mass communications. After all, the success of an ad depends on advertisers' ability to identify and then persuade one person. Indeed, John O'Toole, chairman of Foote, Cone & Belding Advertising, regards advertising as a form of interpersonal communication. He observes, "When the chord is struck in one, the vibrations reverberate in millions." [17]

Advertisers devote considerable attention to research to become familiar with their audience. *Demographic research* refers to the study of human populations. Demographic considerations such as geographical location can play a large role in consumer buying patterns. For example, black is the predominant automobile color on the East Coast, while white and lighter shades of cars are preferred on the West Coast.

Other demographic categories include age, gender, income, education, occupation, race, religion, and family size.

Psychographic research identifies the attitudes, values, and lifestyles shared by groups falling within these demographic categories. Psychographic research enables advertisers to identify the consumption patterns of particular subgroups. For example, you can look forward to the following stages of consumerism after completing college:

- *Young single.* You have moved to your own apartment and begun to make your own buying decisions. A high proportion of this income is spent on clothes, personal care, recreation, and entertainment.

- *Young marrieds, no children.* In general, you become more home oriented. For all but a small proportion of these households, the wife works, providing a higher standard of living for the household. Most consumer buying decisions begin to be made by the female.

- *Young marrieds, children under six.* At this stage, the couple becomes tied down. If the wife quits her job, the family income goes down—although in most cases, the wife continues to work. A move to a larger apartment or house is required.

- *Young marrieds, children over six.* Your children have entered school. At this point, the wife has more freedom for activities outside the home. The children begin to influence purchasing decisions.

- *Older marrieds with children.* Your expenses increase for education, weddings, and the like. You begin to engage in more activities away from home. For instance, you begin to travel more frequently.

- *Older marrieds, no children.* Your children have left home. Smaller living quarters are now required. Your consumption patterns no longer need to consider the children.

- *Older singles.* At this stage you have become widows, widowers, divorcees, and unmarried men or women. You experience a dramatic change in lifestyle as your income is reduced.[18]

Advertisers have discovered that lifestyle has a direct bearing on consumer patterns. For instance, automobile purchases are most numerous among young marrieds with no children and young marrieds with children over six. And because young marrieds with small children are generally less mobile than other groups, they are the most promising prospects for television purchases.

Advertisers can even predict consumer buying patterns on the basis of a consumer's previous purchases. The BBDO Advertising Agency uses a system of *lifestyle indicators (LSIs)* to predict cross-product consumer buying patterns: "[We can] relate the usage of your product to the usage of other products. Through this method we can determine whether your prime prospects drink wine or beer, if they travel outside the U.S., what kinds of cars they drive, what books they read, etc."[19]

As a result, after you have made a purchase, you may be flooded with direct-mail advertising for other types of products that, according to LSIs, might interest you.

Audience research enables advertisers to tailor their message to the needs and interests of the target market. For instance, NBC radio's *Wall Street Report* is sponsored by Audi, an import luxury sedan. "Audiwatch" spokesperson Amy O'Connor urges us to "put Audi on our *shortlist.*" This corporate codeword (meaning a select group that has survived an elimination process) is both familiar and appealing to the upscale audience Audi is trying to attract.

In some cases, products are even modified to meet the needs of a particular subgroup. For instance, Campbell's "Soup for One" is a case in which a product was repackaged to meet the needs of people living alone.

Multiple Audiences. Media programming may also be directed simultaneously at both a manifest and latent audience. For example, ads that appear in women's magazines such as *Cosmopolitan* or *Vogue* are often surprisingly alluring and seductive, given that the target audience consists primarily of heterosexual women. One way to account for this sexually titillating advertising would be by suggesting that the latent audience actually consists of *males*. Women readers project themselves into the role of the model and then respond to the ads from a male perspective. ("How would he like me in this outfit?") This explanation has some rather disturbing implications. For while chic, progressive magazines like *Cosmopolitan* purport to be fashionably liberated, this advertising strategy suggests that women still depend on male approval in our culture.

CONTEXT

Historical Context

In order to reach people in the most immediate manner possible, advertising is uncommonly sensitive to historical events. These events provide a context of meaning for the commercial message. For instance, television ads for Korbel champagne present scenarios of "things we have to celebrate," including family reunions, graduations, and weddings. However, following the conclusion of the Gulf War, the commercial was reedited to include a shot of a yellow ribbon tied around an old oak tree. This additional visual associated Korbel champagne with the celebration commemorating the end of the conflict.

Shifts in advertising strategies also can provide insight into historical context. For instance, the 1990 McDonald's campaign "Food, Folks, and Fun" emphasized the secondary benefits of a trip to McDonald's. However, the 1991 campaign "McDonald's Today" stressed *value* as a response to the economic recession. McDonald's no longer claimed that the food was entertaining (or, for that matter, that it tasted good); its chief virtue was that the food was cheap. The company reduced its prices (59 cents for a hamburger, 69 cents for a cheeseburger) so that families could stretch their limited budgets. In an era characterized by an uncertain economic climate, McDonald's offered itself as a societal bellwether: "Value . . . you can count on."

Cultural Context

Advertising and Popular Culture. Advertising can be regarded as a text that reflects cultural attitudes and values. As an example, advertising can provide insight into cultural attitudes toward women. John Leo notes that the latent messages contained in Newport cigarette ad campaigns contain "coded scenes of sexual aggression" toward women:

The photos always show outdoorsy yuppies horsing around. But amid all this jollity there is a strong undercurrent of sexual hostility, usually directed at women. Many depict women who seem to be off-balance and menaced, or at least the target of berserk male energy. Women are about to be clanged by a pair of cymbals, carried off on a pole, pulled along in a horse collar, or slam-dunked in the face by a basketball-wielding male.[20]

Advertising can also reveal areas of cultural interest and concern. Examples of cultural preoccupations in American advertising would include the following:

Sex. American advertisements reflect our culture's ambivalent, adolescent preoccupation with sex. What are some of the cumulative messages about sex that can be found in American advertising?

- *Sex is a cultural obsession*. The sheer quantity of sexually oriented ads confirms that sex is a national fixation. All products (from perfume to automobiles) have sexual implications. Sex is always on our minds.

- *Sex is dirty*. At the same time, sex must be repressed. Ads encourage a voyeuristic approach to sex. The audience peeks at models on the printed page or screen, which provides much of the sexual tension in the ads. Female models are posed in a posture of innocence, seemingly unaware that they are objects of desire. If they look at us boldly, they fall into the category of "bad girls."

  In general, European advertisements are much more explicit than their American counterparts. Nudity is not uncommon, either in print or television ads. American ads are more prudish.

- *Appearance is everything*. You are sexy only if you look good. We do not accept imperfections, either in our sex objects or, by extension, in ourselves. Consumer items, then, assume a magical quality, transforming people into desirable, sexy creatures.

- *Sex is a youth-oriented activity*. Sex is confined to a narrow stage of life. In advertising, sex ends with marriage. Advertising rarely depicts older adults in sexually suggestive situations.

- *Sex is depersonalized*. People are often reduced to sexual objects. Ads often show only part of a person's body, reinforcing the notion that sex appeal is associated with certain parts of the anatomy. Sex is not presented as an aspect of a larger relationship but an end in itself.

- *Sex is a contact sport*. Sex is a contest, in which people compete for the attention of others. That's why we need all the commodities we can muster. Sex has very little to do with one's partner but instead is an ego-centered performance, undertaken for the approval and admiration of others.

- *Sex is a consumer item*. The sexual style of ads has become its substance: Products are sexy. In the ultimate depersonalization of sex, we are asked to believe that the products advertised in a seductive fashion (e.g., cars) have sexual properties.

Aging. Americans' preoccupation with youth is reflected in advertising. Ads reinforce the ideal of youth by featuring models who are young, healthy, and fit. Julia Smillie, research associate for Citizens for Media Literacy, observes, "Constant exposure to images of youth creates an impression that youthfulness is the norm and that in order to be accepted, [the consumer] must strive to stay young." [21]

An ad for New Age hair color promises that the product will "restore our hair to its natural color," inferring that aging is an unnatural process. Worse yet, an ad for Shiseido skin cream establishes age as an enemy: "The fragile skin around your eyes. This is where time strikes first."

Ads for cosmetics, plastic surgery, exercise equipment, and hair replacement plans make the very ambitious promise of restoring youth. The headline for an Oil of Olay ad declares, "I don't plan to grow old gracefully, I intend to fight it every step of the way."

Cleanliness. American advertising often plays on our cultural insecurities about cleanliness. For instance, ads for Listerine mouthwash historically have been directed at a range of anxieties related to halitosis:

- "Could I be happy with him in spite of *THAT?*' (appeared in 1923)
- "It brought him untold misery; yet only he himself was to blame." (appeared in 1924)
- "Often a bridesmaid but never a bride." (appeared in 1924)
- "Why had he changed so in his attentions?" (appeared in 1924)
- "Their first conversation betrayed the fact that she was not fastidious." (appeared in 1925) [22]

Cultural Myths. American ads frequently tap into cultural myths, including the following:

Progress. According to this cultural myth, new is better. Change is good for its own sake. Advertisers persuade customers that this year's models are superior to last year's. They create new markets by denigrating the old model, breaking last year's promise of quality and durability.

Appeal to mythic past. At the same time, a nostalgic appeal to our mythic past establishes confidence in the product. For example, the highly successful Motel 6 ad campaign positions the hotel chain as a throwback to simpler times. Spokesperson Tom Bodett is a latter-day Will Rogers who offers country wisdom and hospitality in a depersonalized corporate world. With country fiddle music playing in the background, Bodette assures us, "We'll leave the light on for ya."

Individualism. Americans see themselves as rugged individualists, in the mold of John Wayne, Arnold Schwartzenegger, and Norman Schwarzkopf. However, a delicate balance exists between individualism and conformity.

People who are *too* different become cultural rejects (nerds, geeks, etc.). The trick to rugged individualism, then, is to stand out by being the epitome of style. The Marlboro man simply leads the pack of conformists.

Ironically, the way to assert one's individuality in contemporary society is through consumer behavior. The range of individual expression has been reduced to the creative selection of products.

Stephanie Coontz observes that this modern concept of individualism undermines the individual's responsibilities as a member of a larger social network:

Western individualism has always fed daydreams about escaping external constraints and family obligations, but prior to the era of mass consumption, most people had no doubt that . . . the only sure source of self-identity and security lay in relationships with others. Consumer society has increasingly broken down our sense that we depend on others, that we have to live with tradeoffs or accept a package deal in order to maintain social networks.[23]

Cultural Change. Ads can also serve as a useful barometer of cultural change. To illustrate, in a 1992 TV spot for Toyota Tercel, a young man has been commandeered to drive his friends to some unknown destination in his new automobile. He is clearly uncomfortable in this role and lays down a series of rules to protect his new Toyota. ("No eating in the car . . . No fooling around . . . You have to help me wash it afterward.") The voiceover declares, "Because your values may change, but your friends don't." The message here is clear: As part of his upward mobility, this baby boomer now treasures material goods (i.e., his Toyota) even more than his friendship with his old buddies. The commercial makes this statement without apology; according to the ad, this is as it *should* be—part of the maturation of the American consumer. These old friends have become a source of aggravation and embarrassment. The implication is that if they don't grow up (as responsible consumers), they will be left behind.

Worldview. What kind of world is portrayed through advertising?

An optimistic world. There is no problem that cannot be resolved through the acquisition of consumer goods. We see happy people celebrating their good fortune. We can "discover the possibilities" of life and assume control of our own destinies through prudent consumerism.

However, Coontz warns:

The flip side of the urge to have it all is the fear of settling for too little. . . . Some individuals turn even leisure into a form of relentless work as they strive to avoid "missing out" on opportunities. Others are terrified by the possibility of "premature" commitment: The sense that all choice is good and more choice is better is a profoundly destabilizing one for interpersonal relationships.[24]

A material world. The world of ads is reduced to what we can see, feel, touch—and buy. In the here-and-now world of advertising, style has become substance. People discover meaning through the acquisition of material goods. Identity has become a disposable commodity. We can (to all appearances) become anyone we want on the basis of how we look and what lifestyle we adopt. As Andre Agassi, tennis star and pitchman for Canon cameras, observes, "Image is everything." Appearance becomes ascendant; the emphasis is now on youth, looks, and health.

An uncomplicated world. This world offers simple solutions to complex problems: All issues can be resolved by purchasing the right product. The advertising world is populated by uncomplicated people who find fulfillment through laundry detergents and car wax.

World of immediate gratification. A sense of urgency permeates the world of advertising. In commercials, people cannot postpone their gratification for more than 30 seconds. To illustrate, in a McDonald's ad, the merits of the product are sung to the tune "Temptation," enticing us to rush to McDonald's. To revise an old adage, "Nothing worth having is worth waiting for."

A self-absorbed world. In this narcissistic world, satisfaction does not stem from helping others. Instead, pleasure comes from helping yourself to as many products as you can afford. Why buy L'Oreal hair coloring? "Because I'm worth it." Why spend your money at McDonald's? Because "You deserve a break today." A pre-Christmas radio spot for The Cheese Place asks, "Don't we owe ourselves a little self indulgence? So why not be a little selfish before the gift giving begins?"[25]

A class-segmented world. The world of advertising is divided into two groups: the haves and the have-nots. Advertisers for Nike and Reebok have built a market for $150 basketball shoes by convincing teenagers that these items are the keys to status. According to Nike, black males age 13 to 24 accounted for 9.8 percent of the $10.3 billion in annual retail sales of athletic shoes in 1990—nearly a billion dollars.[26] These young consumers feel pressured to keep up with the trends in fashion—often at enormous financial sacrifice.

A world that revolves around the product. Advertisements often promote products as integral to the world depicted in the commercial. Ads suggest that their products are directly responsible for transforming people's lives. For instance, using Grecian Formula will make men look younger, win promotions, and earn respect and admiration.

However, ads may be more subtle, by positioning the product as the center of the world of the commercial. For instance, in Coors Light Beer ads depicting fun at the beach, the product accompanies every activity, implying that the beer is integral to a good time. However, the product is actually superfluous; presumably the partygoers would continue to enjoy themselves whether or not they were drinking beer.

MEDIA LITERACY TIPS

WORLDVIEW

Questions to ask with regard to *worldview* in advertising include:

√ *What kind of world is being depicted in the ad?*

√ *What kind of lifestyle is promoted in the ad?* Consumers may actually be attracted to the lifestyle depicted in the ad, of which the product is only a small part.

√ *What is the role of the product within the worldview of the ad?* Imagine the ad without the appearance of the product to see whether that consumer item is indeed an essential part of that world.

√ *If you did not know what product was being promoted, what would you think was being advertised?* Consumers who are interested in the primary product may also be compelled to purchase the other consumer items depicted in the ad.

Ideology. The world of advertising is still dominated by mainstream culture. Subcultures rarely have been represented in ads. However, advertisers have begun to recognize that subcultures represent a substantial market. For instance, in 1990, the buying power of black Americans was estimated at $263 billion.[27] In response, many ads are now being targeted at the African American community. However, Thomas J. Burrell, president of Burrell Advertising Inc., contends that most ethnic ads reflect only a superficial understanding of black culture. Burrell cites an example in which Canadian Mist liquor directed its attention to the black community through a Canadian wildlife motif:

[The heavy emphasis on scenery, wildlife, and a rural lifestyle] has no relevance to the average black consumer. When they asked us to develop a program for blacks, we had to go in another direction. We focused on style, fashion, and other imagery that blacks are interested in because of their urban environment.[28]

Further, segmented marketing strategies may exploit the condition of cultural subgroups to sell products. John Leo points out that ads for malt liquors subtly target the African American community: "The malt liquors, marketed primarily to poor members of minority groups, use cobra, bull, dragon, tiger, stallion, and pit bull. The idea is to sell wildness and power to the powerless (high alcohol content is part of the same strategy)."[29]

The G. Heilman Brewing Company took this approach one step further, introducing a strong malt liquor with the brand name of PowerMaster. However, this overt promise of empowerment through alcohol generated protests by minority groups, and the Bureau of Alcohol, Tobacco and Firearms withdrew approval for the brand name. But as Leo points out, "So long as this theme is covert, nobody seems to object, but the G. Heilman Brewing Co. has just found out what happens when the fig leaf is dropped."[30]

Media Stereotyping. Because advertisers have a limited amount of time to reach their audience, they rely heavily on stereotypes. Indeed, ads encourage consumers to think of themselves *as* stereotypes (e.g., members of "The Pepsi Generation"). Groups portrayed in ads are depicted in consumer-oriented terms only; that is, heritage and political ideology are stripped away, leaving only lifestyle as the distinguishing feature. Subcultures that are not part of the mainstream are often presented as stereotypical buffoons. A 1992 Wendy's ad campaign depicted various "fringe" groups like hippies, who foolishly wanted such unsavory food as alfalfa sprouts. This caricature had the trappings of the 1960s hippie—the long hair, mannerisms, and language—but was devoid of the political and social convictions that defined members of the counterculture.

MEDIA LITERACY TIPS

IDEOLOGY AND STEREOTYPES

As you analyze ads, ask the following questions with regard to *ideology* and *stereotype:*

- √ To what groups (or subgroups) do the characters belong?
- √ In what settings are they presented?
  - √ Are they the primary or secondary characters?
  - √ Are they at home or at work?
- √ What kinds of products do they promote?
- √ What do the stereotypes reveal about cultural attitudes toward these groups?

Images of Success. In an attempt to present products in their most positive light, ads depict products as part of a successful lifestyle. One common ad strategy involves an appeal to prestige, as in a 1991 print ad for the Mercury Cougar:

> In the Beginning
> You look like everybody else.
> Then something happens
> Maybe it starts with the way you wear your hair.
> Or the colors you put together.
> But pretty soon, you don't look like everybody else.
> You look like you.
> And then something really funny happens.
> Everybody else wants to look like you.

Other ads are more subtle. For instance, in the 1988 ad campaign "Where you're going, it's Michelob," the product serves as a metaphor for success in American culture. Michelob is a premium beer that is targeted at an upscale audience. In the television version of this ad, a variety of people are headed toward a state of being called "Michelob." The first sequence follows two characters ascending a mountain (accompanied to a jingle that begins, "You're on your way to the top"). These upwardly mobile characters overcome odds and are in complete control of their environment. The commercial is choreographed in such a way that all of the characters (mountain climbers, businesspeople, a truck driver, a young couple hustling to meet one another, and people at a barbecue) appear active and purposeful. These fast-paced commercials are characterized by a series of quick cuts. The latent message is that the Michelob lifestyle is exciting and glamorous.

Michelob is equated with self-knowledge, certainty, confidence, and a sense of direction. The song lyrics remind us: "Where you're going, it's Michelob. And along the way you know just where you are and where you're going. You've always known it."

These characters are all young, beautiful, and physically fit—there is not a beer belly in the crowd. The main figures are always in the middle of the frame, the center of attention. Everyone is watching (and admiring) them. And because the use of the personal pronoun *you* projects the audience into the advertisement, we are by extension watching people adoring us.

The culmination of the characters' quest ("Where they're going") is the earthly equivalent of heaven—success, or at least, a frosty Michelob. Michelob is a just reward for hard work and an acknowledgment of achievement. As a metaphor for success, Michelob offers an easy solution to complex problems. Even if you are a total failure, you can maintain the illusion of success by buying a Michelob.

Values Hierarchy. Many ads operate within a traditional values hierarchy in which values such as family, Christmas spirit, and patriotism assume manifest importance. However, these ads often associate traditional values with the purchase of products. For instance, an insurance agency informs us that "America believes in liberty—Liberty Mutual Insurance." The message is that as patriotic Americans we should buy their insurance.

Larry Sabato cites an instance involving a California proposition to restrict smoking privileges in which traditional values were manipulated to support a commercial message:

An alarmed tobacco industry contracted with Woodward & McDowell agency, and a brilliant campaign was produced that succeeded in transferring a threat to a special interest group (smokers) into a threat to everybody's freedom. This was done by transferring the nonsmoking public's ire from the smoker's irritating habits to a more general enemy, the encroaching bureaucracy—always a tempting straw man. With an eye to "big brother," the anti–Proposition 5 spots made clear their theme with a number of recurring slogans: "What will the regulators try to regulate next?" "They're at it again!"; "Let's stop them before they stop us." Of-

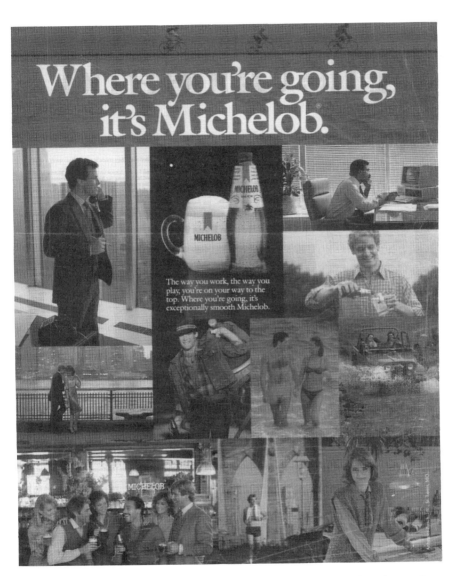

This 1988 Michelob ad offers a composite picture of success in American culture. The ad appeals to the audience by associating the product with these images of success. Advertisement courtesy of Anheuser-Busch Companies, Inc. and Fleishman-Hillard, Inc.

ten the ads did not even make clear the content of Proposition 5; but whatever Proposition 5 may be, the commercials suggested, it is associated with bogeymen and things that go bump in the night.[31]

Thus, manifest values may camouflage a latent, more commercial value system, based on materialism and self-gratification.

MEDIA LITERACY TIPS

VALUES HIERARCHY

Questions to ask in regard to *values hierarchy* include:

√ What manifest values are being used in the promotion?

√ What connection does the product have with these values?

√ What latent values seem to be most prized in the advertisement?

Structure

Ownership Patterns. In the market-driven American media system in which programming is dependent on sponsorship, content is often subordinate to advertising. To illustrate, during radio's golden era of the 1930s the performers took second billing to sponsors: "The Kraft Music Hall" (starring Bing Crosby), "The Pepsodent Program" (starring Bob Hope). This practice changed only after advertisers realized the power of a name performer to attract an audience. As an ABC network executive explains, "The network is paying affiliates to carry network commercials, not programs. What we are is a distribution system for Procter & Gamble."[32]

Edward S. Herman and Noam Chomsky contend that the corporate interests of advertisers often influence programming:

Advertisers . . . choose selectively among programs on the basis of their own principles. With rare exceptions these are culturally and politically conservative. . . . Advertisers will want, more generally, to avoid programs with serious complexities and disturbing controversies that interfere with the "buying mood." They seek programs that will lightly entertain and thus fit in with the spirit of the primary purpose of program purchases—the dissemination of a selling message.[33]

Advertisers can also influence the content of stories that appear in the media. For example, in 1989 Noel Morgan, consumer reporter for Cincinnati's WLWT-TV, met with direct interference while covering a story on used cars: "Morgan says (car) dealers were actually given permission to pre-screen a story he did on cars that were advertised as factory official cars but had, in fact, been rentals. 'The dealers were allowed to put their responses on cue cards and practice them until they got it right,' he said."[34]

Indeed, advertising pressure has prevented a message from reaching the airwaves. PBS station WNET lost its corporate sponsorship from Gulf & Western in 1985 after the station aired a documentary entitled *Hungry for Profit*, which examined the role of multinational companies in the Third World. The chief executive of Gulf & Western explained their decision by claiming that airing the program was not the behavior "of a friend" of the corporation.[35]

Advertising and Government Regulation. The Federal Trade Commission (FTC) was created by Congress in 1914. It is headed by five commissioners appointed by the president. In 1938, the FTC was given the authority to protect consumers from unfair and deceptive advertising. If there is an illegal activity, both the company and the advertising agency may be held responsible.

Although Congress has not provided a comprehensive definition of the term *deceptive,* the FTC considers the following criteria in determining whether an advertisement is deceptive:

- The nature of the misstatements (i.e., Is it likely to deceive someone?).
- The nature of the audience targeted by the ad (e.g., children, senior citizens).
- The significance of the ad to the consumer's decision to purchase the product (i.e., Is it likely to play a material role in the decision to buy?).

Once a company is found guilty of using deceptive advertising, it may choose to comply voluntarily with the recommendations of the FTC; in this case, a consent order may be filed with the court, in which the company agrees to halt the ad without technically admitting guilt. Another option is to seek a thorough litigation. The FTC also may simply notify the public that an offense has occurred. Finally, in some cases the FTC may require corrective advertising, whereby the advertiser must for a reasonable amount of time include corrective statements in its advertisements.

The question remains, however, If regulatory policies and enforcement procedures have been in force for more than half a century, why do misleading ads continue to appear in the media?

Attorney Michael Kahn observes that the law is limited in its ability to define the universe of misleading advertisements:

Laws are composed of sentences, sentences are composed of words, and words are inherently imprecise. Add the imprecision of words to the inventiveness of the human mind, and you will never be able to cover every possible situation in advance. The law sets broad guidelines but cannot cover gray areas. Ads will be invented that do not clearly fall within the category of deceptive ads defined by the court.[36]

As we will discuss later in the chapter, many advertisements are not overtly misleading but instead appeal to the emotions or are associated with cultural values and myths in order to sway the audience.

In addition, Kahn observes that most of the cases of misleading advertising are never brought to the attention of the FTC:

Nothing is officially "deceptive" until declared so by an appropriate tribunal. 90 percent [of allegedly misleading ads] are never brought to anybody's attention. The FTC is a woefully understaffed organization, not set up to handle a large volume of complaints. They are reduced to looking for the worst examples, the ones they can win. For every one they target, there are probably a hundred others out there.[37]

Indeed, many claims are brought to the FTC by competitors seeking to harass one another. For example, the national hamburger chains have waged a series of "hamburger wars" in the courts over claims of deceptive ads, ranging from advertising claims over whether charbroiling is healthier than frying to the relative popularity of Whoppers and Big Macs.

FRAMEWORK

Introduction

In advertising, the introduction is intended to attract the consumer's attention, to lead the consumer into the rest of the ad, and to encapsulate the ad as a whole. The *brand name, packaging,* and *slogan* often serve as the "introduction" to the product advertisement.

Beyond mere identification, a brand name creates an immediate impression and establishes the character of a product. For example, "Hamburger Helper" creates a positive, distinctive image, whereas "Cheap Cereal Filler Meat Supplement" puts a less rosy spin on this type of product.

Selecting brand names has become more complicated in a global market. Some words may be difficult to recall in a foreign language or suffer from an unflattering translation. For instance, "Coca-Cola" in Chinese means "Bite the wax tadpole." Worse yet, the literal Spanish translation for the Chevrolet Nova is "No go."

As a result, the most effective brand names are often *neologisms*—words that have been invented especially for products. According to Ira Bachrach, president of NameLab Inc., neologisms are designed to send universal messages about the essence of the product, as in the case of Honda Acura: "[We] tried to make a name that said, 'Car with high engineering content.' . . . And *acu*, to the extent that it says precision, is an element of engineering."[38]

Packaging can produce a positive first impression and make a product appear distinctive. For example, Beeper Bubble Gum appeals to children by storing the gum in a simulated beeper that they can attach to their belts (just like mom and dad). Individual sticks of gum carry beeper "messages":

- "See you later"
- "Call me"
- "Urgent!"
- "Sorry, line's busy"

Kids are drawn to this unique *packaging,* as though the *product* were different.

At times, packaging can send messages that were not intended by the media communicator. Pat Ross, a teacher at Clark Elementary School in St. Louis, Missouri, observes that Beeper Bubble Gum has been banned from her school because of the latent meaning behind the packaging:

The Beeper Bubble Gum packages had an entirely different association in the inner city neighborhoods. It wasn't just a cute little gadget to wear on their belts like Mom and Dad. The messages "See you later," "Call me," "Urgent," "Sorry, line's busy" were used as a code by drug dealers to indicate whether a sale was going down or not. And further, wearing a beeper in their neighborhood symbolized gang or drug associations.[39]

A catchy slogan is integral to the success of an ad. Five times as many people read the headline than the copy in the body of the ad.[40] Memorable slogans are clever, rhythmical, and alliterative and manage to capture the intended character or spirit of the product.

For instance, "Just do it" is a very sophisticated and effective motto even though the name of the product (Nike) is never mentioned. The slogan lauds athletic effort and tells us that we can succeed despite the odds (or excuses). Buoyed by this pep talk, we are prepared to achieve our goals. The latent message is that Nike athletic footwear will provide essential support in this quest.

From a historical perspective, this slogan also can be regarded as a motivational pitch in the face of economic hard times. It is comforting to hear that effort and perseverance will be rewarded. This public service announcement is a very welcome, attractive—and memorable—message.

Ultimately, the slogan is a not-so-subtle imperative to buy the product: "Just do it."

Slogans may also contain latent meanings for particular subgroups. Referring to the Burger King slogan "Sometimes you've gotta break the rules," Leo comments:

To the well-off, Burger King's [advice] is to allow yourself a fatty hamburger once in a while. But in harsher neighborhoods, (the campaign) seems to identify the product with lawbreaking and freedom from impulse control. The Hispanic agency employed by Burger King got the point right away, declining to translate "Breaking the rules" into Spanish because it implied approval for violating laws or Hispanic traditions.[41]

Leo adds that Merrill Lynch's slogan ("Your world should know no boundaries") "was a totally upscale variation on the same antisocial theme. The latent message suggests that white collar workers have the right to determine which rules and regulations they choose to observe."[42]

Plot

Explicit Content. When a product is unique, clearly superior to its competition, or of public benefit, the advertiser's task is easy. However, if a product is indistinguishable from other brands on the market, the advertiser must devise strategies to make the product appear alluring and distinctive. This task is even more pronounced when a product is harmful to the public, such as alcohol or cigarettes.

Examining explicit content can uncover several types of inconsistencies, fallacies, and incongruities in advertisements:

Ads that appear perfectly reasonable on the surface may be based on an *illogical premise.* To illustrate, a television ad for Coors Light Beer promotes its product as a health drink. As young men and women cavort around the beach in swimwear, the voiceover reminds us that you do not want a beer that will "slow you down." However, a steady diet of beer—regular or light—will hardly keep you trim and fit.

The ad campaign "Newport Lights—alive with pleasure" provides another excellent example. Given the medical evidence about the health hazards of smoking (which by law must be cited in the ads), this claim could hardly be more absurd.

Consumers should remain skeptical of *false and misleading ads.* For instance, on November 27, 1991, a federal judge fined the Ralston Purina Company $12.1 million because of a deceptive advertising campaign for Puppy Chow. The ad cited research claiming that a Puppy Chow diet helped to reduce the likelihood of joint disease and canine hip dysplasia in dogs. U.S. District Judge Stanley Sorkin declared, "Armed with this weapon, Ralston's claims acted like a sponge and literally soaked up the entire market." However, Sorkin found that the research findings did not support Ralston's claims:

Ralston had taken steps to conceal certain of its research that made it quite clear that its dog food formula simply did not work to prevent canine hip dysplasia. Ralston's entire record in this endeavor is not only one of wrongful conduct but of repeated attempts to cover up that conduct once discovered.[43]

Ironically, the suit against Ralston was brought by the Alpo Co., which had been fined by Sorkin for its *own* deceptive ad campaign. Alpo's ads claimed that veterinarians preferred Alpo's puppy foods by a margin of two to one over other brands. Sorkin ruled that these claims were false in that its surveys were flawed.

Some ads present an *incomplete or distorted message,* telling only a half-truth in order to present the product in the best possible light. For example, a Mobil ad justified a price increase by claiming that only 1.7 percent of its wells struck oil. However, Ben Bagdikian points out, "the ad did not explain that this was only true for one small category of drilling and that the average success rate for all drilling is about 60 percent."[44]

Ads often make the *big promise*—that is, claims that are far beyond the capacity of the product. For example:

A fellow confides to his buddy that he is desperately lonely. His friend responds that his troubles can all be traced to his dandruff. If he used Head and Shoulders, his life would turn around. Later, we discover that he has found the woman of his dreams—thanks to Head and Shoulders.

The ad suggests that Head and Shoulders will not merely solve your dandruff problems but in the process will also wash away more substantial problems: loneliness, isolation, and self-doubt.

MEDIA LITERACY TIPS

THE BIG PROMISE

When examining ads, consider the following questions with regard to the *big promise:*

√ What promises does the ad make with regard to the product?
√ Which promises can the product reasonably keep?
√ Which promises are beyond the capabilities of the product?

Hyperbole is a part of the American storytelling tradition and relies on exaggeration or absurd overstatement to make a point. Examples can be found in such tales as George Washington's coin toss across the Delaware River and the legendary Paul Bunyon. In a country of seemingly limitless resources, Americans magnify events and locations for emphasis and dramatic effect. This literary device also reflects the American competitive spirit. Everything must be the best. However, advertising sometimes makes claims (e.g., "Milwaukee's finest beer") that are in fact merely a statement of opinion.

Ads also employ *similes* to promote products. A simile is a literary device that refers to a direct comparison between two things; such comparisons are introduced by *like* or *as*. William Lutz observes that similes are employed "whenever advertisers want you to stop thinking about the product and start thinking about something bigger, better, or more attractive than the product."[45] For instance, a wine that claims "It's like taking a trip to France" is designed to induce the consumer into romantic reverie about Paris instead of thinking about the taste of the wine.

Parity statement refers to ads that are worded in a way that suggests that a product is unique, when what the ad is *actually* stating is that the product is indistinguishable from its competition. For example, Rick Berkoff asserts that the Personna Double II slogan ("There is no finer razor made. Period.") could be rephrased as follows: "Personna Double II: It's no better than its competition. Period."[46]

Unfinished statements make implied claims that advertisers are unable to stand behind. Instead, they leave it to the consumer to complete the statement. Lutz provides the following examples:

- Batteries that "last *up to* twice as long." Twice as long as what?
- "You can be sure if it's Westinghouse." Just exactly what we can be sure of is never explained.
- "Magnavox gives you more." This slogan never details what you get more of.[47]

Qualifier words should also send a white flag to the consumer. However, phrases such as "some restrictions apply" are either quickly flashed on the TV screen or uttered with inhuman rapidity by the announcer, insinuating that this information is inconsequential. Some qualifier words that create the illusion of quality in fact negate this claim: Pevely chocolate-*flavored* ice cream or Hungry Jack Lite Syrup *product*.

The "McDonald's Today" ad campaign cited earlier offers an ironic use of qualifier words. In an era characterized by economic uncertainty, McDonald's offers reassurance: "Value . . . you can count on." However, the ad concludes with a series of qualifiers: "Prices may vary. Taxes not included. Limited time only." These qualifiers undermine the manifest message of stability and only further reinforce the latent message of cultural upheaval.

William Lutz has identified other qualifier words commonly used in advertising:

- *Help*. "The next time you see an ad for a cold medicine that promises that it 'helps relieve cold symptoms fast,' don't rush out to buy it. Ask yourself what this claim is really saying. . . . 'Help' only means to aid or assist, nothing more. It does not mean to conquer, stop, eliminate, end, solve, heal, cure, or anything else. But once the ad says 'help,' it can say just about anything after that because 'help' qualifies everything coming after it. The trick is that . . . you forget the word 'help' and concentrate only on the dramatic claim. You read into the ad a message that the ad does not contain. More importantly, the advertiser is not responsible for the claim that you read into the ad, even though the advertiser wrote the ad so you would read that claim into it."[48]

- *Virtually.* Lutz warns that claims like "virtually spotless" are deceptive. "After all, what does 'virtually' mean? It means 'in essence or effect, although not in fact.' Look at that definition again. 'Virtually' means *not in fact.* It does *not* mean 'almost' or 'just about the same as,' or anything else."[49]

- *New and improved.* An advertiser can present a product as "new" if there has been a "material functional change" in the item. In the same way, a product advertised as "improved" suggests that it has been "made better." However, ads frequently make such claims for products that feature only slight modifications (e.g., changing the shape of a stick deodorant).

MEDIA LITERACY TIPS

EXPLICIT CONTENT

A Consumer Guide to Advertising invites the public to consider the following questions in regard to the *explicit content* of ads:

√ *Can the advertiser support its claims?* Be wary of any claims, and search for independent confirmation, particularly for large purchases like automobiles and appliances.

√ *After watching the ad, do you really know what the product is or does?* As amusing as some ads can be, do they provide us with anything more than a brand name? What about price, value, size, shape and nutritional content? A wise consumer . . . focuses on all of the information needed to make an informed choice.

√ *What's not in the ad?* Sometimes the most important information is not even mentioned in the ad. It could be that the 15- or 30-second spot is just too tight to fit everything in, but it could also be a deliberate evasion or half-truth on the part of the advertiser. . . . Know what you're getting before [making a purchase].[50]

Affective Response. Affective response can be a particularly useful place to begin analyzing messages contained in advertising. Despite working within a very limited format (e.g., a 30-second TV spot), advertisements tap into a reservoir of emotional needs, concerns, and fears, arousing intense emotional reactions on the part of the audience. The advertiser presents a scenario that triggers these emotions and then manipulates these feelings to sell the product.

Some ads simply are intended to evoke a positive emotional response from the audience. Ads featuring puppies and babies are guaranteed to produce a warm reaction. The advertiser hopes that the consumer will transfer these positive feelings to the product. Humorous ads work on a similar principle. Laughter is a positive emotional response; we are grateful to people who make us laugh. It is hoped that this indebtedness will make us feel positively about the product.

Advertisers recognize that products are purchased for psychological as well as product satisfaction. Consequently, ads often strive to accentuate the *emotional benefits* of a product. The phone company is not merely selling a communications system but furnishes the means by which you can "reach out and touch someone" you love. This approach may be used even when the product does not have a logical emotional benefit. For instance, a Christmas radio spot for Kretchmeyer Hams presents the product as a vital part of a family holiday celebration. After dinner, a young man offers a moving toast: "There is no place I'd rather be right now than with my family." This may indeed be true; however, the ham can claim no more responsibility for the emotional richness of the moment than the silverware or canned peas.

Ads may be directed at one of a number of intrinsic psychological motivations:

Guilt. American culture can be described as exceedingly guilt ridden. We feel remorse for any number of real and imagined transgressions. Advertisers capitalize on these irrational feelings to promote their product. For instance, the ad campaign for Michelin tires discussed earlier ("Because so much is riding on your tires") depicts an infant surrounded (and protected) by the product. The latent message is that parents who care about their children must buy Michelin tires. However, this type of affective appeal does not hold up under rational scrutiny: Is the choice of brands critical to being a good parent? (Why not buy new Goodyear tires, for instance?) Does buying Michelin tires automatically make you a good parent? And if you're a responsible parent, shouldn't you worry about the other features of the car as well (e.g., the fuel line or transmission) as well as other drivers and *their* tires? The list could go on and on.

MEDIA LITERACY TIPS

GUILT-PROVOKING ADS

When confronted by *guilt-provoking ads,* ask the following questions:

√ Why am I feeling guilty?

√ How will purchasing the product assuage my guilt?

√ Is the choice of brand important?

√ Could an advertiser exploit these feelings of guilt to sell me other products?

Love. An untold number of products have been promoted in the name of romantic love. Consumer products are positioned as tangible symbols of affection, affirming the depth, sincerity, and permanence of your love.

Some ads position their product as an essential ingredient in the courtship ritual. Using the right product will make you more attractive and desirable (e.g., Norelco shavers: "Making close comfortable"). Giving the proper present can win a person's heart. And some products even promise improved performance in lovemaking (e.g., Big Red Gum: "Make it last a little longer").

These ads emphasize the pleasure that you'll bring your loved one through a thoughtful purchase. But at the same time, this approach is a subtle appeal to the ego of the purchaser: Imagine how grateful your partner will be upon receiving the gift, and how wonderful you are for giving it.

Love between family members is another very powerful psychological motivation. A 1991 McDonald's commercial begins with a young man walking wistfully through a children's playground. He stops at a McDonald's and orders a breakfast to go: "I'm having breakfast with my daughter," he explains to the young woman at the counter. The next scene shows the young man at the hospital, gazing fondly at his newborn child. The ad suggests that Daddy's Egg McMuffin has played a significant role in this deeply personal moment. But however illogical the ad, the very powerful latent message about the connection between father and daughter has reinforced the manifest pitch for McDonald's.

Need for approval. A persistent latent message in advertising is that people can satisfy their need for acceptance through their consumer behavior. As in the Michelob example cited earlier, ads often depict situations in which the person modeling the product is the center of attention. The advertiser encourages the audience to identify with this principal figure, so the audience vicariously receives approval by using the product.

One particularly effective version of this appeal centers around the complex relationship between children and their parents. To illustrate, a television spot for the U.S. Marines begins with a tough-looking young man returning home from boot camp. He is met at the train by his younger brother. The marine immediately asks, "How's Dad?" Behind this rugged facade, the soldier is still a little boy seeking his father's approval for having enlisted in the Marines.

The scene shifts to the marine entering his house. He is dressed in full military regalia. His father looks at him from across the room. Silence. Suddenly, Dad rushes over to his son and embraces him. This reconciliation scene touches young men who may be sorting out their own complex feelings toward their fathers. The underlying message is that by joining the marines young men can find the resolution to this fundamental need for acceptance.

Nostalgia for significant moments. These ads attempt to associate products with the significant moments that touch people's lives. Some ads play on the theme of *initiation*. These ads about first experiences cleverly tie the product into individuals' sense of nostalgia. For instance, an Oreo cookie ad dramatizes the *angst* of a young couple's first date and recalls how the cookie helped ease the tension and make the occasion a success.

Other ads capitalize on significant *rites of passage,* such as birthdays, weddings, and graduations. These "Kodak moments" evoke memories of similar events in the lives of the audience and subtly encourage consumers to think favorably about the product.

Finally, some ads exploit the audience's sentimental attachment to *holidays,* such as Christmas, the Fourth of July, and Thanksgiving. Advertisers try to link their products with holidays ("Kretchmeyer: Your Christmas Ham") in hopes that these good feelings will be transferred to the product. The business community actively promotes holidays like Mother's Day or Valentine's Day as a means to stimulate sales. Many stores use these occasions as excuses for special promotions (i.e., "Halloween Madness sales"). Taking this promotional tack to the extreme, the business community has concocted holidays such as Grandparent's Day as advertising gimmicks to sell their products.

Fixation with death. Sigmund Freud theorized that people experience a primal attraction to death. Freud's theory of the death instinct might help to account for why people race cars, sky dive, and find other ways to live "close to the edge" of death:

Freud postulates that the organism has an innate tendency to revert to its initial state. This instinct, which would lead to self-destruction, has to be diverted outward by the developing organism. . . . The death instinct represents one of the two major classes or drives and motives, which—for psychoanalysts—comprise all motivational processes.[51]

Several ad strategies center around human's love/hate relationship with death:

- *Denial of death.* Castleguard Security system reminds us to "Give the most valuable gift of all . . . the gift of security" in an impermanent world. Advertisements for diamonds are even more blatant, selling immortality in the form of their product. A diamond ensures that love will be permanent, and that the couple will live happily ever after.

- *Loss of control.* A 1990 ad for the Wizard 8000 electronic organizer positions its product as a device that will enable the consumer to assume control of his or her life: "Nothing can help you take control of all the details of your busy life like the Wizard."

- *Abandonment.* A classic TV commercial promoting the Prudential Insurance Agency focuses on the testimony of a grieving widow. She has been abandoned by her husband and now must contend with the emptiness of her life. "We thought it would never happen to us," she laments, realizing that she is not only alone but impoverished as well. In this case, the insurance represents both financial and emotional comfort and security.

- *Longing for the past.* An ad for Tyson chicken reminds us, "So for over 50 years, we've made sure that Tyson's chicken is the leanest and meatiest that they can be." This ad establishes a tradition that makes us feel rooted and safe. At the same time, this return to the past provides us with a sense of confidence in the future.

- *Fear of failure.* Thornton C. Lockwood has analyzed a series of 1988 AT&T ads, which he calls "Slice of Death" advertising. These commercials feature testimonials by businesspeople who have been let down by their current phone system. As described by Lockwood, failure is presented as a form of death in life: "The problem the agency chose to dramatize . . . was phone failure and the problems that creates for business people: loss of credibility with clients, lost sales, demoralized workers, management confusion, and ultimately, even business failure."[52] Significantly, the first test storyboard scenario was even more overt, in which a malfunctioning (and malevolent) telephone swallows a young woman who is taking phone orders at a restaurant.

- *Fear of the unknown.* An ad for "The Travelers" contains a photo with religious overtones: a skyscape, with streaks of light shining through the clouds. The headline reads:

> Financial Serenity
> The Strength to Leap
> Beyond the World of Worry.

Armed with the protection afforded by The Travelers (with its slogan "You're better off under the umbrella"), the audience is prepared to meet whatever challenges lie ahead.

Affective appeals like those cited above offer only a superficial, antiseptic emotional experience that ultimately trivializes genuine emotion. We are spared the complications and consequences that are a part of any genuine emotional commitment. Our involvement need only last for 30 seconds; then we can move on.

Implicit Content. Nowhere is consequence portrayed as more direct and immediate than in the world of advertising. The relationship between the significant events in the narrative is clear. Ads dramatize how products fulfill needs and solve personal problems. Ads show smiling, satisfied consumers who have benefited from the purchase of the product.

Genre

In order to be instantly recognizable, advertisements often borrow from established genres, such as the drama, music video, and sitcom. For instance, Sunday night cable TV spots for health products and self-motivation materials mirror the format of the talk show, complete with host, desk, audience, and a "guest," who hawks the product.

At the same time, advertising is a distinct genre of its own, with a distinct premise, structure, plot, and characters.

Formulaic Premise. In general, the premise for advertisements contains the following elements.

An ad strives to establish a *product identity* for its product. John Ferrill, executive vice president and creative director of Young and Rubicam, explains:

> Every product has a personality. Whether the clients have consciously thought about it or not, people perceive a brand in a certain way. Jell-O is a member of the family; it's friendly, it's fun. Anacin is very businesslike; it gets the job done, but it does it in a very straight, unglamorous, matter-of-fact kind of way. I could name almost any product and you'd have some impressions on . . . really what it is. The brand personality is the description of a product stated as though that product were a person.
>
> If you're trying to write a statement for Oil of Olay, you might characterize the brand as "feminine." You might say she is mysterious, possibly foreign in origin. She understands beauty secrets and the needs of women. She is an authoritative friend.[53]

Repetition is a vital component of advertising, both in terms of frequency of presentation and format.

Advertisements generally attempt to *dramatize the value* of a product. The Earle Palmere Brown Advertising Agency observes, "Advertising that's dramatic gets the attention of the consumer and demands to be noticed. Since the first objective of any advertising is to get itself seen, this is a critical component."[54]

Ads frequently stress the *consumer rewards* involved in using a product. BBDO advertising offers the following insight into the ad strategy employed in its Gillette deodorant campaign:

> The "Product" stance is that it "goes on dry, stays dry." But this did not differentiate this superior performing product until the "You" attitude was added: Control, Aspiration. The resulting themeline, "Never Let Them See You Sweat," and the campaign featuring rising young entertainers, has helped revitalize the brand.[55]

Formulaic Structure. Advertisements are generally structured within the order/chaos/order format:

- A problem is quickly introduced that throws the character's world into chaos.
- The product is presented as a means of solving the problem.
- Order is restored through use of the product.

The conclusion is geared to inspire the consumer to action.

Indeed, some ads first *create* a problem and then offer a solution—in the form of their product. For instance, "ring around the collar" was not an area of tremendous concern until the makers of Wisk brought this situation to the attention of the public.

Print ads offer a variation of this formula, with the visual emphasis on the restoration of order. The problem is either indirectly alluded to (e.g., AT&T's ad "Six Cities. Two Days. Easy") or left entirely to our imaginations (e.g., pictures of beautiful women wearing Mabelline eyeliner). In this case, the consumer is expected to assume that the purchase of the product will transform her into one of the exotic-looking models in the ad.

Formulaic Plot. In television commercials, the product is central to the narrative. The latent message is that the product plays an integral role in our lives.

In one type of ad campaign, the plot is always nearly identical; only the specific nuances differ. For instance, the Sanka coffee commercials featuring Robert Young always consisted of the same basic plot:

Sanka commercials usually involve an irritable young husband, who apologizes for his "coffee nerves," and a tearful young wife. Robert Young suggests the young man try his coffee—Sanka brand decaffeinated. Problem solved, marriage saved, and all is well.[56]

Convention. Conventions compensate for the limited time and space for promoting the product. Costumes, props, and setting provide subtle cues about the product. For instance, an ad that promotes a headache remedy may feature an actor wearing a white lab coat. The unstated message is that this is a medical expert whose advice should be heeded.

Indeed, some ads cleverly establish the product *as* convention. Fashion ads promote a garment not merely as clothing but as a symbol of the status and personality of the individual.

Advertising relies on a stable of stock characters (e.g., The Harried Housewife, Out-of-It Husband, Sex Siren). These stereotypes evoke instant recognition by the audience by drawing on a common cultural understanding and consensus.

MEDIA LITERACY TIPS

ADVERTISING CONVENTIONS

The following questions are useful in considering the role of *advertising conventions:*

√ What conventions are used in the ad?

√ How are these conventions used in the ad?

√ What messages are these conventions designed to convey?

√ How are these conventions used to promote the product?

Logical Conclusion

Advertisements do not always follow logically from their initial premise. As mentioned earlier, ads frequently conclude with a big promise: The product will bring you happiness or success. An example would be the Head and Shoulders ad in which a young man finds romantic fulfillment after washing his hair. At the very least, advertising exaggerates the importance of a product. For instance, the couple jumping in the air to celebrate their purchase of a Toyota would appear to be something of an overreaction.

PRODUCTION VALUES

In advertising, as with all media formats, style reflects content. The originality of the presentation sends a message about the uniqueness of the product and directs us to see (and think about) the product in a new way. Production values can also create a mood that affects how we react to the product. And in some cases, style may make a product look better than it is.

Ad production people are often tempted to show off their artistry and the latest technical innovations. However, Hooper White cautions prospective advertisers that style must be subordinate to the message: "Find out what the advertising is about. Then edit with advertising in mind, not with show biz in mind." [57]

Editing

Copywriters for print advertising strive to keep their messages brief, concise, and simple. John Caples advises ad copywriters to write to the sixth-grade level. [58] At the same time, the effective copywriter elaborates and clarifies, "creating a word picture that makes crystal-clear the specific advantage of every feature." [59] Caples observes that variety in sentence structure avoids monotony and creates a fresh, energetic mood that will carry over to the product. Short sentences "put speed and excitement into your ad" [60] and move the audience to action. Long sentences can furnish useful explanation.

Through *digital imaging* (a computer manipulation technique), photographers can eliminate a model's wrinkles and imperfections. Exposures and colors also can be manipulated in the darkroom to create different impressions.

Television commercials contain a myriad of images and information. Directors, who may shoot as much as 16,000 feet of film, are faced with the challenge of cutting to 45 feet for a 30-second ad. Each second becomes critical. As a result, an enormous amount of attention is devoted to the selection and arrangement of images.

A director can condense a vast amount of information into a limited time frame through editing. For instance, a 30-second Kodak ad is composed of a series of photographs that span a woman's lifetime. In addition, the television soundtrack and picture are commonly speeded up by as much as 25 percent without being noticed by the audience. Dr. James MacLachlan claims that this method increases the unaided recall of the content by 40 percent.[61]

The editing technique of quick cuts is also geared to attract and maintain the attention of the audience. This "MTV" style also sends the latent message that the product is exciting and contemporary.

Color

The selection of bright colors and dramatic color contrasts attracts the attention of the consumer—which is the principal goal of an advertisement. However, the choice of colors also can convey other subtle messages about the product. Otto Kleppner observes:

Color talks its own psychological language: To make a drink look cool, there will be plenty of blue in the background; to make a room look warm (for heating advertisements), there will be plenty of red in the background; springtime suggests light colors, and autumn the dark tones. Thus a clue to the choice of the dominating color may often be found in the mood in which the product is being shown.[62]

In that regard, John Lyons warns consumers, "Be wary of little girl doll commercials shot through pink and green filters."[63] This technique creates a warm, romantic, and traditionally "feminine" tone that subtly influences young girls' response to the product.

Scale

The magnification of images can be a very deceptive ad technique. Extreme close-ups make small products look big. As a result, toys that look impressive and durable on screen may in fact be small and flimsy.

Relative Position

The layout of an advertisement can affect audience response. The product is always prominently displayed, suggesting that it is central to the moment depicted in the advertisement. The actors who model the product are the center of attention—presumably due to the consumer item being advertised.

Figure 7.2
Advertising Space and Gender Roles

According to Erving Goffman, the use of relative position can provide insight into cultural attitudes toward women.

Upper/Lower Space. Men are frequently situated in a high physical place in ads, in contrast to females who are lying down or sitting on the floor. Goffman contends that being relegated to a lower space symbolizes women's social status in a male-dominated world. Photograph by Damon Shell

Attentional Vectors. Women frequently direct their attention toward the male, who is clearly the center of attention. The male has been empowered to the degree that he is free to focus his attention elsewhere. This visual cue instructs the audience to place more importance on the male. Photograph by Damon Shell

Cant. Female models often pose in a "cant" position, in which the head or body is bowed. The latent message of this body language is deference, submission, and subordination. Photograph by Damon Shell

Shielding. Female models are often screened from direct contact with the world of the ad, suggesting that women are dependent and require protection. Women are often stationed behind a barrier or peek out behind another person (generally a male). Women may also be positioned in the background or at the edge of the frame, which suggests a subservient position. Photograph by Damon Shell

---

MEDIA LITERACY TIPS

EFFECTIVE AD LAYOUTS

Otto Kleppner outlines the following criteria for *effective ad layouts:*

√ Is it arresting?

√ Is it clear?

√ Is it orderly?

√ Is the most important idea given the most important attention?

√ Does it invite reading?

√ If the trademark is needed to identify the product, is it sufficiently visible?

√ Does the layout leave the desired impression about the product?[64]

Layouts that display unity and balance produce feelings of harmony and peace that can be transferred to the product. Conversely, imbalance can create a visual tension that attracts the interest of the reader. Unused white space is another subtle visual element that provides relief, suggests a feeling of freedom, and reinforces the messages contained in the ad copy.

Camouflaged Warnings. Product warnings are designed to be as inconspicuous as possible. For example, the disclaimers on cigarette advertisements appear in very small print. The warning is generally separated from the main visual field. And sometimes the print is camouflaged by the color and graphics of the ad.

Product Placement. The appearance of Pepsi-Cola, Texaco, Nike, AT&T, and *USA Today* in *Back to the Future II* was hardly accidental. Manufacturers pay a hefty fee to film studios to ensure that their products are displayed in the film. These brands are cleverly embedded in the narrative so that the audience accepts the appearance of the product as part of the story. To see Michael J. Fox drinking a Pepsi within the context of the plot legitimizes the product and therefore operates as a very subtle form of persuasion.

Is this approach successful? Within a month after Reeses's Pieces were visually displayed in *E.T.,* sales for the candy jumped by 65 percent.[65] As a result, film studios now are demanding large fees for promoting products in film. The Walt Disney Company solicited paid product placements for *Mr. Destiny,* with the following cost structure: $20,000 for a visual, $40,000 for a brand-name mention with the visual, and $60,000 for an actor to use the product.[66]

Movement

In TV advertising, movement can lend a dynamic feel to the presentation, giving the impression that the product is exciting and glamorous. At the same time, the technique of slow motion enables the audience to scrutinize the product demonstration, adding to the dramatic emphasis of the ad.

The direction of the motion can also set the tone for the promotion. For instance, a 1991 television spot for *Sports Illustrated* begins with a sports nut leaning toward the camera to tell us about "a great deal" if we subscribe to the magazine. This movement suggests a familiarity and confidentiality with the audience that inspires trust.

Advertisers now favor the "shaky camera technique" in which the camera jumps around, much like an amateur home video. In contrast with the slick style found in conventional TV spots, this style produces a genuine, "just folks" impression. In addition, Thornton C. Lockwood found that the shaky camera technique employed in the AT&T "business reality" ad campaign "underscored the stress and discomfort the characters experienced" by not using AT&T.[67]

Movement can also be used to draw the attention of the consumer to specific features of the ad. For instance, TV spots for Lipton's Ice Tea typically display an array of beautiful, young people frolicking around a swimming pool. Just as our eyes are drawn to these alluring male and female bodies, these images are replaced by shots of the product and the brand label.

This use of movement even extends into the medium of print advertising. In Western culture, a person glancing at an ad is most likely to focus initially on the upper-right-hand portion of the page. However, art directors often employ the technique of *structured motion* in which the layout is designed to lead the audience through an ad in a predetermined way. Otto Kleppner explains:

The art is to attract attention at the head of the page, and by having optical stepping-stones leading from there to the end, hold the ad together and lead the reader through the copy. Flow may also be helped by the line of direction of the artwork, sweeping across the page. It may be helped by *gaze motion,* that is, having the people in the picture look toward or, perhaps with other elements of the ad, lead the eye to the center of attention.[68]

Figure 7.3 identifies a variety of structured motion patterns—ways in which people look at ads.

Point of View

Advertisers strive to establish a *parasocial relationship* with the audience, making the consumer feel known, appreciated, and special. The Campbell-Mithun-Esty Ad Agency observes, "We must come into our customers' homes and lives as understanding friends and remain as welcome

Figure 7.3
Structured Motion

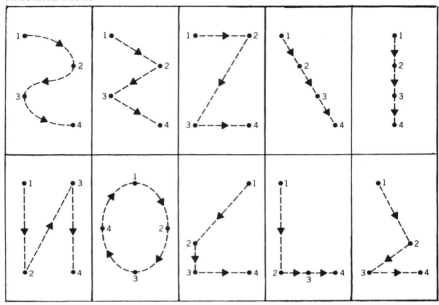

Source: William H. Bolen, *Advertising*, 2nd ed. (New York: John Wiley & Sons, 1984), 209.
Reprinted with permission.

guests because of the honesty and good grace with which we present ourselves." [69]

Ads often emphasize the long-standing relationship between a company
and its customers so advertisers can ask for—and expect—consumer loyalty. The word *trust* is another frequently used word in advertising (e.g.,
Sears: "The brands you want, the store you trust").

While ads are presented through mass media, they often affect an interpersonal tone. It should not come as a surprise that the personal pronoun
you is the most frequent word used in advertising. In that regard, a radio
jingle for Tyson's Holly Farms chicken contains a revealing claim: "I know
what you want before you say it. We know the game before you play it."
Tyson knows you better than you know yourself—and consequently is in
the best position to select your meat for you.

Some ads position themselves as members of the customer's family (e.g.,
Tyson's chicken: "We're family, you and me"). Other advertisers assume
a peer relationship with its audience. For instance, many children's advertisements appear to have been produced by children. Very few of the ads
feature adults. Griffin Bacal, Inc., an advertising agency that specializes in
"youth marketing," declares:

To reach (the adolescent audience), and motivate them, Griffin Bacal talks to them in their own language, on their own terms. Invariably, we take a new and instinctively non-traditional approach to creative work. We pursue the latest techniques in film and video, and develop the most contemporary music and jingles. Breaking rules, stretching guidelines and creating phenomena are the hallmarks of our approach to advertising. At all times, Griffin Bacal advertising thinks young![70]

CBS promos for its 1990 Saturday morning lineup feature kids in the control booth as well as in front of the camera. The young hosts announce that CBS is a place "Where kids are in charge." Presumably, the children are in control of programming as well as writing and producing the commercials. These spots are loaded with trendy dialogue:

Check out kid TV.
We've got all new episodes with those radical rats battlin' the bad dudes and scarfing down the pizza.
It's Teenage Mutant Ninja Turtles.
Then bum a ride on some intense trips through time with a totally new show, "Bill and Ted's Excellent Adventure."
So catch us on Saturday morning.
It's kid TV on CBS . . . where kids rule.

Youngsters accept these messages from their "peers," little realizing that the jargon is written by adults trying to win their confidence in order to sell them products.

Connotation

Connotative Words. Many of the most common and persuasive words used in advertising fall into the following categories:

Commencement words suggest immediacy, importance, and a sense of urgency:
- Introducing
- Announcing
- Now
- Suddenly

Convenience words appeal to the consumers' interest in products that will make their lives easier:
- Easy
- Quick

Transformational words promise new levels of experience:
- Sensational
- Startling
- Amazing
- Remarkable

- Miracle
- Magic
- Revolutionary
- Improvement

Directives tell the consumer what to do:
- Hurry
- Compare

Customer advantage words offer the consumer a feeling of control, vision, wisdom, and superiority:
- Bargain
- Offer
- Free
- Sale

MEDIA LITERACY TIPS

CONNOTATIVE WORDS

A *Consumer Guide to Advertising* cautions the public about *connotative words* commonly found in the food industry:

√ *Natural.* If you think this product is automatically as good for you as fresh broccoli, think again. Read the label: On one box of cake mix "natural" included modified food starches, mono and diglycerides, gum arabic, and so on. (The one exception is meat and poultry labels where natural means "minimally processed.")

√ *Dietetic.* This usually means low in sodium and does not necessarily mean reduced calories.

√ *Light* or *lite.* Could mean anything, and may mean nothing. Don't assume that it's lower in calories unless it's on a meat label.

√ *No sugar.* Yes, but it could have sugar substitutes such as corn sweeteners. Watch for the words containing "glucose, sucrose, fructose, and dextrose."

√ *No artificial ingredients.* What's artificial to you may not be artificial to a food manufacturer! There are no laws that prevent ingredients such as "hydrolyzed vegetable protein" (which involves chemicals) from being included in products listed as containing "no artificial ingredients." [71]

Connotative Image. Visuals can be very persuasive in advertising. *A Consumer Guide to Advertising* suggests that the public consider whether the visual images in an ad correspond with the words:

By playing with . . . visuals, the text can be absolutely accurate, but the image in the mind's eye may suggest something very different. . . . Be suspicious. Don't rely on visual images alone to provide you with accurate information. Listen carefully to the words, read the labels and then decide if this product or service is for you. [72]

What kinds of images are most prevalent in advertising?

- *Products* are always prominently displayed. No matter how sophisticated advertising becomes, the primary goal is still to imprint the product on the minds of the consumer.
- The public is fascinated by pictures of *people*—particularly young, attractive women.
- Images that emphasize the *rewards* of a product are also common. For instance, real estate ads generally show customers either learning about the sale of their home or walking into their new house.
- Pictures of *babies and animals* tap into a wellspring of emotional experiences that are sure to generate a positive reaction in the audience.

Performance

Radio and television advertising depend on performance to make a promotion appealing and convincing. Performers in advertisements fall into several categories:

Actors. Casting directors screen candidates carefully to find actors who will be most convincing in the role. White advises advertising executives:

You should furnish the casting director with a complete written description of the actor you have in mind. Is he or she hard nosed or easygoing, aggressive or passive, funny or serious, quiet or loud? Don't limit the written description to physical details. Be sure to discuss, in writing, the *entire characterization.* You will find that this forces you to clearly identify the character, thereby helping the casting director to find the right actor.[73]

Models. Advertisements frequently feature models—that is, people who display the intended "look" (e.g., glamorous, folksy, or corporate) that will influence the target consumer. However, these images send messages about cultural ideals, which can carry disturbing implications. For instance, according to American University researchers, the female models in fashion and cosmetics ads are, on average, between 13 and 19 pounds underweight. According to the American Psychiatric Association, that falls into the range of anorexia.[74]

Celebrities. Celebrities like Bill Cosby often serve as spokespeople for products. The rationale is that consumers who admire Cosby will accept his recommendation that we eat Jell-O or use Kodak film. We should remember, however, that these performers are paid hefty fees, whether or not they actually use the products they endorse.

Some ads elevate celebrities to positions of undue responsibility and authority. For instance, in a radio spot for Riopan Plus cough medicine, spokesperson Willard Scott reads a letter, addressed to him, in which a person seeks medical advice. Scott's experience as a TV weatherman somehow qualifies him to diagnose her malady and prescribe a cure: "Marlene, it sounds to me like you could use some Riopan Plus II. It's sodium free. Just take it easy and get some Riopan Plus II."

Cartoon characters. Cartoon characters like Charlie Tuna and the Keebler Elves have been created to personalize the company. They must be likable and memorable and project qualities that can be associated with the product. However, these characters are pure fictions and have no connection with product quality or company policy. To illustrate, despite the marketing presence of the Jolly Green Giant, the Birdseye Food Company has been embroiled in a labor dispute with the United Farm Workers. The farm workers organized a grape boycott to draw attention to low wages and health hazards incurred as insecticides were sprayed on workers toiling in the field. There is no small irony in this benevolent corporate symbol representing a company that has been anything but jolly to its workers.

Real people. Testimonials from "average people" lend authenticity and credibility to an ad. The more amateur their performance, the more the audience identifies with them and believes their testimony. This "real people" approach should not be confused with a strategy in which actors *portray* average consumers.

A variation on this strategy involves using company personnel to sell the product. Dave Thomas (Wendy's Hamburger) and Victor Kiam (Shick) are not polished pitchmen; however, the consumer enjoys seeing the corporate heads of companies as "regular guys" who believe in their product.

Attention getters. Every local television station carries commercials by outrageous pitchmen who attract attention by screaming, roller skating, dressing up in ape suits, or simply offering "crazy, crazy low prices." Of course, it is not unreasonable to ask: Why would someone want to buy from someone who is either that crazy or that annoying?

Sound

Music. Music serves a variety of functions in advertising. Music can generate feelings of excitement, joy, and pleasure, which advertisers hope will be transferred to the product. Music also can provide dramatic emphasis, underscoring the advertising message presented by the words and images. Music often establishes a tone (e.g., solemn, whimsical, elegant) that instructs the audience on how to react to the advertising message. And finally, the rhythm and repetition of melodies can trigger the consumer's recall of the product at a later point.

The entertainment value of commercial music can make an ad not merely palatable but enjoyable. The jingles are often well produced; in fact, "I'd like to buy the world a Coke" went on to become a popular hit tune. This entertainment value enhances the chances that the audience will be exposed repeatedly to the commercial message without resistance.

Commercial music also offers a subtle way for advertisers to reach their target audience. For instance, Ford Motor Company's marketing research indicates that pickup truck buyers are more likely to like country and western music than the population as a whole.[75] As a result, Ford truck ads often feature a country music soundtrack in order to appeal to (as well as attract) its intended market.

Advertisers can purchase the rights to popular commercial songs, although the cost can be prohibitive—up to $100,000. This strategy enables advertisers to capitalize on the popularity of a hit tune while sending their commercial message. For instance, a 1991 Toyota commercial supplied the following lyrics to the Monkey's signature hit:

> Hey hey, we're Toyota
> Toyotathon time of the year.
> Savings are better than ever,
> Come on down today.

In some cases, advertisers hire "sound alike" artists to add to the original flavor of the spot. In fact, in 1989 Bette Midler was awarded $400,000 in a suit against the New York advertising agency of Young and Rubicam for using one of her former backup singers to imitate Midler's rendition of "Do You Want to Dance" in a Ford Mercury commercial.[76]

Using *original* music and lyrics can also be an expensive undertaking, but a song that has been especially commissioned for the ad is sure to complement the images and narrative presented on screen. In addition, an original jingle reinforces the message about the uniqueness of the product.

Local productions often rely on older songs, since the copyright law has lapsed and the music has become part of the public domain. These "generic" songs can be found in most local libraries. This music serves many of the purposes of advertising soundtracks; however, because this music appears so frequently in commercials, there is no hope of any product identification with the music.

Background Sound. Sound effects simulate the sounds commonly associated with the product and thereby dramatize the message. Sounds like Coke gurgling, cans opening, and people talking contribute to the verisimilitude of an ad. However, finding sound effects that capture the more elusive qualities of the product can present a challenge for the audio engineer. For instance, White comments on the process of adding sound effects to a General Electric (GE) Halogen Headlight commercial:

When the G.E. Halogen Headlight was first turned on in the graphic picture, we highlighted it with a burst of white sound (an effect quite peculiar to a synthesizer). This burst was followed with a synthetic French horn statement, which became the musical logo for the headlight. This horn statement was reiterated three times as the G.E. headlight was mentioned in the voice track.[77]

Natural sounds, such as the wind blowing or cars passing, are most noticeable in their *absence;* the audience expects to hear the natural sounds that correspond to the environment surrounding the ad. When ads are produced in an artificial setting (i.e., a studio), the media communicator is faced with the challenge of using sound effects to replicate natural sound.

CASE STUDY

Sandra Brands, a graduate student in Media Communications at Webster University, conducted the following media analysis of a print advertisement of Ralph Lauren's Polo Rider boots, using selected keys to interpreting media messages:

An ad in the September 30, 1993 edition of *Rolling Stone* magazine for Ralph Lauren's Polo Rider Boots is not merely promoting the product but is selling a sense of identity for those who wear Ralph Lauren boots.

The image in the ad is of a somewhat well-worn black leather boot with heavy, corrugated soles and two straps with silver buckles. The booted foot rests on the footpad of a chrome-laden motorcycle. Though details on the bike are sketchy, the suggestion seems to be that it is a powerful bike.

The twist in the photo, however, is that across the top third of the ad appears the bottom portion of an expensive, black wool pinstripe suit, complete with immaculate cuffs and precise crease. The pants are hiked up, tucked slightly into the top of the boot and held sway from the side of the motorcycle—a practical consideration that fortunately displays the boot very effectively.

There is little copy—merely a stylized, white banner head that reads "Polo Ralph Lauren" at the top, and a smaller point white title, "The Polo Rider," at the bottom. In fact, it's only guesswork (the size and prominence of the boot) that leads me to suspect that the advertisement is really about the boot.

This advertisement subtly encapsulates cultural mythologies and lifestyle choices for young men. The cultural mythology relates almost immediately to youth—to the rebellious passion of T. E. Lawrence, Marlon Brando, James Dean, Peter Fonda, and today's brooding heroes. It presents a man still able to assert his own personality, to rebel against expectations—"Instead of Oxfords or wing tips, I'll stomp around in these cool, unconventional boots!"—and be his own man. It identifies someone who wouldn't be caught dead in a sedate sedan, a yuppie suburban van, or a hackneyed sports car, but someone who rides to work, in button-down glory, on a motorcycle, long viewed as a reckless, dangerous, and exciting mode of transportation.

The audience for *Rolling Stone* is made up of young men who expect eventually to take their place in corporate America. The Ralph Lauren boots, in combination with the wool pinstripe suit and motorcycle chrome, suggest that this individual has been successful while playing by his own rules. The advertisement is subtle but wildly romantic, and while its drab color scheme makes me wonder if it would be noticed beyond a cursory glance, it is an image that is ultimately seductive: You

This ad promotes the product by offering a sense of identity for those who wear Ralph Lauren Polo Rider boots. Advertisement courtesy of Polo Ralph Lauren

can have it all and still be your own man—and Ralph Lauren can create that identity for you.[78]

NOTES

1. Charles H. Patti and Sandra E. Moriarty, *The Making of Effective Advertising* (Engelwood Cliffs, NJ: Prentice-Hall, 1990), 122.

2. Jim Trelease, *The New Read-Aloud Handbook* (New York: Penguin Books, 1989), 123.

3. Ed Papazian, ed., *TV Dimensions '93* (New York: Media Dynamics, 1993), 343.

4. Interbrand Group Staff, *World's Greatest Brands: An International Review by Interbrand* (New York: John Wiley and Sons, 1992), 5.

5. Tony Schwartz, *The Responsive Chord* (Garden City, NY: Anchor Books, 1973), 69–71.

6. "Surgeon General Criticizes Images from Alcohol Ads," *St. Louis Post-Dispatch*, November 5, 1991, A1, A7.

7. Michael Schudson, *Advertising, the Uneasy Persuasion* (New York: Basic Books, 1986), 92.

8. Patti and Moriarty, *Effective Advertising*, 63.

9. John Curley, "General Dynamics Cleans Up Image," *St. Louis Post-Dispatch*, November 29, 1987, E1.

10. Survey conducted by Video Storyboard Tests, Inc., *USA Today*, October 3, 1991.

11. Deborah Baldwin, "The *Hard* Sell," *Utne Reader* 49 (January–February 1992): 60.

12. Philip Burton and Scott Purvis, *Which Ad Pulled Best?* (Chicago, IL: NTC, 1988), 31.

13. John Vivian, *The Media of Mass Communication* (Boston: Allyn and Bacon, 1991), 245.

14. John Caples, *How to Make Your Advertising Make Money* (Englewood Cliffs, NJ: Prentice-Hall, 1983), 311.

15. Otto Kleppner, *Advertising Procedure*, 6th ed. (Englewood Cliffs, NJ: Prentice-Hall, 1976), 429–434.

16. Everette Dennis and John Merrill, *Media Debates* (New York: Longman, 1991), 182.

17. Patti and Moriarty, *Effective Advertising*, 20.

18. Kleppner, *Advertising Procedure*, 300.

19. Patti and Moriarty, *Effective Advertising*, 53.

20. John Leo, "Hostility Among the Ice Cubes," *U.S. News & World Report*, July 15, 1991, 18.

21. Julia Smillie, interview by author, St. Louis, MO, March 16, 1992.

22. Edgar R. Jones, *Those Were the Good Old Days: A Happy Look at American Advertising* (New York: Simon and Schuster, 1959), 349–53.

23. Stephanie Coontz, *The Way We Never Were* (New York: Basic Books, 1992), 176.

24. Ibid., 176–77.

25. KWMU, 90.7 FM, St. Louis, MO, December 20, 1991.

26. John Leo, "The Well-Heeled Drug Runner," *U.S. News & World Report*, April 30, 1990, 20.

27. Maria Mallory and Stephanie Anderson Forest, "Waking Up to a Major Market," *Business Week*, March 23, 1992, 70, 73.

28. Jeffery L. Kovach, "Minority Sell: Ads Target Blacks, Hispanics, But . . . ," *Industry Week*, November 11, 1985, 30.

29. Leo, "Hostility," 18.

30. Ibid.

31. Larry J. Sabato, *The Rise of Political Consultants* (New York: Basic Books, 1981), 137–38.

32. R. Collins, *Dictating Content* (Washington, D.C.: Center for the Study of Commercialism, 1992), 77.

33. Edward S. Herman and Noam Chomsky, *Manufacturing Consent* (New York: Pantheon Books, 1988), 17–18.

34. Collins, *Dictating Content*, 22.

35. Herman and Chomsky, *Manufacturing Consent*, 17.

36. Michael Kahn, attorney, Gallop, Johnson, and Neuman, interview by author, St. Louis, MO, October 20, 1993.

37. Ibid.

38. Marylin B. Bowden, "The Game of the Name," *Ambassador Magazine*, February 1992, 30.

39. Pat Ross, interview by author, St. Louis, MO, August 11, 1993.

40. Patti and Moriarty, *Effective Advertising*, 5.

41. Leo, "Hostility," 18.

42. Ibid.

43. Adam Goodman, "Ralston Fined $12 Million Over Ads," *St. Louis Post-Dispatch*, November 27, 1991, B1, B3.

44. Ben Bagdikian, *The Media Monopoly*, 3d ed. (Boston: Beacon Press, 1990), 61.

45. Willim Lutz, *Doublespeak* (New York: Harper & Row, 1989), 92.

46. Rick Berkoff, "Can You Separate the Sizzle from the Steak," in *Mass Media Issues*, ed. George Rodman (Chicago: SRA, 1981), 149.

47. Lutz, *Doublespeak*, 95.

48. Ibid., 86.

49. Ibid.

50. Lee E. Norrgard, *A Consumer Guide to Advertising* (American Association of Retired Persons), 6–7.

51. H. G. Eysenck, ed., *Encyclopedia of Psychology* (New York: Herder and Herder, 1972), 247.

52. Thornton C. Lockwood, "Behind the Emotion in 'Slice of Death' Advertising," *Business Marketing*, September 1988, 88.

53. Burton and Purvis, *Which Ad Pulled Best?*, 41.

54. Patti and Moriarty, *Effective Advertising*, 80.

55. Ibid., 55.

56. Hooper White, *How to Produce an Effective TV Commercial* (Chicago: Crain Books, 1981), 23.

57. Ibid., 122.

58. Caples, *Make Your Advertising Make Money*, 370.

59. Ibid., 184.

60. Ibid., 87.

61. White, *Effective TV Commercial*, 118.

62. Kleppner, *Advertising Procedure*, 374.

63. John Lyons, *Guts: Advertising from the Inside Out* (New York: AMA-COM, 1987), 292.

64. Kleppner, *Advertising Procedure*, 380.

65. "How Sweet It Is," *Time*, July 26, 1982, 39.

66. Marcy Magiera, "Disney Plugs Up New Film," *Advertising Age*, October 15, 1990, 8.

67. Lockwood, " 'Slice of Death' Advertising," 86.

68. Kleppner, *Advertising Procedure*, 371–72.

69. Patti and Moriarty, *Effective Advertising*, 62.

70. Ibid., 90.

71. Norrgard, *Consumer Guide to Advertising*, 10–11.

72. Ibid., 7.

73. White, *Effective TV Commercial*, 139.

74. *Adbusters Quarterly*, Summer 1993, 30.

75. David Huron, "Music in Advertising: An Analytic Paradigm," *Musical Quarterly* 73 (Fall 1989): 567.

76. Michael Rubiner, "Style Is One Thing, Defining It Is Another," *New York Times*, July 5, 1992, H23.

77. White, *Effective TV Commercial*, 182–83.

78. Sandra Brands, "Polo Rider: Image and Identity" (paper delivered to Med. 531, Media and Culture, Webster University, September 1993).

CHAPTER 8

AMERICAN POLITICAL COMMUNICATIONS

PROCESS

Introduction

The emergence of the mass media has significantly altered the process by which the public receives messages about political issues and candidates. As discussed in Chapter 2, the traditional communications model has been transformed as follows:

The *channel* of mass communications now determines the choice and image of the *communicator*, the content and presentation of *message*, and the way in which the *audience* receives the information.

Communicator. Media exposure has magnified the importance of the *character* of the political leaders. Candidates must come across as dynamic, charismatic, trustworthy, competent, and likable. Politicians are valued as much for providing leadership for the American people as they are for their positions on specific issues. Boston Mayor Kevin White explains, "What you need in office is a man who can cope with situations as they arise, situations that no one ever thought of." [1]

Political scientist James David Barber has focused considerable attention on the issue of presidential character. Barber devised a formula for predicting presidential performance, based on distinct character types. Barber has identified four character patterns, based on his or her levels of *activity* (activity/passivity) and *enjoyment* (positive/negative affect):

- The *active-positive personality* is distinguished by an industrious nature, combined with the enjoyment of this level of activity. This pattern, typified by Thomas Jefferson, indicates a high level of self-esteem, success in relating to his environment, and achievement orientation.

- The *active-negative personality,* exemplified by John Adams, combines intense effort with a relatively low emotional reward. The active-negative figure is compulsive, and his goal is to obtain and maintain power. As a result, an active-negative president such as Lyndon Johnson or Richard Nixon brought an inherently rigid approach to the presidency, resulting in escalation of policies long after the issues (e.g., Watergate, Vietnam) should have been resolved.

- A *passive-positive* president, such as James Madison, is a compliant figure who combines a low self-esteem with a "superficial optimism."[2] As a result, this personality is looking for acceptance, which can interfere with an aggressive approach to the implementation of policy.

- The *passive-negative* figure, personified by George Washington, "does little in politics and enjoys it less."[3] Withdrawn by nature and possessing a low sense of self-esteem, this personality type regards politics as a civic duty, often serving his term of office with reluctance.

Historically, a president's character type has affected how he has been treated by the press. Roger Streitmatter found that "robust" presidents (those who fell within Barber's active-positive character delineation) received at least 50 percent more newspaper coverage than presidents exhibiting less attractive character traits. Streitmatter also discovered that active-positive presidents received not only more news coverage from the press but also 87 percent more "personal news coverage" related to their daily activities and family.[4]

Barber regards presidential style as an extension of internal presidential character patterns. Barber links style to performance—the way in which the president will perform his or her duties. However, the emerging role of the media suggests a modification of Barber's theory. Style is no longer simply an indication of character but instead is a carefully cultivated persona designed to project the *image* of an active-positive character. This image not only appeals to the American public but, as Streitmatter suggests, attracts favorable media coverage as well.

Media consultants recognize the importance of the active-positive persona. For instance, as George Bush entered the 1992 New Hampshire primary, fewer than 20 percent of the population felt that Bush cared "a great deal" about the problems of people like them. *New York Times* journalist Robin Toner reported that in response "[t]he Bush re-election forces have sent the President forth in a burst of appearances intended to show that he cares about the home front and understands the suffering of the recession."[5] Bush also referred to the Gulf War victory throughout the campaign swing in an effort to remind voters of his courage, energy, and resolve.

Message. Television content must be entertaining and dramatic. As a result, the electoral process has assumed the character of a sporting event. Media analysis invariably centers on "who won" debates, instead of examining candidates' positions on issues.

Complex facts are difficult to digest in a visual medium and must therefore be simplified for television. Political speeches now cater to the 30-second *sound bite*—a brief, catchy, and memorable phrase that will be carried on television news. Who can forget "Where's the beef," "Read my lips," and "He's pulling a Clinton"?

The number of issues must also be kept to a minimum. Rossier Reeves, a pioneer in political advertising, recalls working with Dwight Eisenhower on his campaign: "I attended a speech given by General Eisenhower, and he was all over the lot. I counted twenty seven issues . . . and nobody remembered what he had said. We selected three campaign issues to feature in our campaign ads. I wanted one, but the Republican National Committee insisted on three."[6]

Media consultant Jane Squier warns that it may be a mistake to look to television for the answers to complex questions: "If you want to find [in-depth] information, you need to turn to print and other unpaid media coverage. Otherwise, you are making your choices on the wrong basis."[7]

Audience. Television has blurred traditional differences among political factions. Among Republicans, frequent TV viewers tended to be more liberal than occasional viewers. Among Democrats, heavy TV viewers tended to be more conservative than light viewers.[8] Further, individuals who admit to being frequent TV watchers are more likely to call themselves "moderate" and avoid the labels of "liberal" or "conservative."[9]

Function

The relationship between the media and politicians in America is a confusing mix of conflict and cooperation, support and opposition. For purposes of discussion, it is useful to make the following distinction:

- The media's coverage of politics
- The use of the media by politicians

These *competing functions* are reflected in the often-contradictory, confrontational nature of political communications.

The Media's Coverage of Politics. Media coverage originates in the news industry and focuses on the political life of the nation. Ideally, media coverage is objective and maintains a critical distance from political figures, issues, and events. Some of the purposes of the media's coverage of politics include the following:

The media inform the public about the political life of the nation. The American media educates the public about political affairs and can establish a political agenda for the nation.

The media provide public exposure for politicians. In our mass culture, politicians depend on the media to gain access to their constituency. In addition, media coverage lends legitimacy to aspiring politicians. Quentin Wilson, campaign manager for Congressman Richard Gephardt's bid for the Democratic nomination for president in 1988, relates the story of how Gephardt knocked on doors in the primary state of Iowa with little success. It was not until the congressman's political spots began appearing on television that the citizens of Iowa began taking him seriously as a candidate.[10]

The media influence public attitudes toward politicians and issues. Because of the influence of the media, politicians strive to cultivate the goodwill of the media. To illustrate, President James Buchanan went to great lengths to reconcile differences with James Gordon Bennett, editor of the *New York Herald*, when he came into office in March 1857. A few weeks after his inauguration, he wrote to Bennett's wife, acknowledging her congratulations:

I am glad to learn that Mr. Bennett has promised you "to stick by my administration through thick and thin." Thus far he has given it a powerful support with occasional aberrations, for which I am always prepared and do not complain. He is an independent man and will do just what he pleases—though I know there is an undercurrent of good will towards me in his nature and he is disposed to treat me fairly. The *Herald* in his hands is a powerful instrument and it would be vain for me to deny that I desire its music should be encouraging and not hostile. Mr. B. makes his mark when he strikes and his blows fall so fast and heavy it is difficult to sustain them. . . . It is my desire as well as my interest to be on the best of terms with him.[11]

The media serves as an adversary of the government. At times the media serve as a societal watchdog, making the government accountable to the people. The investigative efforts of reporters (e.g., Vietnam coverage, Watergate, and Irangate) have contributed to the deposing of leaders, policy changes, and reforms in government.

The Use of the Media by Politicians. Politicians may also control the messages presented to the public through the media. One example is political advertising. Candidates produce their own ads and purchase media time. But in addition, politicians strive to set the news agenda for the media to cover. For example, politicians may manipulate media coverage by staging events such as press conferences, speeches, and conventions, which are then covered as news.

This use of the media by politicians falls into the following categories:

The media look to politicians as vital sources of news and profit. The media depend on politicians for programming content. Anything that a significant political figure does is considered newsworthy. Knowing this, politicians in positions of power can withhold access if they are displeased with the way that a reporter (or their news agency) covers a story. For instance, while on an excursion to Colombia in February 1990, George Bush refused to answer questions posed by the press. President Bush was angry because of published reports about how the White House had misinformed the press about a number of critical issues (e.g., the summit, U.S. relations with China, and negotiations on German reunification). Ironically, Bush did not dispute the accuracy of these accounts; rather, he was disturbed because the press was bringing this information to public attention.

The president decided that if he could not rely on the press to tell his story his way, there would be no story to tell. His interview was characterized by punitive "No comments." In response to an innocuous question about whether he was well rested for his trip, Bush responded, "I can't go into the details of that, because some will think it is too much sleep and others will think it's too little sleep."

Press secretary Marlin Fitzwater later attempted to dismiss the episode, contending that the president was "just kidding. He was having fun."

However, in essence Bush was blackmailing the press into presenting the news in a manner that suited the White House.

Politicians also exploit the competition between journalists to pressure reporters into writing favorable stories. Dan Rather recalls that during his tenure as White House reporter, exclusive interviews with President Richard Nixon were offered only to reporters who had written stories sympathetic to the administration.[12]

Politicians use the media to maintain control. Once in office, politicians have learned to manipulate the press to preserve their positions of power. Although previous administrations employed communications consultants during election campaigns, the Reagan administration was the first to adopt this approach after the election. David Gergen, director of communications under both Ronald Reagan and Bill Clinton, observes:

For one of the first times I'm aware of, [the Reagan administration] molded a communications strategy around a legislative strategy. We very carefully thought through what were the legislative goals we were trying to achieve, and then formulated a communications strategy which supported them.[13]

The key to Reagan's communications plan was *information management*. This public relations approach to government/press relations consisted of the following principles:

Plan ahead. Every Friday, the communications team discussed upcoming events from a public relations perspective. As one participant commented, the dominant questions were, "What are we going to do today to enhance the image of the President?" and "What do we want the press to cover today, and how?"[14]

Stay on the offensive. The administration made a point of controlling the agenda. The communications team would prepare its message with an eye on its potential effect on the audience. Two strategies were particularly effective.

Immediately following a presidential decision, press conference, or significant news event, the Reagan communications team would circulate among the press to present the administration's interpretation, or *spin*, on the story in order to manage how information was presented, reported, and received by the public.

Damage control refers to the management of information during a crisis. This strategy was designed to minimize potentially harmful stories relying on the following principles:

- *Consider the broader implications of the story.* The communications team looked at stories from the following perspective: How does information support (or threaten) the goals of the administration?
- *Respond promptly.* The Reagan team was poised to react swiftly to news stories. The communications team then framed a position that downplayed negative aspects of the story.
- *Act with unanimity.* Once an official line was decided on, it was important that the position be presented with consistency.

Manage the flow of information. Recognizing that the news media depends on government as a primary news source, the Reagan team made available information that they wanted conveyed and simply withheld information that they weren't prepared to discuss. As Sam Donaldson observed, "So our options are, do nothing or do it their way." [15]

Limit reporters' access. Limiting access to the president reduced the chances that the administration would lose control of its agenda. It was vital, however, that Reagan maintain the *image* of accessibility. Thus, the president was often in view of the cameras but conveniently out of earshot (e.g., photo opportunities and boarding noisy helicopters).

Speak in one voice. All administration officials presented a unified, official message. Consequently, it was imperative that the Reagan team remain discreet and loyal. This in part accounts for the Reagan administration's obsession with leaks within the administration.

Make it easy on the press. The Reagan communications team provided the media with prepackaged information (which, of course, presented their perspective on events). The working assumption was that the press was inherently lazy and would accept the administration's version of news if it made their jobs easier. As Deputy Chief of Staff Michael Deaver explained, "If you didn't have anything, they'd go *find* something." [16]

Exploit the medium. The Reagan communications team took advantage of the visual nature of television to present their point of view. According to Richard Cohen, senior producer of CBS, Michael Deaver virtually functioned as executive producer for the television networks by setting up visually compelling backdrops and action-oriented events that the networks found irresistible.[17] Hertsgaard explains:

Rather than resist the networks' desire for saturation coverage of the President, the Reagan propaganda apparatus would cater to it. The networks wanted visuals of the President? Fine. But they would be visuals carefully designed to promote the Reagan agenda.[18]

Mislead when necessary. The Reagan team engaged in a "disinformation" strategy in which they deliberately released false information to achieve political goals. For instance, in 1986, the press discovered administration memos confirming that the Reagan administration had released disinformation about Muammar Gadhafi in order to destabilize the Libyan government.

White House officials admitted to the disinformation campaign but minimized its significance (an example of damage control):

We think for domestic consumption there will be no problems. It's Gadhafi. After all, whatever it takes to get rid of him is all right with us—that's the feeling, we think, in the country. On the foreign scene it will cause problems, though. We're constantly talking about the Soviet's doing disinformation. It's going to cause difficulties for us.[19]

Ironically, in a classic example of disinformation, President Reagan flatly denied any government involvement in a disinformation campaign. Reagan declared, "We were not telling any lies or doing any of these disinformation things."

The media support the agenda of the government. Occasionally, American media have crossed the boundary of objective reporting and have collaborated with the government. For instance, in 1961 the *New York Times* learned of the impending Bay of Pigs invasion two days before it was scheduled to begin. President John Kennedy appealed to the paper not to print the story; the *Times* complied. After the failure of the mission, Kennedy later joked that he wished that the *Times* had ignored his request.[20]

Dual Function. Kathleen Hall Jamieson argues that these two separate functions—the media's coverage of politicians versus politicians' manipulation of the media—have begun to merge, much to the detriment of the public:

The differences between news and ads are blurring. News about electoral contests—"free time"—is becoming increasingly adlike. Indeed in 1988 it was no longer unusual to find segments of ads—adbites—broadcast in news stories in ways that heighten rather than diminish their power. Meanwhile, "paid TV," consisting primarily of thirty-second political spots, is becoming increasingly newslike, and in the process further fuzing the line between news and ads. And candidate speeches, press conferences, one-on-one interviews, and debate answers are increasingly tailored with a view toward getting adlike news coverage.[21]

Comparative Media

Television has had an enormous impact on the content of political communications. Because the predominant medium of television is so visually oriented, politicians frequently stage events that make them appear active and dynamic. That explains why politicians routinely appear on the evening news visiting schools, hospitals, and factories.

Television images often overwhelm verbal messages. To illustrate, in 1984 Leslie Stahl filed a news report for CBS in which she discussed Reagan's use of television:

How does Ronald Reagan use television? Brilliantly. . . . Mr. Reagan tries to counter the memory of an unpopular issue with a carefully chosen backdrop that actually contradicts the president's policy. Look at the handicapped Olympics, or the opening ceremony of an old-age home. No hint that he tried to cut the budgets for the disabled and for federally subsidized housing for the elderly.

This script was accompanied by visuals of Reagan in action: "The president basking in a sea of flag-waving supporters, beaming beneath red-white-and-blue balloons floating skyward . . . getting the Olympic torch from a runner, greeting wheelchair athletes at the handicapped Olympics, greeting senior citizens at their housing project."

Stahl recalls that she "worried" about the response from the White House and was astonished when a Reagan official called to congratulate her. He explained:

We're in the middle of a campaign and you gave us four and a half minutes of great pictures of Ronald Reagan. And that's all the American people see. . . . They won't listen to you if you're contradicting great pictures. They don't hear what you are saying if the pictures are saying something different.[22]

Ironically, Stahl fell victim to the central message of her story: It's not what you say. It's what you show. And despite what the public may experience on a day-to-day basis, they believe the images that politicians present.

Unfortunately, the print media have taken a cue from television, seizing on the dramatic and entertaining aspects of our nation's political life. Newspaper coverage of debates emphasizes dramatic exchanges between candidates, often entirely ignoring any substantive news. The tabloids have taken this sensationalized approach a step further, focusing on the private and personal lives of the candidates, such as the *Sun's* allegations of infidelity by Governor Bill Clinton. Ironically, the mainstream press covered this "story" faithfully, all the while condemning this type of "tabloid politics." Sally Quinn declared, "Once again, sensational charges are following a presidential candidate, and the nation is being confronted with questions on moral issues. Once again, issues have surfaced to force us to face basic feelings about fidelity, values, leadership."[23]

Audience

What are the effects of political communication on its audience?

Studies reveal that the media may influence voters on candidates and issues but *only if* allegiances are weak. Between 60 and 65 percent of voters commit themselves to a candidate before the campaign. The remainder make up their minds during the last few days before the election. Although a maximum of 40 percent are open to persuasion, a more realistic estimate of the number of voters who may be affected by a television campaign lies somewhere between 10 and 20 percent of the electorate.[24]

Political messages tend to reinforce previously held views of voters who have strong convictions. For instance, in 1984, pro-Mondale viewers felt that he "won" the first presidential debate. At the same time, the Republican viewers felt that Reagan had emerged victorious.[25] Partisan voters do not turn to the media for answers but rather to support their preexisting point of view.

A clear understanding of audience is critical to modern political advertising. Political consultants rely on psychographic research to anticipate how individuals will respond to political appeals. Campaign teams make extensive use of focus groups to identify the most effective ways to reach their audience. Montague Kern explains, "Buttons and dials are used to test immediate nonverbal responses to televised candidate presentations."[26]

Tracking polls have also become a vital means of identifying voter sentiment. As the campaign progresses, tracking polls are conducted more frequently—often on a daily basis by the end of the campaign. Media consultant Jane Squier notes:

They're taking [the voters'] temperature all the time. Initial polls . . . measure where the voters are, what they're thinking. . . . Their messages are very specifically targeted . . . they know through the polling where they've got to reach voters. . . . There is not a shotgun approach. We are talking about very, very specific targeting. It's easy to do it mathematically. . . . You have a spectrum across the scale of potential voters and you whittle it down . . . and you finally get to the point where you know you have to reach this tiny little group in the middle. These are the undecideds who will or will not vote for your candidate—depending on what happens. And that's who the message has to go to.[27]

CONTEXT

Cultural Context

The mass media industry has transformed the American political system. Today, the media do not merely capture the action but have *altered* the action in a number of respects.

Decline of the Party Machine. The emergence of the mass media has coincided with a decline in party affiliation among Americans. Party loyalties and organizations have declined drastically as candidates are able to get their messages directly to the voters through channels of mass communications. As pioneer media consultant Rossier Reeves observed, "The three major political parties are ABC, NBC, and CBS." (Reeves made his remark before the emergence of CNN as a major news network.)[28] Former Senator Thomas Eagleton (D—MO, 1969–87) sees drastic differences in the two-party system from the time he first entered politics in 1956:

Political ward organizations were the channel by which you got out the Democratic vote. A candidate worked extensively with the ward organizations. . . . You ran as part of the overall ticket. . . . Some billboards might even have "Donkeys vote straight Democratic"—you would never see such a thing today. . . . Contrasting today with '56, the two-party system today is dead. You run strictly as an individual. You don't give a damn about the other candidates on the ticket. If they win, fine. If they lose, fine—tough luck for them. . . . Television has totally changed the American political process and in doing so has helped to destroy the two party system.[29]

The astonishing impact of H. Ross Perot on the 1992 presidential race is an excellent case in point. Operating without the support of a national political organization, Perot attracted enough grassroots support to garner 19 percent of the popular vote. Perot reached the electorate by relying almost exclusively on TV appearances—most notably CNN's "Larry King Live" as well as half-hour paid political ads.

The Rise of the Media Consultant. The political consultant has emerged as a pivotal figure in American politics, assuming many of the roles of the traditional party machine. The primary responsibility of the media consultant is to coordinate both political ads and unpaid media coverage. However, the media consultant has branched out into all phases of a campaign, including media creation and promotion, direct-mail fund-raising, and participation in the formulation of campaign strategies.

Media consultants help candidates clarify their presentations and survive the scrutiny of intense media attention. H. Ross Perot discovered the value of a media consultant when he addressed the National Association for the Advancement of Colored People (NAACP) on July 11, 1992. Disregarding the advice of Ed Rollins (who soon after quit the campaign) and Hamilton Jordon, Perot ad-libbed his remarks. He was mortified to learn that his casual comments ("You people") offended his listeners. According to the *Dictionary of Cautionary Words and Phrases,* which is compiled by a group of professional journalists, this term is used to refer to an outside group and is therefore considered objectionable.[30] On July 16, Perot withdrew from the campaign—only to reenter the race October 1.

Media consultants are advertising specialists who borrow heavily from traditional advertising techniques to "sell" their candidates to the public. However, media consultant Bob Goodman laments that packaging a human being has distinct limitations:

You can't put a candidate completely in a new package. You can take his polyester off and put him in a decent-looking suit. You have him blow dry his hair. You can teach him how to keep his eye on the camera. You can try to inspire certain attributes. But you don't have the complete freedom that you do when you're dealing with a bar of soap.[31]

Some critics regard political consultants as mercenaries who hire themselves out to the largest bid. Top media consultants can command a fee of up to $100,000 for a single political campaign. In addition, consultants must maintain an impressive win-loss record in order to continue to attract clients. Consultants therefore may be reluctant to take chances on candidates who could benefit most from their assistance. Media consultant Sanford L. Weiner admits:

We would all like to think we have only worked for candidates we believed in, and who represented our own individual political thinking. . . . Unfortunately, as with any profession, economics enter the picture. We have all, from time to time, represented clients whom we didn't particularly love, but who could help us pay the overhead.[32]

However, consultants generally offer their services to candidates affiliated with one political party (Republican or Democrat) or to individual candidates they respect.

Top media consultants wield an astonishing amount of power. Where candidates used to solicit the support of the party machine, they now scramble for the services of top media consultants. Candidates often defer to the judgment of the consultant—not only on campaign strategy but on political issues as well. Thomas Eagleton notes:

If you hire any of these big consultants . . . you more or less hand over your mind and soul to what they think is going to sell in the campaign. That consultant works with your pollster and the two decide what goes on the thirty second spot, and what goes on the thirty second spot is supposedly your brain. They'll tell you, "Look, Senator, if you believe there ought to be a cap on social security, for God's sake don't mention it to a soul." . . . So the media consultant sits down and tells you what's marketable and what's dangerous or explosive.[33]

Indeed, consultant Vincent Breglio complains, "some candidates just won't listen, they won't do what they're told" and explains that "the extent to which a candidate is manageable" is a prime consideration in the selection of his clients—an alarming criterion for a national leader.[34]

Candidate Selection. In the media age, a major criterion for selecting candidates is their ability to communicate on television. In addition, a successful candidate must be able to survive the scrutiny of the press. For instance, major campaign issues during the 1992 presidential election included Bill Clinton's trip to Moscow as a student in January 1970, his role in protests against the Vietnam War, and whether he smoked (or "inhaled") marijuana during the 1960s. This media scrutiny limits the pool of potential candidates. It is safe to say that very few people would feel comfortable permitting the press to comb through their past. Indeed, if experience forms character, it can be argued that youthful indiscretions are an important part of growing up. To borrow a line from Groucho Marx, would you vote for anyone whose life was so devoid of experience that he or she could survive this level of media inquiry?

Campaign Finances. The overwhelming expense of a political media campaign necessitates that the candidates have access to money. For instance, the cost of the average winning campaign for the U.S. Senate in 1990 was $3,870,621. The second highest vote-getter in each race spent an average of $1,674,658.[35] Once in office, they must continue to raise money for reelection. Consequently, candidates frequently are forced to devote more of their time to fund-raising than policy formation. Political campaigns depend on the contributions of special interest groups, who in turn expect favored treatment from a candidate. The Federal Election Campaign Act (FECA) of 1971, amended in 1974 and 1976, permits corporations, labor unions, and religious organizations to support political candidates through the formation of political action committees (PACs)— a "separate segregated fund" within a company or as a self-sustaining, though related organization. This legislation enables PACs to donate up to $5,000 to a candidate, circumventing the $1,000 campaign gift limit for individuals.

PACs now have a significant impact on both national and local political campaigns. In 1990, the number of PACs stood at 4,172—almost triple the number of a decade earlier. Their total expenditures amounted to $358 million.[36] (See Figure 8.1.)

Ideological PACs are not distributed along traditional party lines but instead support candidates most willing to support the agenda of the special interest group. For instance, in 1986, the American Medical Association Political Action Committee (AMPAC) gave more than $600,000 to promote two Republican candidates running for House seats: James Eynon of Indianapolis and David Williams of San Francisco. But according to the 1988 *Almanac of Federal PACs,* "AMPAC's real purpose was to finance the defeat of two . . . members of the House Ways and Means subcommittee, which has jurisdiction over the payment of Medicare benefits."[37]

Despite legislation limiting campaign contributions, loopholes still exist under the rubric of "soft money." Barred from donating directly to a political candidate, corporations can contribute to "party building activities" such as dinners. For example, a record $9 million fund-raiser was held for President Bush on April 28, 1992, "with dozens of donors including oil companies, tobacco companies, [and] financial institutions." Individuals were also able to circumvent their legal contribution limit of $1,000 by buying tickets to the dinner. The cost for an individual "plate" ranged from $1,500 to $400,000. In return for a sizable donation, guests gained valuable access to the Bush administration:

Figure 8.1
Political Action Committee Contributions for 1990 (in millions)

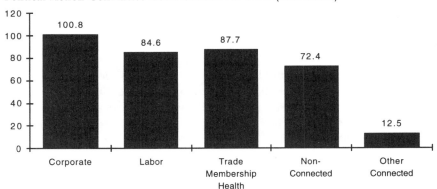

Source: Harold W. Stanley and Richard G. Niemi, *Vital Statistics on American Politics,* 3rd ed. (Washington, D.C.: CQ Press, 1992), 178.

Invitations promised those who raised more than $92,000 a private photo opportunity with Bush and a chance to sit at the head table with Bush or Vice President Dan Quayle. Contributors who bought two tables were promised a private reception with Bush and his wife, Barbara, or a reception held by the Cabinet in addition to lunch with the Quayles and receptions with congressional leaders.[38]

Lobbyists, representing special interests, make every effort to influence the decisions of legislators—including promises of donations or threats to cut off funding. Lobbyists are often former government officials who use their connections to gain access to politicians. For instance, former Reagan aid Michael Deaver found immediate employment as a lobbyist for South Korea, TWA, and Boeing. He was later convicted for "lying to a grand jury and congressional panel about contacts with former co-workers that may have been afoul of the ethics statute."[39] Senator Carl Levin of Michigan declares:

One of the reasons for the lack of confidence [in government] is the widespread belief that government today is too susceptible to the influence of well-connected and highly-paid lobbyists. . . . Lobbyists are seen as part of "the problem in Washington"—as representatives of special interests who are paid well to place their own narrow constituencies above the public interest.[40]

Given the financial pressures of the political system, it is nearly impossible for politicians to avoid financial entanglements that can compromise the performance of their duties.

The Primary System. National media exposure has also rendered the primary system obsolete. This system for nominating party candidates was devised in a less sophisticated media era, when politicians could only gain access to voters by traveling around the country and declaring their positions on issues of local interest and concern. This was also the only means by which voters could hear what the candidates had to say.

Today, state primaries receive national exposure, thanks to extensive media coverage. Candidates can no longer regionalize their messages but are forced to repeat the same general message at each stop. As a result, the national audience quickly loses interest in the primaries. Voter turnout hit a record low during the 1992 presidential primaries. Only 19.6 percent of registered voters bothered to cast their votes. And despite an increase of nearly 6 million people of voting age, 1.6 million fewer people voted in the primaries than in 1988.[41] In response to this voter apathy, candidates often resort to attack ads and peppy slogans to give their campaigns a fresh and dynamic appearance.

Because of the national focus on state primaries, the initial contest in New Hampshire assumes an exaggerated importance. The winner of this primary receives very few delegates (Democratic—18 out of 2,145 needed for nomination; Republican—23 out of 1,105 needed for nomination). More important, however, they become established as frontrunners by the media. Austin Ranney declares:

The result is what politicians call "frontloading" of the presidential candidate selection process. . . . The benefits of this early position are many. The frontrunners, no matter how behind they started, rise rapidly in the public opinion polls, and they find it much easier to raise money and enlist volunteers. Their opponents sink in the polls, find it harder to attract money and workers, and often drop out or "discontinue active campaigning."[42]

The Influence of the Polls. In the past, leaders presented positions and then learned after the election whether their platforms met with public approval. However, with the advent of public opinion polls, leaders now assume the positions that they know are popular with their constituents. In a very real sense, our leaders have become the ultimate followers.

In addition, polls can influence the very outcome of the races they were intended to predict. As an example, during the 1984 Iowa primary, CBS projected Walter Mondale as the Democratic winner *12 minutes* after the caucuses began. State Democratic chair David Nagle complained: "I think [CBS] did a disservice to all the candidates. To the one they projected as the winner, they told his supporters, 'You don't need to go.' And to the others, they in essence told them, 'Don't bother to go. Your guy isn't going to do it.' "[43]

Despite their influence, however, only the results of polls generally are made public, leaving vital information unanswered. To illustrate, much of the early media attention devoted to 1992 Democratic hopeful Bill Clinton was in response to a January 13 poll conducted by the *Boston Globe* and

WBZ-TV. The survey indicated that Clinton held a wide lead in this first primary (29 percent to 17 percent for Paul Tsongas and 16 percent for Bob Kerry). However, these statistics were misleading:

- *Twenty-six percent of the voters remained undecided.* With a 5 percent statistical margin of error, it is conceivable that "Undecided" could have been the leading candidate.
- *Nearly four out of five voters in New Hampshire had, in reality, not yet made up their minds.* Seventy-nine percent of those polled maintained that they had not yet decided for whom they would vote, and expressed a preference for a Democratic candidate *only when pressed* by the pollsters.[44]

Although Clinton was skating on the thinnest of thin ice in terms of this announced lead, the media then began to train the majority of its attention on him. Julia Smillie conducted an analysis of the *New York Times* coverage of the Democratic candidates after the poll was announced (January 13, 1992–January 23, 1992, excluding the Sunday January 19 edition) and discovered the following:

- Clinton was the focus of 65.5 percent of the headlines that referred to the Democratic race—even if other candidates were mentioned in the body of the story.
- Some 50.6 percent of the column inches devoted to all Democratic candidates were focused on Clinton.

It would appear that the shaky results of this poll had a bearing on the amount of media attention focused on Clinton, further reinforcing his status as primary frontrunner.

Further, polls can only capture the mood of the moment and therefore are subject to drastic swings. To illustrate, polls conducted in connection with the 1992 Illinois Democratic senatorial primary reflected a wide range of disparity and inaccuracy, as shown in Figure 8.2.

Finally, as Larry Sabato points out, the methodology used in polling is often defective:

Many polls are just plain wrong—poorly done or poorly interpreted. Several sources of potential error stand out, including prior prejudices and question bias; the construction, analysis, and interpretation of the polling instrument and results, including the sampling and respondent screening processes; and a host of problems with interviewers and respondents.[45]

To illustrate, during the week of October 23–30, 1992, eight separate polls conducted by five firms showed Bill Clinton's lead over George Bush ranging from 2 to 10 percentage points. One of the chief reasons behind this disparity involved the sample. The polls that surveyed *registered voters* (about 72 percent of adults) showed Clinton with a 7 to 13 percent lead.

Figure 8.2
Fluctuation in Poll Results: 1992 Illinois Senate Primary

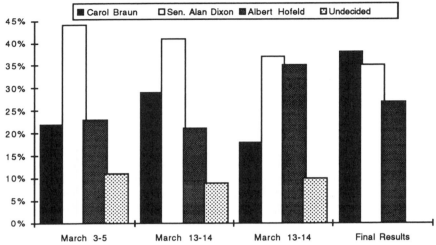

Sources: Chicago Sun Times; Political Media Research of Washington

However, polls sampling *likely voters* (between 50 and 55 percent of adults) saw Clinton with a 2- to 10-point margin. Clinton ultimately won the election by a 5-point margin.

MEDIA LITERACY TIPS

PUBLIC OPINION POLLS

When faced with the results of *public opinion polls,* experts suggest that voters ask the following questions:

√ *How old is the poll?* The fresher, the better. The closer to election day, the better.

√ *What was the size of the sample?* The more, the better.

√ *Who was polled?* Usually, it's a sample of (either) adults, registered voters, or likely voters. Adults: Most reliable, but least relevant, since it includes nonvoters. Registered voters: More relevant, but less reliable, because about 10 percent who say they're registered aren't. Likely voters: Most relevant, but least reliable, because the pollster depends on several "screening" questions to select the sample.

√ *Is the poll state or national?* State polls, usually a few days older, tell you if a presidential candidate is within striking distance of your state's electoral votes. But national polls can detect last-minute trends.

√ *Does it agree with other polls?* Average a candidate's score in similar polls. Averaging the point spread between candidates does not work.

√ *How many days did the poll take?* The more, the better.

√ *Who sponsored it?* Polls paid for by news organizations use safeguards not used by parties in the quick polls that candidates and parties use to guide strategy.[46]

Politics and Popular Culture. Politics has traditionally been the domain of the newspaper or television panel programs such as "Meet the Press" and "Face the Nation." However, the 1992 presidential candidates found that popular media programming was one of the most effective means of reaching the electorate. Larry King's CNN television program became a forum for all of the candidates but particularly for Ross Perot. Candidates found direct, free assess to voters through appearances on talk shows such as "Phil Donahue" and morning news programs like the "Today" show. This popular format was even incorporated into one of the presidential debates, with candidates responding to questions posed by members of the studio audience.

Popular media programming was also a vehicle for reaching younger voters. Bill Clinton appeared on the "Arsenio Hall Show," complete with Ray Ban sunglasses and a sax rendition of "Heartbreak Hotel." Al Gore appeared on MTV, outfitted with a pink tie, to take questions from the audience. The Clinton-Gore team used popular media, such as their theme song (Fleetwood Mac's "Don't Stop Thinking About To-morrow"), to reinforce their political message of youth, change, and hope.

For its part, popular media encouraged participation in the political process. MTV's campaign to "Rock the Vote" was an effort to promote political involvement as hip.

These linkages between popular media and the political process may help to account for a 20 percent increase in voter participation by 18 to 24-year-olds between the 1988 and 1992 presidential elections.[47]

System Favors Incumbents. The current political system clearly favors incumbents (see Figure 8.3). One major reason for this advantage is financial; incumbents have more access to campaign funding. For instance, in 1990, 79.1 percent of PAC money went to incumbents. As Eagleton explains:

The overwhelming tilt in American politics has been in favor of incumbents, for a host of reasons, including money, name identification, and access to the media. It's the inherent built-in advantage that the sitting incumbent has over the challenger who doesn't know where the PACs are located and who can't raise any money and who just sits there, being ignored.[48]

Media and the Balance of Power. The media has greatly augmented the power of the executive branch of government. As Ronald Reagan effectively demonstrated, the president can now circumvent the Congress and appeal directly to the American people through television. Christopher Matthews, former press secretary to Senate Majority Leader Tip O'Neill, notes somewhat enviously, "It is amazing how the monarchy translates so well into the television age and legislatures do not."[49]

Figure 8.3
Incumbent Advantage in Reelection

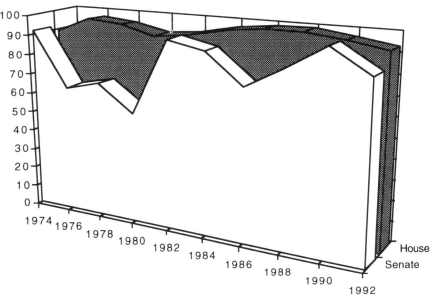

Source: The Guide to Congress, 4th ed., pp. 704–66.

Structure

The structure of the American media industry has a profound impact on political coverage. The ownership of the major news organizations (including ABC, CBS, NBC, *New York Times, Washington Post, Wall Street Journal, Los Angeles Times, Newsweek,* and *Time*) is concentrated within Ben Bagdikian's list of 29 large corporations that own or control the majority of media outlets in the United States. These media industries are often beneficiaries of current political policies; for instance, General Electric (the owner of NBC) made a profit of nearly $10 billion between 1980 and 1984 and yet paid no taxes.[50]

As a result, Bagdikian suggests that the media have an interest in preserving the status quo and are therefore reluctant to criticize the government:

When [newspaper companies] have to choose between, on the one hand, candidates who will dispense governmental favors in the form of corporate taxes and relaxed business regulation, or, on the other hand, candidates who support freedom of information, the record is not encouraging.[51]

For example, Time, Inc., which owns and operates *Time, Life, Fortune, Sports Illustrated, People,* and *Money* magazines, has a political action committee in its own name. Candidates receiving contributions from a Time, Inc. political committee are quite aware that they have become special beneficiaries of the media empire, whose reporting can affect their political careers.[52]

As a product of the system, the press is reluctant to advocate radical changes that might threaten its position. Consequently, they will only push for changes to make the current system work more effectively.

In addition, the imperative to maintain strong ratings often forces the media to treat politics as a form of entertainment. Mark Hertsgaard maintains that this preoccupation with "good time news" led to a pact of complicity between CBS and the Reagan administration in 1981:

It was [CBS News President] Van Gordon Sauter's view that the three network evening newscasts inevitably ended up setting "a national agenda of aspirations, of apprehension, of joy, and purpose." That conception of journalism was all but incompatible with adversarial coverage of the status quo. As a result, the ratings began to climb.[53]

FRAMEWORK

Introduction

Campaign slogans are designed to generate immediate name recognition. For instance, "All the way with LBJ" was a memorable catchphrase. Slogans encapsulate the central themes the candidate wishes to stress. Ironically, however, a slogan occasionally contains revealing latent messages. Gerald Ford pinned his 1976 election hopes on national inertia: "He's Our President—Let's Keep Him." Richard Nixon's pre-Watergate motto "Nixon's the One!" foreshadowed his ouster. And, finally, Pat Buchanan's 1992 primary motto contained this veiled threat: "America First."

Plot. An analysis of plot is a useful way to examine political ads.

Explicit content. Political TV spots generally offer only the *appearance* (or image) of issues. Although 89 percent of political TV ads appearing during the 1984 election contained references to issues, only 16.5 percent were *platform ads* outlining a position on a specific issue.[54] The remainder were *slogan ads* in which the candidate expressed an emotional response toward an issue (e.g., George Bush's statement "I want to be your environmental president").

Politicians often make issues out of emotionally laden themes (e.g., family values) rather than issues. Professor Richard Rosenfeld observes that these themes offer simple solutions to complex problems:

Political positions on the theme of "family values" overlook more complex factors, including poverty, the lack of educational opportunity, and unemployment, as well as hard-earned freedoms and opportunities for women that have made it possible for women to survive outside of relationships with men.[55]

In political communications, facts may be distorted or omitted entirely. For instance, in the latter stages of the 1992 election campaign, President

Bush announced that the government's *estimate* of the nation's gross domestic product had increased by $32 billion, or 2.7 percent, for the third quarter. The president proclaimed, "It shows that the economy is moving. This is good news for the American economy."

However, Philip Braverman, an economist for DKB Securities, charged, "This is an example of pre-election racketeering. The dice were loaded." According to the government figures, $14 billion consisted of computer purchases. In reality, however, only *$2.7 billion* was spent on computers. John Crudele explains, "The government added the extra $11.3 billion because it uses a strange formula to calculate how much 'computing power' people are buying with their money. . . . So don't take economic statistics coming out of Washington too seriously."[56]

Politicians may also confuse the audience by presenting isolated facts as truth. During the third 1992 presidential debate, Governor Clinton pointed to the success of his state of Arkansas as an indication of his leadership:

Mr. Bush's Bureau of Labor Statistics says Arkansas ranks first in the country in the growth of jobs this year—first. . . . Fourth in manufacturing jobs, fourth in the reduction of poverty, fourth in income increase. Over the last 10 years, we've created manufacturing jobs much more rapidly than the national average. Over the last five years, our income has grown more rapidly than the national average. We are second in tax burden—the second-lowest tax burden in the country. We have the lowest per capita state and local spending in the country. We're low spending, low tax burden; we dramatically increased investment and our jobs are growing.

At the same time, President Bush decried Arkansas as "the lowest of the low":

[Clinton] talks about all the jobs he's created in one or two years. Over the last 10 years since he's been Governor, they're 30 percent behind—30 percent—they're 30 percent of the national average, on pay for teachers, on all of these categories Arkansas is right near the very bottom. . . . Admit it! That Arkansas is doing very, very badly against any standard—environment, support for police officers, whatever it is.[57]

In point of fact, both politicians were factually correct. These facts, however, were based on different criteria (percentage of growth versus national ranking). In the face of this bewildering array of information, facts become meaningless. Truth has thus been reduced to a matter of *faith*—whose facts the public chooses to believe.

The rhetorical technique employed in the political arena often consists of the following illogical or one-sided elements:

Attack. Attacking an opponent as a liar for something he or she supposedly did or for something he or she is hiding. Daniel Goleman notes, "This is particularly difficult [to detect], because innuendoes are made that raise doubts without necessarily giving evidence."[58] An example during the 1992 campaign occurred when George Bush attempted to raise questions about Bill Clinton's trip to Moscow as a student. Bush declared, "I don't want to tell you what I really think. To go to Moscow, one year after Russia crushed Czechoslovakia, not remember who you saw there."

One-sided argument. This rhetorical technique consists of politicians arguing that one particular course of action is the only legitimate step, without providing details or support. Goleman reminds voters, "Recognize that a two-sided argument lays out options. Weigh the pros and cons."[59]

Agenda setting. Politicians strive to establish their agenda as crucial and, by extension, other issues as irrelevant. Paul Begala attributed much of the success of the Clinton campaign to "Message management"—that is, he was able to focus his message and set the political agenda for the election. Goleman suggests that citizens ask the following questions:

- "Is this what I think is important?"
- "What of importance is not being talked about?"[60]

Establishing absolutes. Political communications (generated by both politicians and the media) often overstate complex issues to make an impression on the audience. For instance, the 1992 presidential race boiled down to a campaign of tax-and-spend Democrats against read-my-lips-no-new-taxes Republicans.

Kathleen Hall Jamieson identifies a related technique of *apposition* in which a candidate is defined through juxtaposition with the opponent. Campaigns strive to associate their candidate with positive values by positioning their rival in the other extreme (e.g., honesty versus corruption, decency versus immorality).[61]

The emphasis on patriotism that so dominated the 1988 presidential campaign is a graphic illustration of apposition. George Bush made this issue the focal point of his campaign, hammering on the issue of reciting the Pledge of Allegiance in schools. However, the appositional subtext was more significant: If Bush was patriotic, then the inference was that Michael Dukakis must surely be *unpatriotic.*

Affective Response. Many media messages presented by politicians are designed to touch the emotions of the average citizen. Formal media rituals, such as the inauguration, press conferences, and the State of the Union Address, inspire feelings of awe and respect for the members of the government. As mentioned earlier, the selective recitation of facts only stirs feelings of confusion among the electorate.

Media consultant Tony Schwartz claims that the most effective political campaigns are directed at emotions—what he calls the "deep sell." Schwartz uses the public as his "workforce." He first conducts polls to identify their feelings about the candidates and the issues. Then he designs messages that tap into these preexisting emotions. In this sense, political ads do not educate as much as they evoke an intended response.[62]

According to Dr. Anthony Pratkanis, a psychologist who specializes in persuasion at the University of California at Santa Cruz, an awareness of affective appeals in political communications is critical to an enlightened electorate: "Most people think propaganda works on everyone else but themselves. It's helpful to see clearly the message makers' tactics, so you're less likely to be manipulated by them."[63]

Implicit Content. The media have been criticized for a lack of sustained coverage of issues. This in part can be attributed to the "scoop" mentality of the press. Hertsgaard observes, "If information is not new, it is not considered news, regardless of its intrinsic value."[64] Lee Lescaze, reporter for the *Washington Post,* maintains that a story must be followed with some consistency in order to be considered important by the public: "When you've got a good story, you've got to run it more than once in a while. You can't just say it once . . . because the White House writes its story every day."[65]

As mentioned in Chapter 6, the press often fails to draw connections between events or emphasize the consequences of political decisions. Hertsgaard sees this as a lack of sufficient understanding of issues on the part of the media. For instance, Hertsgaard charges the press with "borderline economic illiteracy" in its coverage of Reagan's economic program. Reporters were incapable of grasping the full implications of "trickle-down economics" and could not even raise the critical questions that would lead to a thorough understanding of the issue they were covering.[66]

Genre: Political Advertising

Political advertising can be considered as a genre, with distinct and recognizable functions, plots, characters, structure, and conventions. This genre has become so formulaic that media consultant Charles Gugggenheim complained that he was "disenchanted" with what he called the "cookie-cutter" approach to producing political spots: "They take a technique that works in one state and apply it in another, changing only the name of the candidate."[67]

At all levels, political advertising now dominates news coverage by a ratio of three to one. As a result, political ads can establish the agenda for both the media and the public through sheer saturation. The chief goals of a political ad are:

- To promote name recognition of the candidate.
- To convince the uncommitted.
- To give those who are committed the impetus to vote.
- To present a positive, consistent image.
- To produce and maintain the enthusiasm of the voters.[68]

Political ads share many of the defining characteristics of the advertising genre. Ads must be striking and dramatic in order to build name recognition for the candidate. The structure of the political ad generally falls within the formula of order/chaos/order. From the relative serenity that the audience experiences before the appearance of the ad, a problem is introduced: inflation, despair, the inadequacies of the opposition. The candidate then is presented as a solution to the problem.

Many conventions common to mainstream advertising also appear in political spots. For instance, political ads contain the same proportion of jingles (42 percent) and celebrity endorsements (33 percent) as in consumer product advertising.[69] Politicians make generous use of inclusive pronouns (e.g., wanting to see *"our* kids get ahead") to underscore that they share their constituents' values and concerns. Male voiceovers are also predominant in political ads, with the intention of suggesting authority and inspiring trust and confidence in the viewer.

Conventions such as business suits signify legitimacy, competence, and seriousness. Less formal attire, such as shirtsleeves, indicates a common bond with the people and a sympathy with their circumstances.

Political ads strive to appeal to the self-interest of the electorate, which can be particularly challenging in a mass market. This accounts for the "least objectionable programming" principle in political advertising. Eagleton explains, "The majority of the American people want you to do the right thing without affecting their style of life."[70]

MEDIA LITERACY TIPS

STAGES OF CAMPAIGN ADVERTISING

Edwin Diamond and Stephen Bates have identified four common *stages of campaign advertising:*

- ✓ *Phase one: ID spots.* The first stage of an advertising strategy is designed to instill the name of the candidate in the public consciousness. For instance, a 1988 ad for Paul Tsongas humorously featured children mispronouncing the name of the candidate as a means of ensuring name recognition.

- ✓ *Phase two: argument spots.* This stage is intended to distinguish the candidate from others in the race; what a candidate stands for. However, . . . these "position ads" are often vague, slogan ads, in which the candidate expressed an emotional response toward an issue.

- ✓ *Phase three: attack.* After the candidate has been defined and promoted, it is time to tear down the opposition.

- ✓ *Phase four: "I see an America."* The last stage of a political campaign typically presents the candidate as dignified, thoughtful, and reflective—beginning to act the part of the elected official.[71]

Jane Squier observes that the production of the political ad has become significantly more sophisticated since the 1952 Eisenhower-Stevenson presidential election:

Technically speaking, it's evolved tremendously. We no longer see sixty second spots. We used to do five minute spots. You just don't see those anymore. The kind of production values you see today are very different. You're into the whole glitzy thing. [Political spots] now take a stricter advertising approach.[72]

Squier also notes the trend toward more immediate and timely messages: "One of the major evolutions of the process is that today it's a day-by-day battle. . . . We can technically produce a spot and have it on the air tonight. . . . The producers respond to historical events and daily occurrences."

Affective Response in Political Advertising. Affective political campaigns are directed at a range of emotions:

- Politicians strive to inspire the *trust* of their constituents. During the 1992 presidential campaign, George Bush's principal campaign refrain was "Who do you trust?"

- *Reassurance* appeals promote a sense of confidence about the present. As media consultant Roger Ailes observed, "The candidate who makes the public most secure will win."[73]

- *Patriotic* ads reinforce our faith in our way of life and inspire a sense of pride in who we are.

- Ads for candidates are often designed to inspire *hope* in the audience. Bill Clinton's acceptance speech at the 1992 Democratic Convention concluded, "I still believe in a place called Hope." The statement was an allusion to Clinton's birthplace in Arkansas but also contained a message that responded to the electorate's desire to believe in a brighter tomorrow.

- Political campaigns try to tap into voters' anger, frustrations, and dissatisfactions as a way of marshaling their support. For example, a 1992 Clinton campaign spot introduced a group of factory workers who had been laid off. The workers parade in front of the screen, reciting their names and the number of years that they had been on the job. The last worker declares angrily, "It's not right."

- One particularly effective ad appeal taps into a range of individuals' fears and insecurities. Several examples follow.
    Fear of annihilation. "A young girl holds a flower in her hand, counting as she picks the petals. Suddenly, the picture freezes, and a voice takes over, counting backward. At the count of 'one,' a nuclear explosion is superimposed over the picture of the young girl. Lyndon Johnson's voice then declares, 'These are the stakes; to make a world in which all God's children can live, or go into the

darkness.' " Tony Schwartz, who produced this ad, explains that this famous 1964 campaign ad successfully tapped into the public's fear of nuclear holocaust: "Many people, especially the Republicans, shouted that the spot accused Senator Goldwater [Johnson's opponent] of being trigger-happy. *But nowhere in the spot is Goldwater mentioned.* . . . Then why did it bring such a reaction in 1964? . . . The commercial *evoked* a deep feeling in many people that Goldwater might actually use nuclear weapons. This mistrust was not in the *Daisy* spot. It was in the people who viewed the commercial." [74]

Fear of change. One common approach exploits the voter's anxiety about the future. George Bush's 1992 campaign strategy emphasized the risks involved in making a change. In the second presidential debate on October 15, 1992, the president concluded, "Now let me pose this question to America: If in the next five minutes, a television announcer came on and said there is a major international crisis—there is a major threat to the world or in this country—a major threat. My question is: Who, if you were appointed to name one of the three of us, who would you choose? Who has the perseverance, the character, the integrity, the maturity to get the job done? I hope I'm that person." [75] The message essentially was that even if the voter wasn't satisfied with Bush's overall performance, at least the president was a known quantity.

A variation on this theme raises questions about presidential succession in cases in which a vice presidential candidate is not highly regarded. For instance, a 1968 Democratic spot simply featured the graphic "Agnew for President," accompanied by uproarious laughter. At the conclusion, a voiceover commented, "This would be funny if it wasn't so serious."

Fear of differences. Ads also play on our basic mistrust of differences in American culture. As author George Orwell pointed out in *1984*, an enemy is a very useful political device, providing a target for anger and a way of uniting the country. A good example can be found in the "Willie Horton" ad employed in the 1988 Bush campaign. This ad focused on a Massachusetts inmate (Horton), a convicted murderer who had been released on furlough during Michael Dukakis's tenure as governor. The ad flashed a picture of Horton, an African American, glaring at the audience.

The ad overlooked several vital pieces of information:

- Massachusetts was 1 of 45 states with similar furlough programs.
- During Dukakis's administration, the crime rate in Massachusetts declined by 13.4 percent, while the national crime rate increased by 1.8 percent over the same period.
- Governor Dukakis had canceled the Massachusetts furlough program in April 1988, months before the Willie Horton spots were launched.

Jane Squier contends that the Horton spot effectively exploited racist fears. "If you put it in the most blatant, bottom line terms, the fear is that these black criminals are going to be let out of prison and when they get out they're going to run around and they're going to rape your daughters and wives and sisters. There's no question about it. I mean, to choose the kind of mug shot that was put on the screen. . . . He's a real person, but it's a stereotype they use. It scares everyone who's afraid of black muggers in the night. It's a very basic fear." [76]

MEDIA LITERACY TIPS
AFFECTIVE CAMPAIGN STRATEGIES
Anthony Pratkanis makes the following recommendations for critical analysis of *affective campaign strategies:*   √ "Keep track of your emotions while viewing the ad."   √ "Ask yourself, Why am I feeling (this way) now?"   √ "If you feel yourself getting manipulated this way, turn off the ad." [77]

Political Ads and Cultural Myth. Many political ads capitalize on our cultural self-image—not what we are, necessarily, but how we see ourselves: what we'd *like* to be. As Thomas Eagleton notes, "I think a lot of us . . . are motivated by what we want to believe rather than the actuality of our day-to-day lives." [78]

Mythic past. Ads featuring a nostalgic look backward at mythic America have an enormous appeal, particularly during times of cultural stress. This appeal is designed to project the legacy of the past onto the future.

For instance, America has long been associated with limitless resources. Frontier farmers would work a piece of land until it wore out, burn it, and then move on. However, with the 1976 oil embargo, Americans began to face its limits. For the first time, Americans had to stand in line for gasoline. Today, Americans have been forced to adopt the European system of conservation, recycling, and planned space.

It is not surprising that the public has not been receptive to political messages asking us to accept our limitations. Michael Dukakis's 1988 statement that he would have to make "tough" choices in budget allocations was countered by Bush's more optimistic (and popular) message of *plenty:* We can have it all.

The American Dream. Ross Perot's campaign was based on a pledge to "restore the American Dream" to its children. The American Dream is the promise of opportunity for the individual. Success comes to the deserving through hard work and faith that the system can work.

The romantic ideal. Political spots offer a worldview in which voters are empowered; we can make a difference. Our leaders ask for *our* support. We are momentarily important and in control. Ideals like freedom, hope, and goodness are central to this world of possibilities and prospects.

Insider/outsider. One constant political theme is based on the notion that whoever is in office is corrupt, and that only outsiders can reform the system.

Subgenres. A number of formats—subgenres, if you will—have emerged in political advertising:

- *Humor* is an effective approach to making messages memorable. In addition, ridicule is a socially acceptable means of undermining the accomplishments of an opponent.

- Research reveals that "man in the street" *testimonial ads* generate the highest audience recall of all standard formats.[79] Audience members respond to the sincerity and genuine quality of average citizens. The testimonial is an effective way to influence specific blocks of voters. This approach flatters its audience, inferring that their opinions (and votes) matter. As a result, a TV spot featuring the testimony of an elderly woman may have a significant impact on this subgroup.

- As in advertising, political spots borrow heavily from established television genres. The most striking example of these *TV parodies* is broadcast news: "[Media consultant] Walter DeVries, for instance, is a believer in the 'news look' format, enhancing credibility by presenting political advertisements as mini-documentaries or press conferences, with nonpartisan, factual deliveries sometimes depicting the candidate in the role of an inquiring television news reporter."[80]

  Political ads that parody game shows and sporting events tap into the common understanding and experience of the audience. And in some respects, political ad campaigns unintentionally have evolved into soap operas, since they are ongoing and episodic and deal with character issues familiar to this genre: betrayal, romance, and credibility.

- Although the *negative ad* has been receiving a great deal of attention since the 1988 election, historian Thomas V. DiBacco reports that negative campaigning has long been a part of the American political process:

No campaign was filthier than that of 1884, when Democrat Grover Cleveland was accused of fathering an illegitimate child and the GOP's James Blaine of being on the take. Republicans rushed to make up their verse about the wayward candidate: "Ma, Ma, Where's My Pa?" But Democrats responded, "Gone to the White House, Ha! Ha! Ha!"[81]

However, in recent years negative ads have emerged as a specialized form of political advertising. George Bush's 1992 campaign included a team of opposition research specialists, whose duties consisted of digging for damaging information on opponents that could be used in the campaign.[82] In the past, candidates would resort to negative ads only if they were behind in the latter stages of the campaign. Today, negative ads can be employed from the very beginning of a race, regardless of where the candidate stands in the polls. Although the public does not approve of negative ads, they tend to remember them more readily than less-controversial positive commercials.[83] One objective is "to sever the potential bonds of trust between candidate and voter . . . to make the case that the candidate is different from the voters and therefore not to be trusted."[84] Negative ads can also disrupt an opponents' ability to communicate their positions on issues. Instead, candidates are placed in a defensive position, denying allegations.

This approach, however, is not without risk. The "accuser" may alienate the voters by appearing petty and mean-spirited; people do not like a tattletale. As a result, candidates employ several strategies to avoid voter backlash. Using an opponent's own words or record against him (or her) absolves the candidate of direct responsibility. For instance, a 1960 ad for John F. Kennedy featured a film clip of President Eisenhower responding to a question about what policy contributions Vice President Nixon made to his administration. Eisenhower quipped, "I don't know. . . . If you give me a week, I might think of one." This offhand statement by Nixon's boss was far more damaging than anything the Democrats could cook up.

Another strategy consists of letting surrogates—members of the candidate's staff—play the heavy. An article covering George Bush's 1992 primary campaign provides insight into this approach:

In Georgia, President George Bush's campaign intensified the Republican battle of the airwaves Friday, releasing a new ad that accuses conservative columnist and commentator Patrick J. Buchanan of holding demeaning views toward women.
   In related developments:

- Vice President Dan Quayle hit Buchanan for his opposition to the Persian Gulf War and told an airport crowd in Augusta, Ga., that Bush was the "only true conservative running for president in Savannah."
- Presidential spokesman Marlin Fitzwater, in Houston with Bush, said that Buchanan was "the town bully" and was "out to destroy things."

Bush himself tried to remain above the fray. Asked for his reaction to Buchanan's new attack ads as he started off for a morning jog, Bush said: "I don't want to talk about all that today. It's so nice to get out." Asked if he would hit back at Buchanan, he said, "No, [I'm] going to be nice."[85]

In addition, candidates can subtly send a negative message about an opponent while ostensibly talking about themselves. During the second presidential debate, George Bush made an indirect reference to Bill Clinton's draft record by talking about his own military service:

I remember something my dad told me. I was 18 years old, going to Penn Station to go into the Navy, and he said, "Write your mother"—which I faithfully did—he said, "serve your country"—my father was an honor, duty, and country man—and he said, "tell the truth." And I've tried to do that in public life, all through it. And that says something about character.[86]

Another strategy exploits negative media commentary about opponents. A Bush ad from the 1992 presidential election used a cover of *Time* magazine that asked the question "Why Don't Voters Trust Clinton?" Time/Warner Corporation sued the Bush campaign in an effort to stop the ad, claiming that the Bush people had not received permission to use the cover and that the spot misrepresented the contents of the related article.
   A variation of this strategy consists of candidates *first* leaking information to the press and *then* simply quoting what was reported in the media. Jane Squier comments:

I wouldn't say it's a common, run-of-the-mill thing, but, sure, it's done. . . . I've been in a situation where that very thing happened in a campaign on which I was working, and the debate was whether or not to do that. And it was finally shot down. It was decided not to do that—but it was considered. And there are certainly campaigns where that decision is the reverse.[87]

A recent development in this subgenre involves the "negative-negative" ad campaign. During the 1992 Democratic primary, Bill Clinton's ads pointed out all of the negative tactics being employed by Paul Tsongas to stir up voter backlash and raise questions about the character of his opponent.

PRODUCTION VALUES

In political communications, sophisticated production techniques are employed to clarify ideas, issues, and positions. However, Kathleen Hall Jamieson contends that at times, production values can actually *undermine* the electorate's ability to evaluate political messages:

By flooding us with words, sounds, and images, these stimuli reduce the time that we have to respond and overload our analytic capacity. With that reduction comes a lessened ability to dispute the offered material, a lessened ability to counterargue. Once these defenses are gone, a persuasive message that might otherwise have been challenged or rejected can slip by. Persuasion without benefit of analytic scrutiny of the message is the result.[88]

Editing

The Sound Bite. "Read my lips." Given the time and space limitations of the news media, it is generally difficult to include all of the content of a political speech on the six o'clock news or in the newspaper. Throughout the years, lines have been extracted from speeches and promoted in the media (e.g., Franklin Roosevelt's "The only thing to fear is fear itself").

Recently, however, the emphasis on the sound bite has become more pronounced. For instance, the length of the average sound bite has shrunk appreciably—from 43.1 seconds in 1968 to only 8.9 seconds in 1986. John Tierney explains, "The public's attention span is inexorably shrinking in the age of MTV, which forces anyone in search of an audience—television producers, newspaper reporters, politicians—to deliver shorter, punchier quotes."[89]

Indeed, speech writers are now composing with sound bites in mind. Speeches are constructed around memorable, concise statements that present an idea or attitude in capsule form. Kathleen Hall Jamieson declares that voters should think carefully about messages contained in the sound bite: "It's quite possible to state a coherent position in a few seconds. . . . The problem with sound bites is that the ones chosen for the news often doesn't have any substance." [90]

Editing Techniques. Editing techniques generally are employed to ensure that the audience clearly receives the intended messages in political ads. However, at times editing can *conceal* significant information about a candidate. One famous example involved the 1964 reelection campaign of Senator Clair Engle:

Despite recent brain surgery that had left him with a paralyzed arm and greatly deteriorated verbal and ambulatory skills, his consultants repeatedly filmed and, with difficulty, constructed a forty-two second commercial in which Engle, appearing perfectly healthy, announced his candidacy for a second term. The deception went off with only one hitch; Engle died before the primary. [91]

Creative editing can also be used in negative ads to slander an opponent. In 1950 (at the height of the cold war hysteria), the staff of Republican candidate John Butler circulated fake, composite pictures linking his opponent (Millard Tydings) to well-known communist Earl Browder as a way of discrediting Tydings.

Color

It should come as no surprise that the most common background colors employed in American politics are red, white, and blue. In addition to their patriotic connotation, these warm, uplifting colors evoke positive feelings in the audience. Bright colors are also common to positive political ads.

In contrast, dark colors are frequently employed in negative advertising. One common technique consists of a "dead shot." A black and white photograph referring to the opponent, often shrouded in a black frame, is inserted into the colorful ad, providing a stark visual contrast between the two candidates. [92]

Scale

In American politics, height is often associated with power and authority. As a result, political consultants sometimes manipulate the environment to give their clients the appearance of stature. For instance, a campaign spot for diminutive John Tower of Texas was filmed in an old, reconstructed Senate chamber, using tiny furniture to make him appear larger. [93]

Relative Position

The placement of stories sends distinct messages about political figures. For instance, the *Washington Post*'s coverage of the 1992 Democratic primary during the week of February 20–26 referred to Senator Tom Harkin only in the last two column inches of each article, after the jump cut to the back pages. Each story depicts Harkin as an also-ran whose candidacy was in jeopardy:

- "Amid all the war drums, it looked more and more like Iowa Sen. Tom Harkin soon might be suing for peace." [94]
- "In Minnesota, Harkin remains the favorite. But it is not clear how much a victory there will help him, given the fact that he is from the state next door." [95]

And yet Harkin was actually the Democratic *frontrunner* at this juncture, with three times the number of delegates as the runner-up, Paul Tsongas (46 to 16).

Movement

Movement suggests a sense of direction, purpose, and leadership. This might explain why politicians are frequently depicted walking in the woods, busily engaged in legislation, and interacting with citizens.

Point of View

Despite its lofty goals of objectivity, the press often brings a distinct point of view to its political coverage. Reflecting on the media's treatment of Ronald Reagan, Maynard Parker, editor of *Newsweek,* admits, "I would agree that Reagan has gotten the breaks in terms of press coverage, for the reason that most reporters covering him genuinely like the man and find it difficult to be as tough as they might like." [96]

At the same time, the media sometimes presents a negative slant on a politician they *don't* respect. Referring to the media coverage of Walter Mondale's 1984 political campaign, "CBS Evening News" producer Richard Cohen confesses, "We undercovered Mondale; we weren't fair to him. We thought he was a wimp, we didn't like him and we didn't think he could win." [97]

The press often discloses its point of view by establishing the agenda of important issues and people. To illustrate, in January 1992, before the first Democratic presidential primary, the media promoted Governor Bill Clinton as the frontrunner. On January 25, CNN described Clinton as the "leading Democratic candidate." Clinton was the subject of the cover story of *Time* magazine's January 27 issue, featuring, the headline "Is Bill Clinton for Real?" Under the headline, the tag line read, "Why both hype and substance have made him the Democrats' rising star." And in NBC radio's coverage of President Bush's State of the Union address (January 29), the only reaction from any of the Democratic candidates came from Clinton. The latent message was that Clinton was the official spokesperson for the opposition party.

However, the media also subjects politicians to such intense scrutiny that it often deflates them. During this same week in which the press anointed Clinton as the frontrunner, the media began to zero in on allegations that he had engaged in an extramarital affair. Clinton's accuser, Gennifer Flowers, was paid a fee by the *Sun,* a supermarket tabloid. This accusation was given front page attention by both print and electronic media, putting Clinton in a defensive position early in the race. Despite some glaring inconsistencies in Flowers's allegations, Clinton's vigorous denials, and his efforts to minimize damage, nightly tracking polls in New Hampshire indicated that Clinton's support on the eve of the primary had dropped 14 percent since January 13, and that he now trailed Tsongas.

Political ads attempt to create the appearance of sympathy and intimacy with the public through point of view. Political spots in America rely heavily on close-up shots of the candidates. Close-ups inspire public confidence in the candidate, suggesting that they can withstand intense public scrutiny.

Angle

Political communications makes use of angle in presenting media messages. The camera is often tilted up at candidates in a gesture to evoke feelings of respect and competence. For instance, a campaign ad for Bill Clinton features the testimony of factory workers who had been laid off after years of service. These workers expressed their personal frustration with the economic policies of the Bush administration. The camera is directed up at the workers, which suggests that Clinton takes them (and their problems) seriously. The camera style thus reinforces Clinton's campaign theme of "people first."

Connotation

Connotative Words. Politicians choose their words very carefully to maximize their impact. Connotative expressions fall into several categories:

- *Traditional vernacular* like *home* and *family* respond to the public's thirst for stability and meaning in modern society. As such, these words are thrown

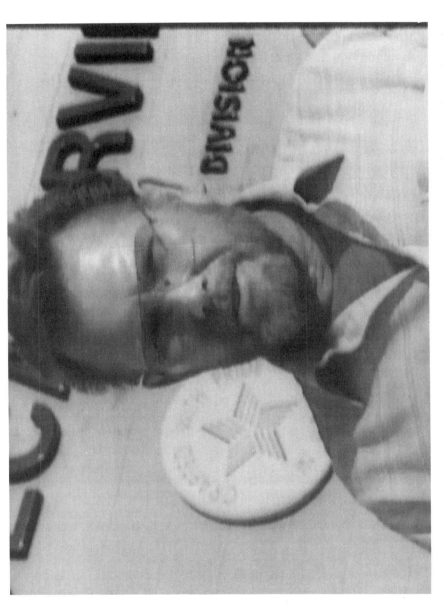

This TV spot for Bill Clinton makes use of angle to lend credence to this factory worker's complaints about the state of the economy under the Republican administration. Photo courtesy of the Clinton/Gore Creative Team

around generously by politicians. For instance, during a campaign stop in Arlington, Virginia, George Bush told the congregation at a black church, "You're learning the value of family—church family, personal family. And never underestimate its importance." [98]

- *War rhetoric* has been applied to a variety of issues, from the "War on Drugs" to the U.S. trade imbalance. References to war suggest a sense of mission, clear heroes and villains, and glory.

- *Drug rhetoric* is a very powerful metaphor to describe any social or political ill. To be "hooked" on anything conjures up images of immorality, dependency, and weakness on the part of the abuser. In his 1992 State of the Union address, George Bush described welfare as a "narcotic" that could get out of control.

- *Patriotic jargon* has always been a staple in American politics. To illustrate, the 1988 presidential election degenerated into a contest to see which candidate was truly the most patriotic, as witnessed by the Pledge of Allegiance nonissue.

- Although the Constitution guarantees separation of church and state, it is always a good bet to interject *religious rhetoric* into political speeches wherever possible. Like a minister, priest, or rabbi, President Bush concluded his 1992 State of the Union address with the following benediction:

  And so we move on, together, a rising nation, the once and future miracle that is still, this night, the hope of the world.
  Thank you. God bless you.
  God bless our beloved country.

- The *macho vernacular* in politics often reflects the male-dominated perspective of American culture. The coverage of political life often assumes the character of sporting events, with "frontrunners" and "knockout blows." During the 1988 race, journalists speculated whether the "wimp factor" would damage George Bush—raising the issue of Bush's manhood in the public consciousness.

  An even more striking example of macho vernacular occurred during the Clinton-Gore cross-country bus tour in July 1992. In chronicling the tour, reporters Robert L. Koenig and Bill Lambrecht manufactured a competition between the two candidates:

  When they played miniature golf on Saturday, Gore stroked a hole-in-one on the first hole. Clinton, bearing down, got a two. Later, when Clinton and Gore threw around the football . . . , Gore's passes had the most zip and the best spirals. [99]

  "The regular guys who play touch football and miniature golf have been failed by Bush and Quayle," said Gore, who at 44 is one year younger than Clinton, trimmer, and a better athlete. [100]

  This macho vernacular suggests that political leadership ability is defined by who is the biggest and strongest.

  Political leaders often revert to the sensibility of adolescent boys. For instance, after the 1984 vice presidential debate, George Bush bragged that he had "kicked Geraldine Ferraro's ass." In 1986, Bush's press secretary referred to Democratic Senator Paul Simon as a "weenie."

Political rhetoric sometimes reflects the homophobic nature of American culture. For instance, a tabloid supporting Jesse Helms's 1984 reelection bid for the Senate ran an article about his opponent, entitled: "Jim Hunt Is Sissy, Prissy, Girlish and Effeminate," claiming that in college Hunt had "a lover who was a pretty young boy." [101]

Jamieson notes that even an association with a homosexual can make a politician a target of innuendo:

> When LBJ aide Walter Jenkins was arrested during the 1964 campaign for soliciting a male in the men's room of the YMCA, California Republicans created a bumper sticker that read, "Johnson Is King and Jenkins Is Queen." One of Goldwater's TV ads claimed snidely that Jenkins was "Johnson's *closest* friend." [102]

Labels. Labels send very clear signals about candidates and issues. Anthony Pratkanis explains the effectiveness of labels by citing the term *granfaloon,* which was coined by novelist Kurt Vonnegut. A granfaloon creates a we/they sensibility by promoting a false and arbitrary sense of belonging to a group: "You see it in Governor Clinton's talking about 'the rich,' in President Bush's use of 'those liberals,' and Ross Perot's invoking 'Washington insiders.' It works once voters identify as part of the 'we' you're trying to create." [103]

Pratkanis suggests, "Be wary of anyone who gives you a label; ask, 'Why are they dividing the world up this way?' Do not succumb to hating vague categories of people; rather, think of people as individuals." [104]

Euphemisms. Neutral rhetoric is designed to minimize the impact of potentially damaging information. Columnist Clarence Page cites examples of euphemisms used during the Gulf War: "During what Pentagon officials called an 'armed situation' in the Persian Gulf . . . 'hard' and 'soft' targets, otherwise known as buildings and human beings, were 'degraded,' 'neutralized,' 'attrited,' 'suppressed,' 'eliminated,' 'cleansed,' 'sanitized,' 'impacted,' 'decapitated,' and 'taken out.' " [105]

Code Words. Politicians often rely on carefully selected *code words,* which have clear and distinct messages for audiences. As an example, Anna Quinlin identified code words used by David Duke, former Ku Klux Klan Grand Wizard who in 1988 ran for governor of Louisiana (and then was a Republican candidate for president in 1992):

> If you don't speak "white supremacist," here's a handy guide: "the liberal social welfare system which encourages the rising illegitimate welfare birthrate" means "poor black people are having babies on your tax dollars." Reporters Bill Walsh and James O'Byrne add, "When [Duke] says 'we,' he means white people. When he speaks of welfare cheats, he means black people. When he speaks of 'New York Interests' he means Jewish people.[106]

MEDIA LITERACY TIPS

CONNOTATIVE WORDS

Newt Gingrich, Minority Leader of the House of Representatives, published a campaign guide for Republican office seekers entitled "Language: A Key Mechanism of Control." In the booklet, he listed a series of "Optimistic, Positive Governing Words" for effective campaigning, including:

√ Environment	√ Peace
√ Freedom	√ Fair
√ Flag	√ We/us/our
√ Family	√ Humane
√ Charismatic	√ Candid
√ Caring	√ Youthful
√ Empowerment	√ Courage
√ Children	√ Moral

Gingrich's booklet also identified "contrasting words" with which to attack opponents:

√ Betray	√ Sick
√ Pathetic	√ Lie
√ Hypocrisy	√ Liberal
√ Permissive	√ Self-serving
√ Corrupt	√ Special interest
√ Wasteful [107]	

Derivation of Terms. The use of language does not simply describe events; sometimes connotative words can actually define public attitudes toward issues and candidates. As a result, pinpointing when a term began to appear in the media can provide considerable insight into media messages.

Sometimes word choice is dictated by politicians and then picked up by the press. Take, for example, the 1992 House of Representatives bank "scandal." In reality, the House "bank" was a collective enterprise; the funds were made up of the salaries of the House members, so no taxpayers' money was endangered by any overdraft.

However, the term *scandal* suggests impropriety, disgrace, abuse, and possible violation of the law. Where did this term originate? When the story of the House overdrafts first broke in the *New York Times,* it was simply referred to as a *case* ("24 May Be Named in House Bank Case," March 7, 1992) and then as an *affair* ("Adding Up the Casualties of the House Bank Affair," March 12).

However, Republican Newt Gingrich (who, ironically, had himself written overdrafts) began dramatizing the seriousness of the situation to discredit the Democratic majority during an election year. The headline for the March 17 *Times* announced, "Gingrich Takes No Prisoners in the House's Sea of Gentility." In the lead paragraph, the House bank affair was finally transformed into a scandal: "Above the low confessional groan coming forth from Capitol Hill in the aftermath of the House bank scandal, one ebullient war cry rings out [Gingrich]." Thus, one man with a partisan agenda created an atmosphere that was then picked up by the media and magnified into a major incident.

At other times, the news media blindly adopts the vernacular of campaign advertising. For instance, Jamieson found that much of the terminology used by the press to describe Michael Dukakis's record on crime was lifted from Bush's negative ads. Terms like dispensing "weekend passes" and references to Dukakis's "revolving door" policy originated in the infamous "Willie Horton" spots. In this case, the messages conveyed through "objective" news coverage were derived from the advertising machine of one of the political candidates.

Connotative Image

Many photographs of politicians appearing in newspapers and magazines are the result of *photo opportunities*. Events such as George Bush buying socks for Christmas or Bill Clinton and Al Gore tossing a football have been staged to give photographers the opportunity to snap pictures. Content has become subordinate to image. As Jane Squier observes, "The politician's staff asks the question, 'What would the message be if they took this picture?' "

On first blush, it is easy to dismiss these pictures as pure public relations fabrications. However, as politicians devote more of their agendas to creating photo opportunities, these sessions have begun to reflect the reality of their day-to-day experience.

Political symbols fall into these general categories:

- *Primary personal experiences* show a political figure at home and play, surrounded by family members. Jane Squier observes, "You've got Bush with his grandchildren and wonderful music behind it. . . . The message is, 'Oh, he's a good family man and he cares about family values. He's a grandfather. . . . But really, it doesn't have anything to do with the major issues in the campaign." [108]

- *Place symbols* associate a politician in a setting that evokes positive responses. Congressional candidates are filmed amid easily recognizable landmarks from the home state. Candidates also situate themselves in front of monuments, parks, and other sources of national recognition and pride.

- By posing with the elderly, middle class, or Hispanics, candidates become symbolic members of the group—if only for the moment in which the photo is snapped. These *"just folks"* images send this message: "I am with you, I share your concerns, I support you . . . Now, please support me."

Politicians are also depicted in a variety of situations that draw connections with the people, as when Clinton jogged in the streets of Washington, D.C. during his first visit to the nation's capital as president-elect in November 1992.

- We expect our leaders to be courageous and resolute in times of crisis. Consequently, *strength symbols* such as shots of our armed forces and candidates engaged in sports frequently appear in political spots.

- Many political symbols associate American political life with a highly regarded male institution—*sports*. Television footage of presidents jogging, throwing out the first pitch of the major league baseball season, or congratulating winners of sports tournaments suggests that the talents and skills that are essential to success in sports are also vital to the world of politics.

- *Patriotic symbols* such as American flags and eagles are familiar props in political communications. Although these symbols remain in the background, they serve as reminders of the politician's loyalty and commitment to the country. Senator Eagleton recalls the stirring use of patriotic images employed in 1984 when Ronald Reagan visited Normandy:

  It was the anniversary of the Normandy invasion, and there's President Reagan up there with the flags, waves splashing around. It was a beautiful day, a panoramic vision of the Normandy beach, and he's giving this speech on courage and patriotism when the U.S. came to the rescue of the free world. It was marvelous.[109]

- *Success images* such as footage of the Gulf War remind the voters about the achievements of the candidates.

- No president was more adept at using *warmth and sincerity symbols* than Jimmy Carter. The connotative properties associated with Carter's cardigan sweater—the informality, warmth, and comfortable appearance—convinced the electorate of his sincerity and conviction. One might even argue that Jimmy's brother Billy was a symbol of the president's down-home character.

- Politicians frequently rely on *symbols of hope* to convey their messages. Children are a universal symbol of innocence and hope for the future. Ever since the days of Caroline and John-John Kennedy, television audiences have come to expect shots of children in political campaigns.

- Politicians also frequently rely on *competence symbols*. Politicians are often shown in professional settings, busily engaged at work (for their constituents). Shots of the Senate, White House, or official ceremonies are common. We often find candidates in their offices, surrounded by bookcases filled with impressive-looking volumes. The implication is that the politician has actually *read* these books and is a wise and learned person.

- Negative political ads frequently rely on *negative symbols* to reinforce their messages. For instance, showing opponents in limousines and expensive clothes is an effective way of depicting them as rich and pampered beneficiaries of the political system who are out of touch with the concerns of the average citizen.[110]

Performance

As mentioned earlier, performance has assumed an enormous significance in contemporary American politics. Indeed, John Tierney's "Political Memo" column in the *New York Times* on the 1992 democratic primary campaign reads more like a theater review than a political analysis:

Mr. Clinton is doing well in the air war, partly because his ads have been on so often, but also because he looks most at home in front of the camera. He seems more calmly authoritative than most television news announcers. . . .

The ads for Senator Bob Kerry of Nebraska show him on a hockey rink, where he talks about trade. . . . His gaze might be a little too intense. . . .

The advertising for Senator Tom Harkin of Iowa shows him in shirtsleeves trying to rouse a crowd by shouting, "Let's have resource-based economics!" He has the exuberance of a good stump speaker, but . . . his passion can be disconcerting on the small screen. . . .

The most noteworthy aspect of the spots for former Senator Paul Tsongas of Massachusetts is what's missing: his voice. . . . His message tends to get lost in his mushy diction and vague sentences.[111]

Media consultants coach politicians on phrasing, intonations, facial expression, eye contact, and body language, often relying on "electronic response" mechanisms to measure viewer reactions to politicians' nonverbal cues.[112] Media consultants also employ focus groups to gauge the public response to the most minute detail of a politician's appearance. Referring to candidate Bill Clinton, Elizabeth Kolbert notes:

Clinton focus groups have sometimes divined danger in astonishingly everyday things. Clinton's hair, for example. Early groups were disturbed by the Governor's blow-dried coiffure; there was too much of it, and it seemed to stand unnaturally on end. The candidate eventually switched to a new, less-stylized-looking cut. Then there was the problem of Clinton's smile. Groups that watched video-tapes of the candidate sometimes thought that he was "smirking." Clinton has been working on this, too.[113]

The "issue" of Clinton's hair reemerged in August 1993. President Clinton engaged the services of an expensive Hollywood hairstylist, setting off media debate about "whether President Clinton is living up to his carefully groomed image as a regular kind of guy."[114]

Sound

Next to the visual image, Jane Squier considers music to be the "single most important element" in a political spot. A soundtrack underscores important points and provides dramatic emphasis. Music also can establish the tone of an ad. Light music signals a humorous ad. Reassurance and hope ads commonly feature romantic music.

Negative adds also depend on music to influence voters. As Kern observes, " 'Scary' music and sounds . . . shake patterns of belief and tap existing uncertainties."[115] In 1984, John Franzen developed a series of negative ads with "dissonant sound effects, such as clocks ticking increasingly loudly to raise the question of what the Republican incumbent had done 'for you,' and dripping faucets to raise the toxic wastes issues."[116] These sound effects remained discordant, denying viewers the resolution they desired. Franzen's goal was to leave the viewer with a feeling of dissatisfaction that would then be transferred to the opposing candidate.

The tone, volume, and pace of the voiceover may also communicate messages about a candidate. Some voices are authoritative; others are friendly. Negative ads are often characterized by a threatening or ominous intonation.

CONCLUSION

It is undeniable that the evolution of the mass media has had an enormous impact on the American political process. Information about issues is readily available to the public; in fact, it is sometimes difficult to ignore. In addition, continuous media exposure gives constituents unprecedented access to public figures.

However, long ago, Greek philosopher Plato warned that rhetoric would eventually displace epistemology in the political process. Rhetoric is defined as "the persuasive use of language to influence the thoughts and actions of listeners." Plato felt that in democratic societies the people tend to become more concerned with what they *believe* than what is true. Consequently, persuasion (how something was communicated) can overshadow knowledge (content). The main features of rhetoric, according to the Greek philosopher, are repetition and style. Modern politicians have learned to use these traditional rhetorical devices through the media in order to manipulate public thought and behavior.

Media literacy can enable citizens to become aware of how the channels of mass communication can be used to discourage debate, conceal information, and mislead the public. At the same time, media literacy can enhance public discourse on our political system.

NOTES

1. Tony Schwartz, *The Responsive Chord* (Garden City, NY: Anchor Books, 1973), 103.

2. James David Barber, *The Presidential Character* (Englewood Cliffs, NJ: Prentice-Hall, 1972), 13.

3. Ibid.

4. Roger Streitmatter, "The Impact of Presidential Personality on News Coverage in Major Newspapers," *Journalism Quarterly* 62 (Spring 1985): 66–68.

5. Robin Toner, "Bush Campaign Scrambles to Put Forth a More Caring Candidate," *New York Times,* January 19, 1992, 14.

6. Bill Moyers, "A Walk Through the Twentieth Century: The Thirty Second President," Public Broadcasting Service, August 8, 1984.

7. Jane Squier, former vice president, The Communication Company, interview by author, St. Louis, MO, February 24, 1992.

8. Leo Jeffres, *Mass Media: Processes and Effects* (Prospect Heights, IL: Waveland Press, 1986), 278.

9. George Gerbner, Larry Gross, Michael Morgan, and Nancy Signorielli, "Political Correlates of Television Viewing," *Public Opinion Quarterly* (Spring 1984): 294.

10. Quentin Wilson, campaign manager, Congressman Richard Gephardt, interview by author, St. Louis, MO, February 12, 1988.

11. John Tebbel, *The Media in America* (New York: Thomas Y. Crowell, 1974), 180.

12. Dan Rather with Mickey Herskowitz, *The Camera Never Blinks* (New York: William Morrow, 1977), 222.

13. Mark Hertsgaard, *On Bended Knee* (New York: Farrar Straus Giroux, 1988), 108.

14. Ibid., 35.

15. Ibid., 27.

16. Ibid., 52.

17. Martin Schram, *The Great American Video Game* (New York: William Morrow, 1987), 33.

18. Hertsgaard, *On Bended Knee,* 53.

19. Bernard Weinraub, " 'Disinformation' Risks Reagan's Credibility," *St. Louis Post-Dispatch,* October 4, 1986, B1.

20. John Tebbel and Sarah Miles Watts, *The Press and the Presidency* (New York: Oxford University Press, 1985), 184–85.

21. Kathleen Hall Jamieson, *Packaging the Presidency,* 2d ed. (New York: Oxford University Press, 1992), 10.

22. Schram, *American Video Game,* 24–26.

23. Sally Quinn, "Tabloid Politics, the Clintons, and the Way We Now Scrutinize Our Potential Presidents," *Washington Post,* January 26, 1992, C1.

24. Jeffres, *Processes and Effects,* 267–68.

25. Donna Rouner and Richard M. Perloff, "Selective Perception of Outcome of First 1984 Presidential Debate," *Journalism Quarterly* 65 (Spring 1988): 141.

26. Montague Kern, *30-Second Politics* (New York: Praeger, 1989), 25.

27. Squier, interview by author.

28. Larry J. Sabato, *The Rise of Political Consultants* (New York: Basic Books, 1981), 135.

29. Thomas Eagleton, former U.S. senator (D—MO, 1969–87), interview by author, St. Louis, MO, April 1, 1992.

30. 1989 Multicultural Management Program Fellows, *Dictionary of Caution-*

ary Words and Phrases: An Excerpt from the Newspaper Content Analysis Compiled by 1989 Multicultural Management Program Fellows (Columbia: University of Missouri School of Journalism, 1989).

31. Sabato, *Political Consultants,* 144.

32. Ibid., 26.

33. Eagleton, interview by author.

34. Sabato, *Political Consultants,* 38.

35. Ray Hartmann, "The Green Stuff," *The Riverfront Times,* July 8–14, 1992, 2.

36. Edward Zuckerman, *Almanac of Federal PACs* (Washington, D.C.: Amward Publications, 1992), ix.

37. Ibid., 375.

38. "Record Fund-raiser Held for President," *St. Louis Post-Dispatch,* April 29, 1992, C1.

39. "Deaver's Wrong Turn in a Limousine," *U.S. News & World Report,* December 28, 1988, 12.

40. Robert L. Koenig, "Senator Offers Legislation to Close Lobbying Loopholes," *St. Louis Post-Dispatch,* February 28, 1992, A16.

41. "Voter Turnout for Primaries Was Worst Ever," *St. Louis Post-Dispatch,* July 12, 1992, A9.

42. Austin Ranney, *Channels of Power* (New York: Basic Books, 1983), 95.

43. Associated Press, "TV Networks Accused of Interfering with Iowa Caucuses," *St. Louis Post-Dispatch,* February 21, 1984, A9.

44. Michael Berlin, "Let the People—Not the Press—Decide," *St. Louis Post-Dispatch,* January 26, 1992, B3.

45. Sabato, *Political Consultants,* 93.

46. "Experts Guide Voters on Weighing Polls," *St. Louis Post-Dispatch,* October 30, 1992, C4.

47. *Rock the Vote 1992 General Election Statistics* (Beverly Hills, CA: Rock the Vote, 1993).

48. Eagleton, interview by author.

49. Hertsgaard, *On Bended Knee,* 51.

50. Ibid., 86.

51. Ben Bagdikian, *The Media Monopoly,* 3d ed. (Boston: Beacon Press, 1990), 8.

52. Ibid., 94–95.

53. Hertsgaard, *On Bended Knee,* 174.

54. Kern, *30-Second Politics,* 48, 51.

55. Richard Rosenfeld, associate professor of criminology, University of Missouri at St. Louis, interview by author, St. Louis, MO, August 12, 1992.

56. John Crudele, "The Gross Domestic Product Hoax and Other Flimflams," *St. Louis Post-Dispatch,* November 2, 1992, BP7.

57. "Transcript of 3d TV Debate Between Bush, Clinton and Perot," *New York Times,* October 20, 1992, A20.

58. Daniel Goleman, "Voters Assailed by Unfair Persuasion," *New York Times,* October 27, 1992, C1.

59. Ibid.

60. Goleman, "Voters Assailed by Unfair Persuasion," C1.

61. Jamieson, *Packaging the Presidency,* 47.

62. Moyers, "Thirty Second President."

63. Goleman, "Voters Assailed by Unfair Persuasion," C1.

64. Hertsgaard, *On Bended Knee,* 340.

65. Ibid., 126.

66. Ibid., 123.

67. Edwin Diamond and Stephen Bates, *The Spot: The Rise of Political Advertising on Television* (Cambridge, MA: MIT Press, 1984), 301.

68. Kern, *30-Second Politics,* 57.

69. Sabato, *Political Consultants,* 175.

70. Eagleton, interview by author.

71. Diamond and Bates, *The Spot,* 302–45.

72. Squier, interview by author.

73. Sabato, *Political Consultants,* 7–8.

74. Schwartz, *The Responsive Chord,* 93.

75. "Transcript of 2d TV Debate Between Bush, Clinton and Perot," *New York Times,* October 16, 1992, A14.

76. Squier, interview by author.

77. Goleman, "Voters Assailed by Unfair Persuasion," C1, C8.

78. Eagleton, interview by author.

79. Moyers, "Thirty Second President."

80. Sabato, *Political Consultants,* 123.

81. Thomas V. DiBacco, "Dirty Campaigns—So What's New?" *St. Louis Post-Dispatch,* April 22, 1992, C3.

82. Douglas Harbrecht, "Political Mudslinging Enters the Information Age," *Business Week,* April 27, 1992, 32.

83. Kern, *30-Second Politics,* 26.

84. Ibid., 94.

85. "Tsongas, Clinton Compete in West," *St. Louis Post-Dispatch,* February 29, 1992, A1, A8.

86. "Transcript of 2d TV Debate Between Bush, Clinton and Perot," *New York Times,* October 16, 1992, A11.

87. Squier, interview by author.

88. Jamieson, *Packaging the Presidency,* 60.

89. John Tierney, "Using Ads to Cast Star of White House Series," *New York Times,* January 19, 1992, A1.

90. Ibid.

91. Sabato, *Political Consultants,* 162–63.

92. Kern, *30-Second Politics,* 99.

93. Sabato, *Political Consultants,* 163.

94. Tom Kenworthy and Maralee Schwartz, "South Taking on Aura of Political War Zone," *Washington Post,* February 28, 1992, A18.

95. Dan Balz, "Tsongas Shows Surprising Strength in Colorado," *Washington Post,* February 29, 1992, A12.

96. Hertsgaard, *On Bended Knee,* 47.

97. Ibid., 260.

98. "Bush Visits Black Church, Praises 'Value of Family,' " *St. Louis Post-Dispatch,* January 27, 1992, B1.

99. Bill Lambrecht, "Clinton Making Early Hit with Six-Day Road Show," *St. Louis Post-Dispatch*, July 19, 1992, A7.

100. Bill Lambrecht, "Team Mates," *St. Louis Post-Dispatch*, July 20, 1992, A7.

101. Jamieson, *Packaging the Presidency*, 84.

102. Ibid., 83.

103. Goleman, "Voters Assailed by Unfair Persuasion," C8.

104. "Persuasion: A Consumer's Guide," adapted from Dr. Anthony Pratkanis, *New York Times*, October 27, 1992, C8.

105. Clarence Page, " 'Sluggish Recovery' Is Bush Doublespeak," *St. Louis Post-Dispatch*, December 3, 1991, B3.

106. Jamieson, *Packaging the Presidency*, 90–91.

107. Newt Gingrich, "Language: A Key Mechanism of Control" (pamphlet), Washington, DC: GOPAC, 1990.

108. Squier, interview by author.

109. Eagleton, interview by author.

110. Kern, *30-Second Politics*, 100.

111. Tierney, "Using Ads to Cast Star of White House Series," A14.

112. Kern, *30-Second Politics*, 16.

113. Elizabeth Kolbert, "Test-Marketing a President," *New York Times Magazine*, August 30, 1992, 60.

114. Paul Richter and Greg Krikorian, "Sartorial Splendor May Cut Into Clinton's Image," *Los Angeles Times*, May 21, 1993, A1.

115. Kern, *30-Second Politics*, 2.

116. Ibid., 35.

PART III

ISSUES AND OUTCOMES

CHAPTER 9

ISSUES IN MEDIA COMMUNICATION

This chapter examines the following media-related topics from a media literacy perspective:

- Media and violence
- Media and children
- Media and social change
- Global communications

MEDIA AND VIOLENCE

A 39 year-old man who wanted to "scare" his wife was being held Tuesday on suspicion of setting fire to her shortly after he watched a television movie about a woman who had burned her abusive husband. Police said the husband told them that he had watched the NBC movie "The Burning Bed." The movie starred Farrah Fawcett in the true story of a battered wife from Michigan who killed her husband by setting fire to his bed while he slept. She was acquitted after a jury found her temporarily insane. "He told us he watched the show and decided to scare his wife with fire," an arresting officer reported in a police complaint.[1]

Everyone has heard or read about incidents in which violent media programming has led to violence in real life. However, violence in the media is a complex issue that does not offer any simple solutions.

Definitions of Violence in the Media

Numerous studies find a high degree of violence throughout almost all television programming. For example, one study tabulated the occurrences of violence in prime-time television during one broadcast week:

- 382 "acts of crime or violence" were committed between the hours of 8 and 11 P.M.
- 51 of the 67 prime-time shows studied contained at least one instance of crime or violence.
- 132 people were involved in violent actions.
- Some 56 people "died."[2]

The National Coalition on Television Violence (NCTV) has found that an average of 9.5 violent acts per hour appeared on prime-time television during the 1989–90 season. At the same time, Saturday morning network programming, directed at children, featured 20 violent acts per hour. Indeed, the cartoon "Dark Water" (Fox Network) contains a staggering 109 violent acts per hour.[3] By the age of 18, a typical child has witnessed an estimated 200,000 acts of violence, including 25,000 murders.[4]

But despite all of these statistics, no universal consensus exists with regard to what constitutes a violent act in the media. Is a pie in the face a violent act? A vicious verbal assault? And what about the *style* of a presentation? Mabel L. Rice, Altha C. Huston, and John C. Wright contend that the frenzied camera movements, severe angles, and extreme close-ups employed in commercials and music videos convey violent messages:

The forms of television can . . . take on connotative meaning, either because of their repeated association with certain content themes or because of their metaphorical similarity to real-world objects and symbols. For example, rapid action, loud music, and sound effects are often associated with violence in children's programs. . . . The forms themselves may come to signal violence or sex typing to children, even when the content cues are minimal or nonexistent.[5]

The NCTV admits that the criteria for defining violence in the media are subjective: "It is acknowledged that no single set of guidelines . . . will ever meet with the full agreement and approval of all concerned parties, and some elements of subjectivity and arbitrariness inevitably enter into any such system based on observational analysis."[6]

Thus, when faced with articles citing the amount of violence in the media, it is important to consider the criteria used in the tabulation of the data.

MEDIA LITERACY TIPS

MEDIA VIOLENCE GUIDELINES

The NCTV has proposed a set of guidelines for identifying television or movie violence, which includes the following criteria:

  I. Agent and Victim
     Violent acts must include an agent, who commits the violence, and a victim, toward whom the violence is directed. They may be one and the same.
 II. Overt Force
     Violent acts must include the use of overt force, or an immediate and direct threat thereof, in a coercive (aggressive and/or compelling) manner.
III. Intent
     Violent acts must be committed with deliberate and hostile intent.
IV. Exceptions
     A. Accidents
     B. Anger and Emotional Displays
     C. Animals and Other Non-Human Agents/Victims. "Sanctioned" forms of violence towards animals (e.g., hunting, fishing, slaughter, branding) will NOT count.
     D. Horseplay, Pranks, etc. Generally, typical "horseplay" (pillow fights, pie fights, playful wrestling, etc.) will NOT count as violence UNLESS there is hostile intent.
     E. Property Damage. Aggression strictly against property or inanimate objects (no victim) and which poses no direct threat to human beings will NOT count as violence.
     F. Pro-social "Violence." Physical acts carried out solely with the intention of aiding the individual to whom the act is done are called by some people as "pro-social" violence and will NOT count.
     G. Slapstick Comedy, Sport and Other Non-dramatic Violence
        1. All violent acts are to be judged by the same consistent set of guidelines whether they appear in a comedic, documentary, or dramatic context. Thus, identical violent acts are scored the same whether they appear in a comedic, documentary, or dramatic context.
        2. Physical action that is a normal, sanctioned part of a legitimate sport (fencing, football, basketball, etc.) . . . will NOT be counted. Violent action that is NOT a normal or sanctioned part of a sport, stunt, etc. (such as a hockey brawl) WILL, however, count.
     H. Threats
        1. Purely verbal or gestural threats will NOT count as violence.
        2. However, direct and immediate threats toward a victim that involve a weapon . . . or other evident force . . . WILL count.[7]

Possible Explanations for Violence in the Media

Several possible explanations exist for the prevalence of violence in the media:

Human nature. Undeniably, a side to human nature exists that is attracted to violence. You may recall that as a child it was fun to build something with blocks; however, it was often even *more* enjoyable to tear them down. Audiences, of course, have the choice of watching nonviolent programming but enjoy watching programs that contain violence.

Media as reflection of culture. Violence is deeply ingrained in American culture. Richard Rosenfeld, author of *Crime and the American Dream,* declares, "The U.S. is in a category by itself in terms of homicide and serious interpersonal violence. American culture is saturated with violent images and examples that reflect the violent nature of U.S. culture." [8]

However, the media still present an exaggerated amount of violence. One in 10 television characters is involved in violence in any given week. In contrast, the chances of an individual encountering violence in the United States is only about 1 in 100 *per year.* [9]

Media as industry. In order to attract the largest possible audience, media programs generally feature the unusual and exciting. Nobody wants to watch policemen involved in the uneventful routine of their jobs, like filling out forms, walking the beat, or selling tickets to the policeman's ball. Successful police dramas like *Lethal Weapon III* (1992) are packed with shootouts, car chases, and mass destruction—to the point that the audience regards violence as a part of the policeman's typical day.

Characteristics of media. As motion-oriented media, film and television often stress external action, or plot. And since plot generally involves some conflict between characters or events, the action that takes place is often violent in nature.

Cumulative Messages: Media Violence

Audiences have been inundated with programs that, when seen as a whole, present some very clear cumulative messages about violence in American culture:

- *The world is a violent place.* Studies show that heavy watchers of television regard the world as a far more violent place than people who watch less TV. [10]

- *Violence is an effective solution to problems.* The world is divided into absolutes (good versus evil), and direct action is the best way to combat injustice. Significantly, a pilot study by Kathleen Heldenbrand conducted in a content analysis class at Webster University found that in Saturday morning cartoons "good guys" engaged in *twice* as many acts of violence as "bad guys." [11]

- *Sometimes the ends justify the means.* In many media presentations, the moral issue is no longer whether violence is right or wrong, but rather whether it is justified. To illustrate, a popular sub-genre in entertainment programming is the Retribution film; at the beginning of these films the hero is either personally mistreated or discovers a social injustice. At this point, the protagonist becomes the primary perpetrator of violence. These heroic figures (Stallone, Schwarzenegger, and others) are never held accountable for the damage they inflict on people and property. Within the context of the film the violence is justifiable, as the end justifies the means.

- *Violence is associated with masculinity, power, and sexual energy.* Real men are distinguished by their ability to inflict violence. Women are attracted to the strength and power of protagonists engaged in violence. Consequently, in film entertainment, violent incidents frequently are followed by scenes with a romantic or sexual orientation.
- *The value of human life is minimized.* Victims of violence often function as chess pieces, removed from the board and forgotten in the flow of the narrative.
- *Violence is safe.* Acts of violence never hurt members of the audience.
- *Violence is glamorous.* Killings and bombings are frequently shot in slow motion, from many angles. The explosions resemble a fireworks display.
- *Violence is gratifying.* Often in films, the primary message *is* violence. Plot and character merely provide context and rationale that lead up to a crescendo of violence. Mark Crispin Miller observes that the audience often shares the excitement and pleasure that accompanies the violent scenes:

> Screen violence is now used primarily to invite the viewer to enjoy the feel of killing, beating, mutilating. There is no point to Rambo's long climactic rage . . . other than its open invitation to become him at that moment—to ape that sneer of hate, to feel the way it feels to stand there tensed up with the Uzi.[12]

The Effects of Media Violence

Five theories offer a range of perspectives on the effects of media violence on individuals:

The arousal theory. This school of thought maintains that violent programming stimulates aggression in audience members that can lead to violent behavior. The research of scholars like Bandura, Ross and Ross supports this theory.[13]

Studies show that the likelihood of screen-triggered aggression is increased if the violence depicted on screen:

- Is realistic and exciting, like a chase or suspense sequence that sends adrenalin levels surging.[14]
- Succeeds in righting a wrong, like helping an abused or ridiculed character get even.[15]
- Includes situations or characters similar to those in the viewer's own experience.[16]

Surely the most graphic illustration of the arousal theory of media violence can be found in the Los Angeles riots on April 30, 1992, following in the wake of the Rodney King verdict. Significantly, the riot was initially triggered by the media. A bystander videotaped the beating of King by officers, which would not otherwise have been brought to public attention.

In response to the news that the jury acquitted the police officers involved in the incident, Los Angeles erupted in violence. At least 58 people were killed and 2,383 injured. Thirteen TV station traffic helicopters furnished national coverage of the destruction, which further inflamed the situation. In Miami, Atlanta, Seattle, and San Francisco, protests turned violent, and hundreds of people were arrested. Two people in Las Vegas were killed.

The cathartic theory. Paradoxically, violent programming may at times provide a healthy release for our aggressions. After watching a violent program, the audience may feel drained and purified, purged of our violent impulses.[17] In that regard, media violence could be regarded as positive and constructive.

The opiate theory. After watching enough programming, people may become passive and incapable of feeling anything. Fred Emery and Merrelyn Emery contend that watching television is a dissociative medium that "as a simple, constant, repetitive visual stimulus gradually closes down the nervous system of man."[18] Couch potatoes who fall asleep on Sunday afternoons while watching the brutality of NFL football would support this theory.

Cumulative effects theory. Most researchers have focused their attention on the immediate impact of media-carried violence on behavior. However, some studies suggest that cumulative media messages regarding violence may have long-term, *indirect* effects on individuals. For instance, N. M. Malamuth and J.V.P. Check found correlations between exposure to sexually violent media content among male college students and aggressive attitudes, as reflected in the belief that women enjoy forced sex.[19]

Studies also suggest that the cumulative media messages with regard to violence may have a long-term impact on the individual in the following ways:

- Becoming less sensitive to the pain and suffering of others.
- Being more fearful of the world around them.
- More likely to behave in aggressive or harmful ways toward others.[20]
- Thinking of aggressive behavior as normal.[21]

The no-effects theory. This theory holds that media violence has a minimal effect on audiences. The violence is obviously fictitious and is not taken seriously. And graphic acts of violence depicted in the media causes audiences to become repulsed, rather than attracted to violence.

Which of these theories about the effects of media violence on individuals is correct? *All of them.*

Studies conducted on the effects of media violence are not definitive. To illustrate, in 1982, the National Institute of Mental Health released a ten-year follow-up to the U.S. surgeon general's study of television and violence, concluding that "violence on television does lead to aggressive behavior by children and teenagers who watch the programs." [22] However, scholars and broadcasters hastily pointed out that "no one study definitively proves its case for or against the link between TV violence and aggression. Rather, it is the *accumulated* evidence from hundreds of research projects that indicates this relationship." [23]

Many factors contribute to an individual's response to media violence apart from the media presentation. To illustrate, in 1981 John Hinkley attempted to assassinate President Ronald Reagan in reaction to the film *Taxi Driver*. But although an entire audience watched *Taxi Driver*, John Hinkley was the *only* one who was moved to attack the president. Other members of the audience may have felt purged, drowsy, or simply entertained.

Many other factors can contribute to an individual's response to media violence, including:

Personality profile. An individual's psychological makeup may affect how they respond to violent programming. Some studies suggest that aggressive children may be attracted to media violence, which causes them to be even more aggressive.[24] Other personality variables that may influence response to media-carried violence include:
- Introvert versus extrovert
- Stability versus instability
- Tender versus tough-mindedness [25]

Identification with media content. Sometimes a media presentation strikes a responsive chord within an individual. For example, you might react more strongly to the way that the character behaves if the character on-screen resembles your ex-boyfriend or ex-girlfriend. Some studies have found that the reaction to filmed violence can depend on a person's identification with the characters in the film.[26] As a result, women may react strongly to films in which a woman is being victimized by violence.

Recent experiences. What kind of a day did you have today? If you are in a foul mood, you might react differently to a program than if you were in a jolly frame of mind.

Immediate environment. Sometimes what is going on around you can color how you respond to a particular media presentation. Is someone sitting directly in front of you in the movie theater, blocking your view? Are kids running up and down the aisles? Can you hear the dialogue in the film?

Gender. Some studies suggest that gender may be a factor in determining how people respond to violent programming.[27] However, Richard Frost and John Stauffer caution that these results must be seen in a broader societal context: "Since the great majority of violence in the real world is committed by males, their arousal responses to dramatized violence may differ from those of females." [28]

Social class. According to Frost and Stauffer, inner-city subjects are significantly more aroused by viewing violent programming than a sample of college students.

These findings support the theory that when media content is generally congruent with the real-life experience of the audience, the result is a marked amplification of the reality of media messages. Since the environment of the inner-city residents is indeed more violent than that of the college students, the former's significantly higher arousal levels to violent stimuli may be connected to their real-life surroundings.[29]

Content attributes. Barry Gunter found that the following qualities of a program could affect how the audience responded to violent content in the program:

- *The fictional setting of a portrayal.* Violent acts committed within a realistic setting were more disturbing than similar acts depicted in fictional entertainment genres, such as westerns, science fiction, or cartoons.
- *The types of characters who were involved as perpetrators and victims of violence.* Viewers reacted dramatically when the content depicted men inflicting violence on women.
- *The type of violence depicted.* Some forms of violence are more disturbing than others. For instance, shootings and stabbings were regarded as more "serious" forms of violence than explosions or unarmed combat.
- *The amount of attention focused on the suffering of victims.* Visibly harmful violence was deemed to be more disturbing to viewers than violence with no observable consequences.[30]

Legislative Solutions

In the United States, deciding on a course of action in regard to media violence is a very complex matter. Led by Senator Paul Simon, Congress has pressured television executives to voluntarily curb the amount of violence in children's programming. In July 1993, the four major networks (NBC, CBS, ABC, and Fox) agreed to add an audience advisory to programs that, in their judgment, contain excessive violence.

Citizens groups such as the NCTV have expressed reservations about this step. First, determining which programs should include viewer advisories remains a concern. For instance, cartoons—the most violent programming, according to the NCTV—are excluded from this voluntary warning system. And second, because this is a voluntary system, unsupervised children (or, for that matter, parents who *are* supervising their children) are free to ignore the warning.

However, no completely satisfactory solution exists to this complex issue. Because there is no definitive way to predict how people might react to violent programming, it is impossible to monitor who will be able to cope with this type of content. As mentioned above, questions remain about how to define violence in media. And finally, in a democracy, it is always dangerous to censor information. Ultimately, audiences must assume responsibility by becoming aware of the possible impact of media violence and developing a sensitivity to media messages about violence.

MEDIA AND CHILDREN

No discussion of media literacy would be complete without some discussion of the influence of media in the lives of children and some strategies for helping youngsters to become media literate.

Television has emerged as a major factor in the lives of children. For example:

- The average child aged two to five watches over 27 hours of television a week.[31]
- Children are exposed to an average of 20,000 television commercials each year.[32]

However, children often lack the capacity to understand the messages being conveyed through television. W. Andrew Collins found that young children have a short attention span, which affects their ability to decode content:

- Six-month-old infants gaze at the set but only sporadically.
- One-year-olds watch about 12 percent of the time that the set is on.
- By the age of two, children watch about 25 percent of the time that the set is on.
- Between the ages of two and three, children's attention span jumps to 45 percent of the time that the set is on.
- By the age of four, children are watching 55 percent of the time that the set is on, "often even in a playroom with toys, games, and other distractions."[33]

A study conducted by the National Institute of Mental Health found that five-year-old children have difficulty deciding what is real or fantasy on film. The children embellished stories with their own ideas, added people and objects not in the film, and had a hard time telling when a story ended. Nearly half (14 of 30) of the children thought a person on television had spoken directly to them and 6 had actually answered back. By the age of ten, children are generally able to identify cartoons as fantasy and can distinguish between "funny" and "serious" violence. However, they have difficulty deciding whether situation comedies are real or make-believe.[34]

As mentioned in earlier discussions of implicit content, young children are often unable to identify the motives behind an act of violence. As a result, they may not judge media violence on the basis of any moral standard but rather on whether or not the behavior is successful. As David Considine and Gail Haley observe, "The media, therefore, potentially provide a model that tells children 'might is right' and 'the end justifies the means.' "[35]

Worldview

Children's programming presents a distinct worldview, including:

A *homogeneous world.* The world of children's programming offers a distorted picture of the composition of American society:

- 3.7 percent African Americans (as opposed to 11 percent in the general population of the United States)
- 16 percent women (as opposed to 52 percent)
- 3.1 percent Spanish speaking (as opposed to 6 percent) [36]

A world filled with stereotypes. During spring semester 1992, Professor Linda Holtzman of Webster University conducted a class that examined stereotypes in children's Saturday morning television. After monitoring children's Saturday morning television programs, the class discovered that of 75 major characters, only 6 were women. Only 1 of those 6 female characters exhibited qualities that were not categorized as "traditional"—and she was a villain! [37]

A violent world. As mentioned earlier, children's programs have been found to be far more violent than programming directed at adults. The National Coalition on Television Violence has reported that violence on Saturday morning cartoons increased by 11 percent between 1990 and 1991 and is now *three times higher* than violence shown during prime-time programming. [38] Violence is depicted as a natural part of life and justifiable to achieve a worthwhile goal.

An absolute world. The world of children's programming is populated by good guys and bad guys. Issues are clearly divided into right and wrong. Programs offer simple solutions to complex problems.

A world run by children. Adults are presented as ignorant, close minded, or inept. Adults are incapable of either understanding or participating in the extraordinary adventures of the children. Kids are best served by bonding together in peer groups and keeping information from their parents.

Children and Advertising

Children represent a tremendously lucrative market for goods and services. Children between the ages of 6 and 14 spend approximately $6 billion yearly. [39] This figure does not include the considerable purchasing influence that children exercise on their parents. And because these children represent a future adult consumer market, advertisers strive to develop brand loyalties and consumer buying habits at an early age. James McNeal observes that it is therefore not surprising that marketing researchers think of children as "consumers in training": "All of the skills, knowledge, and behavior patterns that together we call consumer behavior are purposely taught to our children right along with toilet training, toddling and talking." [40]

Advertising can have a decided impact on young people. Studies by Thomas Donohue, Lucy Henke, and William Donohue found that by the age of three, children understand both the intent of television commercials and the sophisticated concept of audience segmentation (i.e., that advertisements are targeted to specific groups). [41]

To illustrate, in 1992 the American Medical Association (AMA) and the surgeon general singled out the "Old Joe" Camel cigarette ad campaign for contributing to a serious health problem among children. Despite the tobacco industry's contention that the Old Joe ads were not directed at children, the AMA study disclosed the following:

- Of all the three-year-olds asked, 30.4 percent recognize Old Joe and know that he is selling cigarettes.
- Of all the six-year-olds asked, 91.3 percent recognize Old Joe and know that he is selling cigarettes.
- "Old Joe" is recognized by more children than adults.
- The camel's image was as familiar to six-year-olds as Mickey Mouse. [42]

Spokespeople for R. J. Reynolds Tobacco Company contend that there is no proof that these ads persuade young people to smoke Camels: "We reject the notion that advertising leads to initiation of smoking. Numerous studies around the world have shown that peer pressure and parental influence are the leading factors in underage use of tobacco products." [43]

However, the AMA study also found that

- Camel's share of the underage smoking market increased from 0.5 percent to 32.8 percent during the first three years of the Joe Camel Campaign. This represents an increase from $6 million in profits to $476 million. [44]
- Camels are smoked by a higher percentage of children who smoke than of adults, matching closely the brand recognition.

Incoming AMA president Dr. John L. Clowe declares, "Every day 3,000 children pick up their first cigarette because advertising says it's cool: smoke and you'll be popular."

Public Media, Inc. has produced a videotape entitled *Buy Me That: A Kid's Survival Guide to TV Advertising* that raises some essential questions about advertising that children should consider:

- *"Do commercials use tricks?"* Commercials sometimes exaggerate the capabilities of toys to make them appear more enticing. For example, some products may appear more sturdy in ads than they really are.

- *"Can toys really talk (move or sing)?"* If they move or talk on TV . . . don't be so sure. This may only be a way of dramatizing the imaginative possibilities of the product.

- *"How do they make food look so good?"* Stylists often manipulate food to make it look particularly appetizing or interesting on television. In some cases, the product itself is not even used in the demonstration; for instance, the ice cream that appears on television is actually a combination of shortening, sugar, and food coloring.

- *"How do they make games look so easy?"* In television commercials, product demonstrations always appear effortless. Through skillful editing, nobody ever makes a mistake. Consequently, children may be frustrated once they attempt to use the product on their own.

- *"What does 'Parts sold separately' mean?"* Young children who cannot read the fine print at the end of an ad may be disappointed when they do not receive all the accessories displayed in the ad.

- *"What's wrong with 900 numbers?"* Children who are invited to call 900 numbers to talk with their favorite rock stars find only a prerecorded message promoting upcoming albums or concert appearances. And since the payment for this service is delayed, young fans may not realize that this activity is extremely costly.

- *"Are celebrity sneakers better?"* The relationship between a product and its celebrity spokesperson can be confusing to children. Celebrities like Michael Jordan are paid to endorse products, whether or not they really use them. Ads suggest that a celebrity's use of a product is the secret to his or her performance; however, Michael Jordan's skills are not dependent on the shoes he uses. And finally, it must be made clear that buying Air Jordans cannot turn a youngster into another Michael Jordan.[45]

MEDIA LITERACY TIPS

CHILDREN'S ADVERTISING

John Lyons offers some additional suggestions in regard to children's advertising:

- √ Resist cereals named after monsters or cartoon characters.
- √ Resist anything that insinuates that it's made with fruit when it isn't.
- √ Be wary of little girl doll commercials shot through pink and green filters.
- √ Beware of toy figures shot at severe angles that distort the scale and make a tiny toy appear huge.
- √ Scorn any product whose commercial . . . makes one kid look "out of it" to his peers if he doesn't have the toy. Scorn . . . companies who work guilt trips on parents.[46]

Media Literacy Strategies

Several strategies can help children become more sensitive to media messages:

Moderation. The Roman dramatist Plautus surely must have been thinking about television viewing when he declared, "In everything the middle course is best: all things in excess bring trouble to men."[47] Studies show that watching too much television reduces other activity. Six- to 11-year-olds who were frequent TV watchers put in much less effort on schoolwork than light viewers.[48] Another study found that sixth graders who watched less than one hour of TV daily scored 7 percent higher on academic achievement tests than classmates who watched four or more hours each day.[49]

Tactics to combat the overuse of television include the following:

- *Make sure that the TV is not constantly on.* Adults often leave the TV set on as "background" noise even though they are not watching. As a result, TV watching becomes accepted as a normal part of the daily routine.
- *Watch by the show, not by the clock.* In its excellent educational packet *Parenting in a TV Age (PTA)*, the Center for Media Literacy recommends that parents and children make clear choices *in advance* about what program the child should watch: "If you've set limits, they'll learn to prioritize and watch what they *really* like."[50]

  This strategy also sends the message that people should be in control of the television. The individual can decide when to watch, what to watch, and how to watch.
- *Set limits.* Parents should establish clear limits on how much TV their children should watch per day. The *PTA* also recommends that parents should set the conditions for watching sensitive content like violence and sex in advance: "For example, 'You can watch *Terminator 2* if you spend an hour discussing it with me afterwards.' "[51]

Participate with your child. Parents who use the TV as an electronic babysitter are absent during a time in which their children are exposed to many ideas. Watching television can be a shared activity, providing a common reference point and serving as the springboard for future discussions.

Discuss TV industry considerations. Aimee Dorr, Sherryl Graves, and Erin Phelps suggest that one way to promote TV literacy among young children is to discuss the following industry considerations that affect media content and presentation:

- Plots are made up.
- Characters are actors.
- Incidents are fabricated.

- Settings are often constructed.
- Programs are broadcast to make money.
- Money for programs comes from advertisers purchasing airtime.
- Ads are to sell products to the viewer.
- Audience size determines broadcaster income.[52]

Discuss the reality/fantasy of entertainment programming. Dorr, Graves, and Phelps recommend that parents raise the following issues about the reality/fantasy of television content:

- Entertainment programs are made up.
- Entertainment programs vary in how realistic they are.
- Viewers can decide how realistic they find entertainment programs.
- Television content may be evaluated by comparing it to one's own experience, asking other people, and consulting other media sources.[53]

Talk back to your TV. Talking back to the television transforms a passive activity into an active, two-way interaction. This is a way for children to learn about parents' perspectives and encourages critical viewing on the part of the child.

Present TV postulates. PTA suggests that parents stress the following postulates about TV:

- *You are smarter than your TV.* Encourage kids to challenge the premise of programs. Point out inconsistencies in content. Ask how the program compares to their personal experience and understanding of the world. This healthy skepticism encourages children to come to independent conclusions about the information presented on television.

- *TV's world is not real.* PTA suggests that parents and children watch a cartoon together and list all the things that could not happen in real life. This exercise reinforces the notion that much of what we see on television is true only on the tube. This activity can also be applied to other types of media programming, such as situation comedies.

- *TV keeps doing the same things over and over.* Encourage children to look for patterns and similarities in programming. Children can then learn to anticipate these occurrences in future programming. For instance, once a child becomes sensitive to the introduction of ominous music in a program, he or she is less likely to become frightened by it. Discovering patterns together can be a good starting point for discussion: *Why* does this music appear during particular points of a program?

- *TV teaches us that some people and ideas are more important than others.* PTA suggests, "Let your child use the remote control to flip through channels and count the number of different kinds of people on the screen at that instant. . . .

Or keep a tally of 'bad guys' in shows . . . noting the sex and race of bad guys. Are there any patterns?" [54]

Encourage an active selection of programming. Videotape, public television, and cable channels furnish a range of options with regard to media programming. The selection process requires that the children become active, critical viewers before they watch. Parents and children have the opportunity to discuss why the child would enjoy watching a particular program. In addition, this process enables parents and children to select a program or tape that both would enjoy watching together.

Keys to Interpreting Media Messages

Several keys to interpreting media messages are particularly helpful in generating discussions with children about media content.

Explicit content. It is very important for adults to ascertain what a child *thought* occurred during the course of a program. Asking the child to give a plot synopsis of the story ("what happened") provides an opportunity for adults to clarify any misconceptions, fill in gaps, and learn about the child's interests and concerns.

Affective response. Asking children to tune in to their feelings can be a very useful way to begin to talk about a media presentation:

- How did you feel during particular points of the story?
- How did you feel about certain aspects of the program? For instance, "Did you like (a particular character)? Why?"

Implicit content. Asking children to explain *why* things occurred in the story encourages them to examine the relationship between events and the consequences of actions. Children also find it interesting and worthwhile to explore the motives of characters. ("Why do you think he behaved like that?")

Function. Discussing the function of a program with a child often helps to put the content into a broader perspective. For instance, asking a child why an entertaining ad has been produced can make him or her a more critical consumer. Nobody likes to think of themselves as being "suckered" into doing something they don't want to do. It can be far more satisfying to learn to resist the ad message than succumb to it.

Logical conclusion. At the conclusion of a program, ask the child the following questions:

- Did you like the ending? Why or why not?
- If not, how *should* the program have ended? Why?
- How would you have *preferred* for the program to end? Why?

These questions can lead to a discussion about personal feelings and values.

Audience. It can be particularly enlightening for children to try to identify the intended audience. It has been estimated that only 10 percent of children's viewing time is spent watching children's television programming. The other 90 percent of children's viewing time is devoted to watching programs designed for adults.[55] And this statistic does not include instances in which younger children are watching programs geared for *older kids.*

It is, therefore, worthwhile to examine the content, style, and strategies of media presentations to determine the target audience. Looking at the advertising can also provide insight into the intended—and appropriate—audience.

MEDIA AND SOCIAL CHANGE

The media have been criticized at various times for (1) taking too active a role in promoting social change and (2) obstructing necessary changes in our culture. However, the media are, of themselves, neutral; that is, newspapers, television, and so on, merely provide a channel through which a communicator can reach his or her audience. Consequently, the media's role with regard to social change depends on the following:

- The intentions of the communicator
- The predilections of the audience
- The capabilities of the medium

Media as Agent of Social Change

Media and the American Revolution: Case Study. The American Revolutionary War is an excellent case study in which the media served as an impetus to social change.[56]

According to John Tebbel, by 1750 newspaper publishers had grown so numerous that the Crown had given up trying to license them. Newspapers were becoming closely allied with the growth of business in prerevolutionary America. Circulations and advertising made a few publishers reasonably rich. As a result, newspapers increasingly were becoming invested in the growth of the economy and of colonial society.

In 1765, England imposed a Stamp Act on the colonists. Britain had drained much of her financial reserves during the French and Indian War, saving the Protestant colonies from Catholic France. Consequently, England felt that it was appropriate that the colonies assume some of the financial burden. The stamp tax was levied on all segments of the population but was most damaging to businesses relying on newsprint and legal documents. Ironically, the two most offended segments of the population were those capable of doing the most harm to England—newspaper publishers and lawyers.

In response, some publishers suspended operations, upsetting the business community (which had grown reliant on newspapers for advertising), as well as the general readership. However, the majority of publishers evaded the law. Some published without masthead or title. Others published without the required tax stamp on each issue, explaining editorially that the publisher had tried to buy stamps but had found none available.

Motivated by self-interest, these young editors mounted an effective campaign against the British. They became advocates for democracy, charging that the Stamp Act was an assault on their freedom of the press. Tebbel observes, "They argued with fervor and dedication, if not with much devotion to the truth."[57] One paper claimed that the British were planning to impose a tax on kissing.

This public relations effort on the part of the publishers was critical to the revolutionary movement. Newspapers kindled patriotism in cities, where British tax collectors, civil servants, and soldiers were visible. Newspapers were delivered in wagons to the isolated settlers in the "frontier" regions of the Ohio Valley, which otherwise would not have received news for weeks or months. As a result, the English presence in the colonies began to meet with an organized resistance, leading to the American Revolution.

Media and Revolution in Eastern Europe. More recently, media technology emerged as an essential element in the democratic reform movement in Eastern Europe. According to ABC's Ted Koppel, new technologies such as the video camera, VCR, and communications satellites have empowered political groups to wage propaganda wars at levels once available only to governments: "The media does more than simply record events. It is a weapon. . . . [New media technologies] undermine what every dictatorship requires—silence. . . . You [could] keep people out but not their ideas, message, or image."[58]

To illustrate, during the revolution in Poland in 1989, the democratic movement relied on media that were difficult to intercept—3 million VCRs and 10,000 private satellite dishes—to develop solidarity among the populace. These media also provided irrefutable evidence about the status of the revolt to the outside world, attracting world attention and sympathy. After the communist regime in Poland was toppled, President Lech Walesa acknowledged, "Fifty percent of the victory is owed to media."[59]

Media as Impediment to Social Change

Other critics point out that the media can *obstruct* social change. Edward Herman and Noam Chomsky argue that the U.S. media operate according to a propaganda model that supports the status quo: "The propaganda model traces the routes by which money and power are able to filter out the news fit to print, marginalize dissent, and allow the government and dominant private interests to get their messages across to the public."[60]

The propaganda model consists of the following elements:

- *Size, ownership, and profit orientation of the mass media.* The American mass media industry prospers within the current system. As a result, media conglomerates benefit from the status quo policies of business and government.

- *The advertising license to do business.* Because the American media system is market driven, media communicators are dependent on sponsorship to produce programming. Consequently, media executives are reluctant to present content that might offend powerful advertisers. Herman and Chomsky declare, "In addition to discrimination against unfriendly media institutions, advertisers also choose selectively among programs on the basis of their own principles. With rare exceptions, these are culturally and politically conservative."[61]

   Because advertisers are selective about the types of presentations they choose to support, they can exert enormous influence over programming decisions.

- *Sourcing mass media news.* Much media content is shaped through the use of sources, who often represent government and corporate interests.

- *Flak. Flak* refers to responses to media content, which can take the form of letters, phone calls, petitions, lawsuits, and legislative initiatives. Herman and Chomsky distinguish between individual feedback and "serious flak"—organized efforts by groups with political agendas. Indeed, some groups (e.g., the American Legal Foundation, the Capital Legal Foundation, the Media Institute, the Center for Media and Public Affairs, and Accuracy in Media) have been formed with the expressed purpose of influencing media content. The authors observe that "the ability to produce flak, and especially flak that is costly and threatening, is related to power."[62]

   These groups are often well funded and can produce serious flak through contacts with the White House, heads of networks, or ad agencies. These groups may also generate their own media campaigns in response to programming, or back politicians who support their points of view.

- *National security as a control mechanism.* Since the 1950s America has used the ideology of anticommunism to control the information that reaches the public. Since the thawing of the cold war, this rationale has been replaced by broader appeal of national security.

The Media and the Gulf War. A case study that illustrates how the media can obstruct social change can be found in the media coverage of the Gulf War. Public perceptions and attitudes toward the Gulf War were manipulated through a carefully designed communications strategy. This strategy was essential to the U.S. government's marshaling of support for the military action, both at home and abroad. Media coverage was also a consideration in key military decisions. Secretary of Defense Dick Cheney and Commander of the Joint Chiefs of Staff Colin Powell were reluctant to engage in a land war featuring hand-to-hand combat, principally because the resulting gore and loss of American life would not play well on television.

The Gulf War communications strategy consisted of the following elements:

- *Censorship policy.* The "journalistic pool" system was fundamentally no 'different than the censorship policy of Iraq. The U.S. government insisted that all reports be carefully screened twice, on the pretext of military security. Much of the censorship, however, focused on maintaining a positive image of the war. Content was altered by censors (e.g., changing a report that the pilots were "giddy" with excitement to "full of pride") that had little to do with the issue of security.

    More important, the government controlled the *access* to information by the media before it had a chance to be screened. Officers monitored interviews with personnel stationed in the Gulf, influencing the integrity of the interview.

    In this information vacuum, the public was left with secondhand reports about the war. The government furnished the media with waves of interviews, briefings, and press conferences—all of which presented a uniform, official perspective on the war.

- *The call to conformity.* The communications strategy was designed to reinforce the notion that complicity was equated with patriotism. Paradoxically, individuals who exercised their democratic right to question policy were considered anti-American. Support of the war and the government policy was, then, clearly defined as an act of faith.

- *Patriotic rhetoric.* Patriotic rhetoric incited intense feelings of nationalism and coerced the public to support the conflict without question. In his State of the Union address, George Bush declared, "Our cause could not be more noble." He cited the Bible, Abraham Lincoln, and Thomas Aquinas in his speech and stated, "The U.S. and its allies were 'on the side of God.' "

- *Euphemisms.* Many of the terms employed to describe the campaign itself presented an antiseptic portrait of the war. Expressions like "collateral damage," "surgical strike," and "carpet bombing" originated with the government but were passed along without question by the media.

- *Demonization of the enemy.* Emotionally charged terms were applied to the enemy. George Bush called Saddam Hussein the "Butcher of Baghdad" and compared him to Adolf Hitler. The goal was obvious: It is easier to fight someone you hate.

In the absence of hard news, the media devoted much of its remaining time to "experts"—that is, former government officials who elaborated on, but basically reinforced, the same party line. Reporters were often reduced to the role of facilitators or, worse, cheerleaders for the official government line. For instance, NBC's Tom Brokaw made the following observations in his news coverage of the Gulf War:

- "Can the United States allow Saddam Hussein to live?"
- On Saddam: "This guy talks tough and swings back very feebly indeed."
- On whether the media should show caskets coming home: "Do you think that's in the best interest of the U.S.?"

A March 11, 1991, editorial in the *PR News* attributed much of the success of the Gulf War campaign to "information management":

The victorious Gulf War owes much to PR, but that is appreciated by only a minimal part of the general public. Here is a unique opportunity for the public relations profession to tell the story and get due credit for a job well done. It was *brilliant PR advice* which guided President Bush in assembling and winning support from an international coalition of allied nations. . . . It was skillful PR approaches that earned for him an unparalleled reputation as Commander in Chief. And it was that leadership which earned him just about the highest rating in public favor for any U.S. President. . . . And the superb job of rationing the news to keep it from helping the enemy, making effective use of pools despite resentment of reporters, and nevertheless provided a continuous flow of information to the public. . . . Of key importance to the PR field is that the function has earned recognition for its power at a unique moment in world history. We hope President Bush will continue to enjoy his stunning leadership and direct it at an effective economic war to conquer our crippling recession.[63]

The Media and the Women's Movements. A comparison of the media coverage of the women's movements provides insight into the factors that determine whether the media accelerates or inhibits social change. There have been two women's movements in America during the twentieth century: the woman's suffrage movement, which began in 1908, and the feminist movement, which originated in 1968. Francesca M. Cancian and Bonnie L. Ross tabulated the number of articles devoted to women and women's issues appearing in the press during the time period surrounding these two movements in order to address the following questions:

- What is the causal relation between the movement and the media?
- Which changes first, the quantity of news coverage or the strength of the movement?
- What is the time lag between the two events?[64]

The authors found that during the rise of the women's suffrage movement, the increase in media attention was almost immediate and played a direct role in the success of the movement. Several factors can account for the responsiveness of the press. The movement was characterized by dra-

matic tactics, such as open-air meetings and parades, which lent themselves to media coverage. In addition, the leaders of the suffrage movement made a devoted effort to cultivate the favor of the media. Finally, the authors note that the suffrage movement did not threaten the male-dominated society: "The suffrage movement was not revolutionary . . . but focused on the single goal of getting the vote." [65]

In contrast, the 1960s feminist movement at first was largely ignored by the press; media coverage lagged behind the movement by several years. The authors offer several explanations for the initial lack of attention by the press:

- *The 1960s movement emphasized issues rather than events.* The feminist movement originated largely through the organization of consciousness-raising groups and women's liberation organizations. These activities did not lend themselves to media attention (the more dramatic bra-burning demonstrations occurred later in the history of the movement).

- *The feminist movement was perceived to be antinews organizations.* Some of the leaders of the feminist movement were openly hostile toward the media, feeling that coverage was biased, demeaning, and exploitative. Consequently, these leaders were far from receptive to media attention.

- *The feminist movement posed a threat to the power elite.* The authors maintain that the media only cover those movements and issues that are acceptable to the establishment. "Once a movement is accepted by the government, big business, labor leaders, and other members of the political establishment, it will receive considerable media coverage." [66]

- *News organizations were antimovement.* News organizations, which were dominated by males, were threatened by the radical goals of the feminist movement. M. B. Morris contends that the press attempted to subdue the movement in its early stages—first by ignoring it, then by undermining its serious intent through frivolous coverage, and finally by "publicizing its least offensive goals and de-emphasizing its revolutionary aims." [67]

By late 1969 and early 1970, media coverage of the women's movement began to increase. Cancian and Ross suggest that by that time the movement had gradually grown in popularity and notoriety, until it crossed some "threshold level" of respectability. At that point, the authors note that the media coverage contributed to the growth of the movement: "There is considerable support for believing that the media blitz caused the movement to grow much faster than it had previously." [68]

Cancian and Ross's study underscores the paradoxical role of the media with regard to social change. Under some circumstances, a social movement is covered promptly by the press, promoting public awareness. At other times, media coverage may lag behind the beginning of a movement, inhibiting social change. However, once a movement has become mainstream and nonthreatening, media attention often follows; and this coverage can further accelerate growth and popularity of the movement.

GLOBAL COMMUNICATIONS

As the twenty-first century approaches, the media have truly reached global proportions. Media technology has become so sophisticated that these channels of mass communication are capable of transcending national boundaries. Several keys may help put these messages into perspective.

Process

Function. The purposes of global communications include the following:

To foster global community. Media technology such as the communications satellite can serve as a channel that brings different cultures together. One of the first instances of this "global village" concept occurred in 1952, when the coronation of England's Queen Elizabeth was broadcast overseas and celebrated worldwide.

To disseminate information. Enormous differences exist in the way that various countries produce and distribute the news. Comparing the coverage of a current event in a variety of international newspapers reveals dramatic differences in presentation, content, and even different cultural definitions of news. For example, news about the Third World and Asia in Western papers (when it appears) tends to be sensational, while coverage of Western items shows more balance between political coverage and sensational stories.[69]

To serve political interests. Propaganda refers to the systematic development and dissemination of information to propagate the views and interests of a particular group. Harold D. Lasswell identified four principal strategic aims of propaganda in war:

- To mobilize hatred against the enemy
- To preserve the friendship of allies
- To preserve the friendship and, if possible, to procure the cooperation of neutrals
- To demoralize the enemy[70]

However, propaganda is also deployed during peacetime to promote national interests; pave the way for diplomatic initiatives; and encourage trade, tourism, and investment. Significantly, one of the most effective *indirect* forms of American propaganda is entertainment programming. International audiences are decidedly fans of American films, television, and music. The unbridled energy and freedom of expression send positive cumulative messages about America.

To promote economic development. In recognition of international markets, companies are developing communications strategies to cultivate markets and influence consumer patterns abroad.

Context

Cultural Context. The relationship between international media and culture has many facets:

Media as cultural text. Media programming is a principal vehicle through which cultures learn about one another. Unless you have personally visited another country, what you know about that culture is derived primarily from the media. International media, then, serves as a text that provides insights into the activities, lifestyles, and concerns of other cultures.

In addition, the media is a fruitful place to examine a country's attitudes toward other nations. For example, the Asia Society reports that American textbooks contain some disturbing messages about the East:

- Portray Asia as "catching up with the West"
- Equate Westernization with modernization
- Praise and describe by Western standards
- Emphasize Asian problems and neglect Asian strengths[71]

National stereotyping. National stereotyping refers to the generalized conception associated with members of a particular country. As mentioned previously, these stereotypes generally are not very flattering. For instance, an episode of the English comedy "Faulty Towers" depicts Americans as vulgar, materialistic, and shallow. American advertising often pokes fun at other nationalities as a way to flatter the American consumer in comparison. For example, a Wendy's Hamburgers ad campaign portrayed Russians as ugly, ignorant peasants; the implication is that Americans are blessed with both the taste and freedom of choice to buy Wendy's Hamburgers.

Media and cultural identity. In some traditional cultures, the channels of mass communications have introduced new and different ideas that have disrupted the established values system. To illustrate, in his study of the effects of Western media on Indonesia, Asep Sutresna found that younger Indonesians are losing touch with traditional Indonesian culture: "Young Indonesians are not familiar with traditional cultures anymore, such as ephics which contain Indonesian ancestors' philosophy of life. They are not familiar with the figures in those ephics or traditional stories. They tend to view these cultures as being for rural people's consumption."[72]

The widespread presence of the media has led to a schism between generations. Sutresna explains, "Young Indonesians tend to view the traditional values and ethics as too strict and obsolete. Those are their parents' values and ethics."[73] Instead, the younger generation has adopted Western values, including the definition of success: "Success for young Indonesian means becoming rich, popular, independent, and individualistic."[74]

The infusion of these Western values through the media can be very threatening to the established order. To illustrate, consider the following article:

Angry Brazilian Mutilates Ears of Feminist Wife

TERESINA, Brazil (UPI)

A machine operator angered by the new feminist ideas his wife learned from television sliced off her earlobes. His explanation: "A woman who wants to be like men doesn't need a place to wear earrings."

The man, Osvaldo Pereira da Silva, was being held in the jail of Teresina, 1,300 miles northwest of Rio de Janeiro. He refused to let his wife undergo plastic surgery to repair her mutilated earlobes, the Jornal do Brasil reported.

"Women were born to bear children, take care of their husbands and children, and not to gossip in neighbors homes," da Silva said, adding that his wife had got "new feminist ideas by watching so much television."

His wife, Conceicao Maria Vierira Barros, tried last week to withdraw a complaint against her husband and said she would be willing to sell the television set. She called the television "that terrible thing that started changing my head."

She wore a scarf to hide her scarred ears and said she was "ready to forget everything and take care of the house and my husband."

Some neighbors approved of da Silva's attack. "That's the only way that she will learn to respect men," said Joao Policarpo, a vendor in the city's central market. Policarpo said he allowed his wife to go out of the house to buy household items only when she was accompanied by him or their children.[75]

Global Hegemony. The worldview presented through the media reflects the ownership pattern of news organizations. Four of the five major news agencies are Western; and these agencies account for 90 percent of the global news flow.[76] This dominance has come under increasing criticism by the international community. Developing countries in particular have accused the United States of promoting its ideology by monopolizing media programming on a global scale. Through the United Nations Educational, Scientific and Cultural Organization (UNESCO), these countries have called for a New World Information and Communication Order to respond to the following inequities:

1. The flow of information is unequal, with too much information originating in the West and not enough representing the developing nations.
2. There is too much bias against, and stereotyping of, the developing or "less developed" countries.

3. Alien values are foisted on the Third World by too much Western (mainly American) "communication imperialism."

4. Western communication places undue emphasis on "negative" news of the Third World—disasters, coups, government corruption and the like.

5. Finances are unequally distributed around the world for technology and communication development.

6. The Western definition of "news" (meaning atypical and sensational items) is unrealistic and does not focus enough attention on development news (items helping in the progress and growth of the country).

7. Communication and journalism education in universities is too Western-oriented, and too many textbooks used in the Third World are authored by First-World writers, especially by Americans.

8. Too much of the world's information is collected by the big five news agencies, all but one representing the First (advanced capitalist) World.[77]

Defenders of international news coverage maintain that the current system reflects the principles of free speech. Countries are free to develop their communications systems to the best of their abilities. And finally, no one is forcing Third World countries to consume the American-generated media content.

Structure. A country's media system often reflects its economic, political, and cultural orientation. Consequently, an interesting way to approach the study of a foreign country is to examine its media system. To illustrate, consider the following brief descriptions:

- *The American media system.* The American media industry is shaped by the relationship between its capitalistic economic structure and democratic political system. The American media are owned by individuals and corporations, which make programming decisions in hopes of maximizing their profit. As mentioned earlier, this structure often inhibits the range of views expressed in the media.

  At the same time, however, the public assumes a large role in determining content in this market-driven economy, by deciding which programs to watch or which newspapers to purchases. And the democratic political system is designed to ensure that opinions and ideas are brought before the public.

- *The People's Republic of China.* The People's Republic of China operates within a socialistic economic system; consequently, the media are owned by the state. Information is tightly controlled as a means of maintaining order and serving the interests of the communist government.

- *The Netherlands.* In this social democratic country, this media industry is based largely on the principles of "accessibility, variety, non-commercialism, and cooperation."[78] Operating costs are taken from tax revenues. Programming time is distributed among many social and political groups on the basis of the number of members in their group. Production facilities (complete with crews) are made available upon request.

Shifts in a country's media system are often a microcosm of broader societal changes. For instance, as the former Soviet Union moved toward democracy, Soviet President Mikhail Gorbachev introduced the policy of *glasnost,* or openness, which encouraged more freedom of expression in the press, including criticism of the authorities. And as part of the movement toward a market economy, in July 1990, Gorbachev ordered the privatization of the nation's radio and television industries.

NOTES

1. Associated Press, "Movie Tied to Burning of Woman," *St. Louis Post-Dispatch,* October 10, 1984, 10A.

2. Verne Gay, "Acts of Violence & Crime Tallied in *Variety* Study," *Variety,* August 15–22, 1989, 39, 44.

3. National Coalition on Television Violence, "Violence in Cartoons Increases," *NCTV News,* 12 (June–August 1991): 7.

4. Ibid.

5. Mabel L. Rice, Altha C. Huston, and John C. Wright, "The Forms of Television: Effects on Children's Attention, Comprehension, and Social Behavior," in *Television and Behavior: Ten Years of Scientific Progress and Implications for the Eighties,* vol. 2, *Technical Reviews,* ed. David Pearl, Lorraine Bouthilet, and Joyce Lazar (Rockville, MD: National Institute of Mental Health, 1982), 26.

6. National Coalition on Television Violence, *TV or Movie Violence Monitoring Guidelines* (Champaign, IL: National Coalition on Television Violence, 1993), 1.

7. Ibid., 2–4.

8. Richard Rosenfeld, associate professor of criminology, University of Missouri at St. Louis, interview by author, St. Louis, MO, August 12, 1992.

9. John Vivian, *The Media of Mass Communication* (Boston: Allyn and Bacon, 1991), 300.

10. Joseph R. Dominick, *The Dynamics of Mass Communication,* 3d ed. (New York: McGraw-Hill, 1990), 512.

11. Kathleen Heldenbrand, Med 315: Content Analysis—Cartoons, Webster University, St. Louis, MO, Summer 1992.

12. Mark Crispin Miller, "Hollywood; the Ad," *The Atlantic Monthly,* April 1990, 53.

13. A. Bandura, D. Ross, and S. A. Ross, "Transmission of Aggression Through Imitation of Aggressive Models," *Journal of Abnormal and Social Psychology* 63 (1961): 575–82.

14. Robert M. Liebert and Joyce Sprafkin, *The Early Window: Effects of Television on Children and Youth,* 3d ed. (New York: Pergamon Press, 1988), 140–41.

15. Ibid., 157.

16. Ibid., 147.

17. Seymour Fesbach and Robert D. Singer, *Television and Aggression* (San Francisco: Jossey-Bass, 1971).

18. Fred Emery and Merrelyn Emery, *A Choice of Futures* (Leiden, Netherlands: Martinus Nijhoff Social Sciences Division, 1976), 82.

19. Neil M. Malmauth and James V. P. Check, "The Effects of Mass Media Exposure on Acceptance of Violence Against Women: A Field Experiment," *Journal of Research in Personality* 15 (1981), 436–46.

20. G. S. Lesser, *Children and Television: Lessons from Sesame Street* (New York: Vintage Books, 1974), 4.

21. Liebert and Sprafkin, *Early Window*, 140.

22. Lesser, *Children and Television*, 3.

23. Ibid.

24. Charles W. Turner, Bradford W. Hesse, and Sonja Peterson-Lewis, "Naturalistic Studies of the Long-Term Effects of Television Violence," *Journal of Social Issues* 42 (1986): 51–73.

25. Richard Frost and John Stauffer, "The Effects of Social Class, Gender, and Personality on Psychological Responses to Filmed Violence," *Journal of Communication* 37 (Spring 1987): 29–46.

26. Charles W. Turner and Leonard Berkowitz, "Identification with Film Aggressor (Covert Role Taking) and Reactions to Film Violence," *Journal of Personality and Social Psychology* 21 (1972): 256–64.

27. Joanne R. Cantor, Dolf Zillmann, and Edna F. Einsiedel, "Female Response to Provocation after Exposure to Aggressive and Erotic Films," *Communication Research* 5 (October 1978): 395–412.

28. Frost and Stauffer, "Responses to Filmed Violence," 30.

29. Ibid., 41.

30. Barrie Gunter, *Dimensions of Television Violence* (New York: St. Martin's Press, 1985).

31. A. C. Nielsen Company, *Nielsen Report on Television 1990* (Northbrook, IL: Nielsen Media Research, 1990).

32. John P. Murray and Barbara Lonnborg, *Children and Television: A Primer for Parents* (Boys Town, NE: Boys Town, 1991), 5.

33. W. Andrew Collins, "Cognitive Processing in Television Viewing," in *Television and Behavior: Ten Years of Scientific Progress and Implications for the Eighties*, vol. 2, *Technical Reviews*, ed. David Pearl, Lorraine Bouthilet, and Joyce Lazar (Rockville, MD: National Institute of Mental Health, 1982), 11.

34. Ibid., 47.

35. David Considine and Gail Haley, *Visual Messages: Integrating Imagery into Instruction* (Englewood, CO: Teacher Ideas Press, 1992), 80.

36. Jim Trelease, *The New Read-Aloud Handbook* (New York: Penguin Books, 1989), 127.

37. Linda Holtzman, Med 315: Content Analysis—Cartoons, Webster University, St. Louis, MO, Summer 1992.

38. National Coalition on Television Violence, "Violence in Cartoons Increases," 1.

39. *Parenting in a Television Age: A Media Literacy Workshop Kit™ on Children and Television* (Los Angeles: Center for Media Literacy, 1991).

40. James U. McNeal, *Children as Consumers* (Lexington, MA: Lexington Books, 1987).

41. Thomas R. Donohue, Lucy L. Henke, and William A. Donohue, "Do Kids Know What TV Commercials Intend?" *Journal of Advertising Research* 29 (October 1980): 56.

42. Paul M. Fischer, Meyer P. Schwartz, John W. Richards, Jr., Adam O. Goldstein, and Tina H. Rojas. "Brand Logo Recognition by Children Aged 3 to 6 Years," *Journal of the American Medical Association* 266 (December 11, 1991): 3145.

43. "Cigarette Ad Targets Young, Doctors Say," *St. Louis Post-Dispatch,* March 10, 1992, A7.

44. Ibid.

45. *Buy Me That: A Kid's Survival Guide to TV Advertising,* produced by Consumers Union, 28 min., Films Incorporated Video, 1990, videocassette.

46. John Lyons, *Guts: Advertising from the Inside Out* (New York: AMA-COM, 1987), 292.

47. Kate Louise Roberts, ed., *Hoyt's New Cyclopedia of Practical Quotations* (New York: Funk & Wagnalls, 1922), 520.

48. Murray and Lonnborg, *Children and Television,* 2.

49. Ibid., 2–3.

50. *Parenting in a Television Age,* Handout #1.

51. Ibid.

52. Aimee Dorr, Sherryl Browne Graves, and Erin Phelps, "Television Literacy for Young Children," *Journal of Communication* 30 (Summer 1980): 73.

53. Ibid.

54. Jay. F. Davis, "Five Important Ideas to Teach Your Kids About TV," *Children & Television: Growing Up in the Media World,* no. 52/53 (Fall-Winter 1991): 16.

55. Nicholas B. Van Dyck, "Families and Television," *Television & Children* 6 (Summer 1983): 3–11.

56. John Tebbel, *The Media in America* (New York: Thomas Y. Crowell, 1974), 39.

57. Ibid.

58. Ted Koppel, "Television: Revolution in a Box," ABC News Special, 1989.

59. Ibid.

60. Edward Herman and Noam Chomsky, *Manufacturing Consent* (New York: Pantheon Books, 1988), 2.

61. Ibid., 17.

62. Ibid., 26.

63. "The Victorious Gulf War Owes Much to PR . . . ," *PR News,* March 11, 1991, 1.

64. Francesca M. Cancian and Bonnie L. Ross, "Mass Media and the Women's Movement," *Journal of Applied Behavioral Science* 17 (1981): 11.

65. Ibid., 18.

66. Ibid., 25.

67. Ibid., 18.

68. Ibid., 20.

69. W. James Potter, "News from Three Worlds in Prestige U.S. Newspapers," in *Current Issues in International Communications,* ed. L. John Martin and Ray Eldon Hiebert (New York: Longman, 1990), 280.

70. Harold D. Lasswell, *Propaganda Techniques in the World War* (New York: Peter Smith, 1927), 195.

71. The Asia Society, "Asia in American Textbooks," in *Toward Internation-*

alism, ed. Elise C. Smith and Louise Fiber Luce (Cambridge, MA: Newbury House, 1987).

72. Asep Sutresna, "International Communication and Popular Culture in Indonesia" (Paper presented to MED 531, Media and Culture, Webster University, May 1993), 6.

73. Ibid., 7.

74. Ibid.

75. "Angry Brazilian Mutilates Ears of Feminist Wife," *St. Louis Post-Dispatch,* July 14, 1985, A2.

76. John C. Merrill, John Lee, and Edward J. Friedlander, *Modern Mass Media* (New York: Harper & Row, 1990), 428.

77. Ibid., 426.

78. Ministry of Foreign Affairs, *The Kingdom of the Netherlands: Facts and Figures, The Mass Media* (The Hague, Netherlands: Ministry of Foreign Affairs, 1983), 3.

CHAPTER 10

OUTCOMES

The Aspen Institute National Leadership Conference on Media Literacy has considered the critical issue of *outcomes:*

Is media literacy important only to the extent that it enables one to be a better citizen in society? What is the role of ideology in the process? To what extent is an individual "media literate" if she just appreciates the aesthetics of a message without going further with it? [1]

Potential outcomes for media-literate individuals include:

CRITICAL AWARENESS

- *Become well informed in matters of media coverage.* Read the newspaper on a daily basis. Check several sources of information (e.g., both newspapers and television) to examine the coverage of issues.
- *Be aware of your everyday contact with the media and its influence on lifestyle, attitudes, and values.*
- *Apply the keys to interpreting media messages to derive insight into media messages.*
- *Develop a sensitivity to programming trends as a way of learning about the culture.*
- *Keep abreast of patterns in ownership and government regulations that affect the media industry.*
- *Consider the role of the media in individual decision making.* Think carefully about the possible role of media messages on specific decisions or behavior. In what ways have the media affected the purchase of consumer items, the selection of candidates, the choice of activities, or standards of conduct?

DISCUSSION

The keys to interpreting messages provide a framework for discussing media programming with friends, colleagues, and children.

CRITICAL CHOICE

In the United States, technology has provided the public with a measure of control in the selection of media presentations. Videotapes and audio cassettes enable people to choose what they wish to receive. Cable television and digital cable radio offer a wide range of programming options. Modern distribution systems allow for the dissemination of a variety of periodicals throughout the country. And computer technology provides immediate access to a variety of information. As a result, the audience can become their own programmers and assume responsibility for their personal media usage.

SOCIAL ACTION

You may choose to respond to the messages you receive through the media by engaging in several types of activities:

- *Cancel your subscription or turn off objectionable programming.*
- *If you have concerns about a newspaper article, write a letter to the editor.*
- *If you have objections to a television or radio program, write to the general manager of the station.* FCC regulations require that stations keep all public correspondence on file. Consequently, station management must make a formal acknowledgment of your point of view.
- *Register a complaint with the FCC.* The FCC may respond to public complaints by investigating broadcast stations. On the basis of their findings, the FCC is authorized to levy fines on stations. In extreme cases, the FCC can suspend station operations, refuse to renew a station's broadcast license, or even withdraw a station's current license. However, the First Amendment (freedom of speech) provides considerable latitude for the expression of ideas—even those that are in "poor taste."
- *Attempt to meet in person with the staff of the newspaper, TV, or radio station.*
- *Organize a petition drive.* Media organizations are always more impressed by complaints by numbers of people than the opinions of one individual. However, the list of names on a petition also may be easily dismissed, since it takes relatively little effort on the part of the people signing the petition.
- *Organize a grassroots letter-writing campaign.* An effective letter-writing campaign was orchestrated by Carol Rubin-Schlansky of Richmond Heights, Missouri, in response to the placement of an objectionable ad during her young daughter's favorite television program. Rubin-Schlansky contacted the station

manager but found him unresponsive. She then composed a complaint letter, leaving it unsigned, and distributed copies to friends and acquaintances. They were instructed that if they agreed with her position, they should sign their names and mail the letters on *the same day.* This strategy had a definite impact. The station manager admitted, "Anytime you get 50 letters about something, it gets your attention." He then conceded that his station would be more likely to move potentially objectionable ads to a later time block.

Rubin-Schlansky declared, "It doesn't take much to sit down and write a letter. It doesn't take much to go up to [the copy store] and run off 100 copies of something. It doesn't take much to do what I did." [2]

- *Picket the media organization.* This strategy can draw public attention to the station and the problem. The trick is to attract the attention of the media through this action.

- *Organize a boycott against the advertisers of the program or newspaper.* Media organizations are very sensitive to the concerns of their advertisers who, in turn, strive to maintain the goodwill of the public. Consequently, taking out an ad in the paper explaining your concerns and listing the program's advertisers can be an effective action step.

- *Promote the instruction of media literacy throughout the school system (K–12) by contacting members of your board of education, PTA, and principals.* Some educational organizations are beginning to recognize the need for media literacy classes. For instance, the National Association for the Education of Young Children has called for "the development and dissemination of curriculum for teachers to improve children's critical viewing skills." [3]

- *Join media literacy organizations so that you will have access to information about media content not commonly available to the public.* Addresses for some media literacy organizations are listed below.

The Association for Media Literacy
40 McArthur Street
Weston, Ontario M9P3M7
(416) 394–6992

Center for Media Literacy
1962 South Shenandoah Street
Los Angeles, CA 90034
(310) 559–2944

Citizens for Media Literacy
38½ Battery Park Avenue
Asheville, NC 28801
(704) 255–0182

The National Telemedia Council
120 E. Wilson Street
Madison, WI
(608) 257–7712

Strategies for Media Literacy
1095 Market Street, Suite 410
San Francisco, CA 94103
(415) 621–2911

MEDIA LITERACY RESOURCES

Bright Ideas; Media Education (1990), Avril Harpley. Scholastic Books, 2931 E. McCarty, Jefferson City, MO 65102; (800) 325–6149, $14.95. A sourcebook of dozens of activities to teach critical thinking and use of mass media. Elementary school materials.

Creating Critical Viewers (1992), Pacific Mountain Network, GPN, P. O. Box 80669, Lincoln, NE 68501–0669; (800) 228–4630, workbook: $15.95; video and workbook: $39.95. Covers the news, stereotypes, the how and why of commercials, plus exercises in editing. Middle school up.

Media & You: An Elementary Media Literacy Curriculum (1991), Educational Technology Publications, 700 Palisade Avenue, Englewood Cliffs, NJ 07632; (201) 871–4007, $29.95. Practical classroom activities (and handout masters) on what are media, production techniques, advertising, news, and entertainment.

Media Literacy Project (1992), KRCB Television, 5850 LaBath Avenue, Rohnert Park, CA 94928; (707) 585–8522, $15. Workbooks with audio- and video-tapes on communication and television issues that connect media literacy ideas to other curriculum plans. Elementary school materials.

Media Literacy Workshop Kits™, a continuing collection of curriculum kits on media themes. Contains extensive leader's guide and background resources plus handout masters; some with videos. Titles include: *Living in the Image Culture,* a media literacy "primer," $29.95; *Break the Lies That Bind,* sexism in media, $27.95; *News for '90s,* values in the news, $21.95; *Parenting in a TV Age,* parent education program on children and TV, $27.95; *Selling Addiction,* tobacco and alcohol advertising, $44.95; *Images of Conflict,* learning from the media coverage of the Gulf War, $44.95; *Citizenship in a Media Age,* media in the democratic process, $27.95; *TV Alert: A Wake-up Guide for Television Literacy,* $57.95; *Global Question: Exploring World Media Issues,* $44.95. Youth and adult. Center for Media and Values, 1962 S. Shenandoah, Los Angeles, CA 90034.

Visual Messages: Integrating Imagery into Instruction (1992), David Considine and Gail E. Haley, Libraries Unlimited, P. O. Box 3988, Englewood, CO 80155; (800) 237–6124, $26.50. The first comprehensive guide to media literacy education published in the United States. Provides background and activities for dozens of topics from why study television to advertising, violence, and stereotyping. Some elementary; mostly high school/adult.

NOTES

1. Aspen Institute, National Leadership Conference on Media Literacy, Queenstown, MD, December 7–9, 1992.

2. Eric Mink, "Mother's Anger Turns into Primer on Activism," *St. Louis Post-Dispatch*, April 11, 1993, C14.

3. "National Association for the Education of Young Children Position Statement on Media Violence in Children's Lives," *Young Children* 45 (July 1990): 19.

GLOSSARY

active-negative personality Political scientist James David Barber devised a formula for predicting presidential performance, based on distinct character types. Barber has identified four character patterns based on his or her levels of activity (activity-passivity) and enjoyment (positive-negative affect). The active-negative character combines intense effort with a relatively low emotional reward. The active-negative figure is compulsive, and his or her goal is to obtain and maintain power.

active-positive personality Political scientist James David Barber devised a formula for predicting presidential performance, based on distinct character types. Barber has identified four character patterns based on his or her levels of activity (activity-passivity) and enjoyment (positive-negative affect). The active-positive personality is distinguished by an industrous nature, combined with the enjoyment of this level of activity.

advertorials Advertorials are ads that appear in newspapers in the form of editorial content.

affective response In contrast with print, visual and aural stimuli initially touch us on an emotional, or affective, level. Media communicators can influence the attitudes and behavior of audiences by appealing to their emotions and evoking an affective, or emotional, response.

affective strategies Media communicators can influence the attitudes and behavior of audiences by developing communications strategies designed to appeal to the emotions of the audience. For instance, ads frequently are directed at emotions such as guilt or the need for acceptance to sell their product.

agenda setting Even if newspapers don't tell us what to think, they do tell us what to think *about*. An issue can become a topic of national debate through the news media.

angle Angle refers to the level at which the camera is shooting in relation to the subject. The choice of angle can affect the audience's attitude toward the subject. A person filmed from a high angle looks small, weak, frightened, or vulnerable. In contrast, a person filmed from a low angle appears larger, more important, and powerful.

arousal theory of media violence A theory of media violence effects, this school of thought maintains that violent programming stimulates aggression in audience members and can lead to aggressive behavior. An illustration of the arousal theory is John Hinkley who, after watching the film *Taxi Driver* in 1981, attempted to assassinate President Ronald Reagan.

artistic expression Artists are often able to find a creative outlet through their work. Novelists, painters, or experimental videographers express themselves through their art and share their artistic vision with the audience.

audience attention span Attention span can be a factor in audience interference. Communication is an active process that demands concentration and energy. Occasionally, members of the audience will just tune out the speaker and take a brief rest.

audience identification Audience identification is perhaps the most pressing challenge facing a media communicator. Media communicators devote enormous resources to developing a clear sense of audience. Different sectors of audience have distinct, identifiable interests and look for specific objectives or gratifications in media programming, based on their stage of life. Audience identification can affect content, style, and communications strategies.

audience interference Audience interference refers to instances in which the audience obstructs the communication process. Several factors may influence the way in which individuals select and process information, including selective exposure, selective perception, selective retention, attention span, and the ego of the audience member.

biased interviewing techniques A reporter can slant a story through the type of questions he or she poses to subjects while conducting research for the story. Types of biased interviewing strategies include compliance as assertion, leading or loaded questions, hypothetical questions, and presenting questions with "either/or" choices.

big promise The big promise refers to an ad strategy in which an advertisement makes claims that are far beyond the capacity of the product.

broadcasting Broadcasting is a concept tied to the early stages of American media. Because the overall audience was limited, the mass communicator had to produce general programming that would appeal to the mass culture.

camouflaged warnings Product warnings are designed to be as inconspicuous as possible. For example, the disclaimers on cigarette advertisements appear in very small print. The warning is generally separated from the main visual field. And sometimes the print is camouflaged by the color and graphics of the ad.

cathartic theory of media violence A theory of media effects that holds that violent programming may at times provide a healthy release for our aggressions. After watching a violent program, the audience may feel drained and purified, purged of our violent impulses. In this sense, media violence could be regarded as positive and constructive.

channel interference One of the sources of communications interference. Channel interference occurs when a glitch in the channel prevents the audience from understanding the message. In mass communications, channel interference occurs when the television picture suddenly goes blank or the sound becomes inaudible. Channel interference can also result from using an inappropriate channel to send a particular type of message.

character development By the end of a narrative, characters often have changed dramatically. Focusing on these changes can provide insight into media messages.

code words Code words are terms that have clear and distinct messages for targeted audiences.

color A visual element that can have a powerful effect on the way that audiences respond to a media presentation.

commencement words Commencement words suggest immediacy, importance, and a sense of urgency (e.g., *introducing, announcing, now, suddenly*).

communications model The basic communications model consists of the following elements: the *communicator,* who delivers the message; the *message,* which is the information being communicated; the *channel,* the passage through which the information is being conveyed; and the *audience,* which consists of the person or people who are receiving the message.

communicator interference One of the sources of communications interference. Communicator interference occurs when the communicator makes it difficult for the audience to understand the message. For instance, the communicator may not know what he or she wants to say or may send mixed messages to the audience.

comparative media Comparative media refers to the characteristics that distinguish one medium from another. The effective media communicator takes advantage of the unique properties of each medium to convey media messages.

competing functions Competing function refers to instances in which media productions attempt to fulfill several competing functions simultaneously, which undermines the effectiveness of the presentation.

compliance as assertion In this biased interviewing technique, reporters may come prepared with a point of view (and a quote) ready to include in an article and is only asking for the *consent* of the subject. In this case, reporters may phrase a question, "Would you agree that . . . ?" or "Would you say that . . . ?" or "So what you are saying is . . ."

connotation Connotation refers to the meaning associated with a word beyond its denotative, or dictionary, definition. The meaning of a connotative word is universally understood and agreed upon.

connotative images Images appearing in photographs, film, or video that possess universal associative properties.

consequences Events in a media presentation that are caused, directly or indirectly, by a character's actions. A media-literate viewer may ask if the consequences of a character's actions are accurately depicted.

content analysis Content analysis is a quantitative methodology that can be employed to look for patterns in messages, symbols, language, art forms, and potential biases in the media.

context Context refers to those surrounding elements that subtly shape meaning and convey messages. Elements of context include historical context, cultural context, and structure

convenience words Convenience words appeal to the consumers' interest in products that will make their lives easier (e.g., *easy, quick*).

convention A convention is a practice or object that appears so often in the media that it has become standard. Conventions furnish cues about people, events, and situations.

conventional setting Conventional settings refer to a standard background against which the action takes place. The conventional setting for a sitcom is the home or workplace.

conventional trappings Conventional trappings include props and costumes that are common to a genre. These trappings furnish the audience with clues about the action.

critical studies Critical theorists argue that the worldview presented through the media does not merely *reflect* or *reinforce* culture but in fact *shapes* thinking by promoting the dominant ideology of a culture. The media largely present the ideology of the dominant culture as a means of maintaining control. In that sense, the media can create (or *re-create*) representations of reality that reflect the dominant ideology.

cross-cutting Cross-cutting is an editing technique in which footage from different locations is juxtaposed to give the impression of events occurring at the same moment.

cultural context Anthropologists study ancient civilizations by unearthing artifacts in order to reconstruct a portrait of the society. In the same way, the study of media productions furnishes a means of understanding culture.

cultural myths Cultural myths are sets of beliefs that may not be true but nevertheless tell us about how we see ourselves and our culture.

cultural preoccupations The relative importance that a culture places on particular issues as reflected through media content; for example, the amount of attention given to sexually oriented content.

cultural studies A critical approach to communication analysis that regards the media as a reflection of multiple realities (e.g., cultural subgroups).

cumulative effects theory of media violence This theory of media violence effects maintains that cumulative media messages regarding violence may have long-term, *indirect* effects on individuals.

cumulative messages Messages often appear in the media with such frequency that they form new meanings, independent of any individual presentation. Examples would include messages regarding gender roles, definitions of success, and racial and cultural stereotypes.

customer advantage words Customer advantage words offer the consumer a sense of control, vision, wisdom, and superiority (e.g., *bargain, offer, free, sale*).

damage control Damage control refers to the management of information during a crisis. This strategy is designed to minimize potentially harmful stories.

deep background In journalism, information provided by a source that puts a story into a broader perspective and guides a reporter in a particular direction.

demographic research Demographic research refers to the study of human populations. Demographic considerations such as geographical location can play a large role in consumer buying patterns. Other demographic categories include age, gender, income, education, occupation, race, religion, and family size.

description This common communication function occurs when a communicator provides details, elaborates on general statements, or offers concrete examples as a way of enhancing the understanding of the audience.

designated spokesperson Sometimes the press anoints a spokesperson to represent a particular cause. They may be leaders of an organization or an "expert" (e.g., university professor). But whether these people actually enjoy the support of a broad constituency is open to question.

dialogue Dialogue is written material that is intended to *sound* like conversation. A script may contain a great deal of information and complex layers of meaning. This material is presented very rapidly, like speech, so that the audience member easily can confuse the message being delivered.

directive response Media content such as advertising, political spots, and public service messages have very specific cognitive, attitudinal, and behavioral response objectives on the part of the media communicator.

directives Directives tell the consumer what to do (e.g., *hurry, compare*).

disengagement This function applies to situations in which the objective is to discourage extended conversation.

dissemination schedule The dissemination schedule refers to the amount of time that it takes for information to reach the audience, when conveyed through a particular medium.

editing Editing refers to the selection and arrangement of information.

editorial content Editorial content refers to news content—everything in the newspaper that is not paid space.

ego A factor in audience interference, in which the audience member focuses on those aspects of a conversation or media presentation that relate to him/her, ignoring the rest of the message.

elite art Elite art is directed at a select, educated audience. The responsibility for comprehending and appreciating the content rests with the audience (as opposed to the artist, as is the case with popular art). Elite art is defined by the following characteristics: exclusivity, aesthetic complexity, historical context, and exploration.

embedded values Media content often reflects the value system of the media communicator, as well as widely held cultural values and attitudes. Values may be embedded in the text through such production techniques as editing decisions, point of view, and connotative words and images.

emotional benefits Advertisers recognize that products are purchased for psychological as well as product satisfaction. Consequently, ads may focus on the impact that the product has on the consumer.

emotional catharsis One of the possible functions of a communications exchange, this would include spontaneous expressions of love, passion, anger, pain, happiness, or the release of tension.

entertainment One of the possible functions of a communications exchange, this refers to communication that is devoted to amusing ourselves and others, often as a tool of persuasion.

environment Environment refers to the physical surroundings that can affect communication.

environmental interference One of the sources of communications interference. Environmental interference refers to distractions that occur in the setting in which the information is received.

euphemism Euphemisms are words that have an innocuous connotation; these neutral terms often are substituted for language that could offend the audience.

explicit content Explicit content consists of events and activities in the plot that are displayed through visible action. The viewer constructs meaning by selecting the essential pieces of explicit information in the story.

exploration One of the possible functions of a communications exchange, this refers to instances in which media communicators are actively composing their message during the course of the presentation. Mass communicators generally present polished information that has been prepared in advance. However, media communicators are sometimes subject to slipups when they work without a script.

expression One common function of communication is to inform the listener of the speaker's frame of mind. In these situations, speakers might talk about what they are thinking at that moment, how they are feeling, or their attitudes toward people and issues.

extreme close-up (XCU) Film and television can *approximate* the first-person perspective through use of the extreme close-up camera shot. This shot studies a character's reaction to events and people.

extreme long shot (XLS) The extreme long shot, which is used in film and television, takes in a wide expanse of visual information and often establishes the setting at the beginning of a scene. This shot provides broad context for the subsequent action.

false and misleading ads In some cases, ads make false claims that are intended to mislead the consumer.

false function Media programs may offer the appearance of serving one function while actually fulfilling other purposes. Examples include "infotainment" TV programs like "Entertainment Tonight" and "A Current Affair," which are entertainment programs presented in a news format. People may look to these programs for legitimate news, although their predominant functions are to amuse and titillate.

feedback Part of the communications process, feedback furnishes an opportunity for the audience to respond to the communicator. Listeners ask questions or comment to better understand what the communicator is trying to say. Feedback also provides vital reassurance for the communicator.

file photos File photos are pictures that are kept by newspapers and published when the need arises. Consequently, some photos that accompany newspaper articles may have been taken long before the event being covered.

first-person point of view The first-person point of view presents the action through the eyes of one character. The reader's understanding therefore is colored by the predispositions and values of the first-person narrator.

flak Flak refers to organized responses to media content, which can take the form of letters, phone calls, petitions, lawsuits, and legislative initiatives, with the expressed purpose of influencing media content. Part of Herman and Chomsky's propaganda model.

formula Formula refers to patterns in *function, premise, structure, plot,* and *character.* Individual programs generally conform to the formula of the genre.

formulaic function A genre shares a common manifest objective. For instance, the primary function of the sitcom is to entertain or amuse the audience. In addition, a genre may contain shared latent functions.

formulaic plot Only a finite number of general plots, or stories, appear within a given genre. While these general plots appear regularly, the embellishments, detail, and small nuances within these plots keep each episode fresh and interesting.

formulaic premise A formulaic premise refers to an identifiable situation that characterizes a genre.

formulaic structure A genre generally fits within an identifiable, unvarying structure, or organizational pattern. In many genres (including the sitcom), the standard formula is order/chaos/order.

framework Framework refers to various structural elements of a production, including introduction, plot, genre, and logical conclusion.

function A simple communication activity may be motivated by many purposes, or functions, which include expression, description, education, information exchange, persuasion, entertainment, creative expression, artistic expression, ritual, performance, emotional catharsis, disengagement, and profit.

genre A genre is a standardized format that is distinctive and easily identifiable. Examples include horror films, romances, sci-fi, situation comedies, westerns, and the evening news. A genre is not confined to one medium. For instance, at one time or another, westerns have appeared in print, on radio, television, and film.

gestalt A natural predisposition to order. For example, human beings tend to look for balance, that is, equal distribution around the center.

hard news Hard news stories deal with topical events and issues that have an impact on the lives of the readers. The principal function of hard news is to inform. This information provides readers with a vital connection to the nation and the world.

hegemony The imposition of an ideology within a culture is referred to as hegemony. Critical theorists like Stuart Hall argue that the worldviews presented through the media do not merely reflect or reinforce culture but in fact shape thinking by promoting the dominant ideology of a culture.

hermeneutics Hermeneutics refers to the study of the methodological principles of interpretation. The study of media has a hermeneutic, or interpretive, function, furnishing a means of understanding culture.

historical context Media content often derives its significance from the events of the day. As a result, understanding the historical context can provide insight into media messages. At the same time, media presentations can furnish information into the period in which it was produced, as well as serving as providing perspective on cultural changes.

hybrid media As media technology has evolved, existing media systems have begun to overlap, creating hybrid channels of mass communications. One example is the VCR, which now presents film on television.

hyperbole An ad strategy that relies on exaggeration or absurd overstatement to make a point.

ideology The manner or the content of thinking characteristic of an individual group or culture.

illogical ads Advertisements that appear perfectly reasonable on the surface often do not hold up under logical scrutiny.

implicit content Implicit content refers to those elements of plot that remain under the surface, including motivation, the relationship between events, and the consequences of earlier action.

incomplete/distorted message This type of ad strategy tells only a half-truth in order to present its product in the best possible light.

indirect feedback mechanisms Since immediate responses are not observable, most mass communications feedback is delayed and cumulative. Media organizations depend on a variety of indirect audience feedback mechanisms, including ratings, generated revenue, delayed audience response, audience research, critical response, and intuition.

information exchange This function occurs in interpersonal communication when all parties benefit from an exchange of information.

information management This public relations approach to government/press relations, first used by the Reagan administration, emphasized the following principles: plan ahead, stay on the offensive, manage the flow of information, limit reporters' access to the president, speak in one voice, make it easy on the press, exploit the medium, and mislead when necessary.

infotainment Entertainment programming that has taken on the trappings of journalism.

instruction This communication function refers to occasions in which the purpose is either (1) to inform someone about a subject with which he or she is unfamiliar or (2) to furnish *additional* information about a subject with which the audience is already acquainted.

interference Interference refers to those factors that can hinder the communications process (e.g., communicator interference, channel interference, and audience interference).

internal structure The internal structure of a media organization consists of the following elements: the resources of the production company, the organizational framework (i.e., different departments, lines of responsibility), and the process of decision making.

interpersonal communication Interpersonal communication refers to face-to-face interaction with another person.

intrapersonal communication Intrapersonal communication takes place within ourselves. It is the basis of all forms of communication.

introduction The introduction often acquaints the audience with the most important information, primary characters, and premise of the media presentation. The opening of a film, television, or radio program may serve as a preview of the entire presentation.

jump In journalism, a jump refers to the continuation of a story to another page.

label Labels are connotative words or phrases that describe a person or group. Labels often appear with such frequency in the media that they no longer simply *describe* but in fact *define* the group.

latent function Latent function refers to purposes behind the communication of information that may not be immediately obvious to the audience.

latent message Latent messages are indirect and beneath the surface and consequently escape our immediate attention. Latent messages may reinforce manifest messages or may suggest entirely different meanings.

lifestyle indicators (LSIs) Lifestyle indicators refer to a type of advertising research that predicts consumer buying patterns on the basis of a consumer's previous purchases.

lighting The amount of light used in a visual medium can affect the mood. Brightly lit presentations evoke a feeling of security and happiness, while a dimly lit presentation creates an atmosphere of mystery and apprehension. The source of the light can also convey messages.

logical conclusion The assumption behind the concept of logical conclusion holds that the conclusion of a presentation must be a logical extension of the initial premise, characters, and worldview, free of intrusion by the artist. In light of this, it is striking that the conclusions to popular media presentations so frequently violate this principle of logical progression. Conclusions are often false, confused, or simply illogical when considered within the flow of the program.

manifest message Manifest messages are direct and clear to the audience. We generally have little trouble recognizing these messages when we are paying full attention to a media presentation.

mass communication In mass communication, messages are communicated through a mass medium (e.g., radio or television) to a large group of people who may not be in direct contact with the communicator.

media literacy The author's definition of media literacy emphasizes the following:

- An awareness of the impact of the media on the individual and society.
- An understanding of the process of mass communication.
- The development of strategies with which to analyze and discuss media messages.
- An awareness of media content as a "text" that provides insight into our contemporary culture and ourselves.
- The cultivation of an enhanced enjoyment, understanding, and appreciation of media content.

media messages Media messages are the underlying themes or ideas contained in a media presentation.

media presentations Media presentations refer to the specific programming that is produced within each medium—for instance, particular films (e.g., *The Fugitive*), newspapers (e.g., the December 3, 1993, edition of the *Washington Post*), or television programs (e.g., the October 12, 1993, episode of "Roseanne").

medium A channel of mass communications that enables people to communicate with large groups of people who are separated in time and space from the communicator. Examples of media include print, photography, radio, film, and television.

medium shot (MS) The medium shot, which is used in film and television, is analogous to the third-person perspective in print. This shot often includes several actors interacting in the shot.

motivation Those reasons that compel a character in a media presentation to behave in the ways that they do. If a character's motivation is poorly presented, the character's actions may not make sense to the viewer.

multiple function A communications exchange may serve more than one function at a time. While these functions are often compatible, at other times they may be in conflict.

multiple realities This term is used in cultural studies. It refers to a phenomenon in which media content is subject to different interpretations, depending on the experience and orientation of the audience member.

mythic reality Mythic reality refers to cultural myths that assume a degree of reality over time as people buy into it. The danger presented by mythic realities is that people sometimes make decisions on the basis of these myths.

narrowcasting Narrowcasting is a concept tied to the evolution of American media. Over time, the consumer media market has become so large that it is now profitable to direct messages at specialized interests, tastes, and groups.

natural sound Natural sound consists of the noises that normally occur within a given setting (e.g., crowd noise at a baseball game). Natural sound is frequently added to the audio tracks of media presentations to add a feeling of verisimilitude.

neologism Neologisms are words that advertisers invent for products—for example, Acura.

newspaper chain A series of newspapers in different locations throughout the country owned by one large company.

no-effects theory of media violence This theory holds that media violence has a minimal effect on audiences.

nonverbal performance skills Nonverbal skills refer to communications vehicles other than language. Nonverbal communication elements include gestures, facial expressions, posture, and dress.

not-available ploy In this journalistic bias technique, an article including the statement that the subject was unavailable for comment implies that the subject was uncooperative, ducking the reporter, or had something to hide. This statement often neglects to clarify the circumstances: whether the person was in town, when the person was contacted, where the person was contacted, how often the reporter attempted to reach the person, and the time frame in which the reporter attempted to contact the subject.

omniscient camera The omniscient camera, which is used in film and television, is analogous to the omniscient narrator in print. This all-seeing or all-knowing camera enables the director to focus on characters in different settings (unbeknown to the other characters).

omniscient point of view The omniscient or all-knowing point of view enables the author to enter the heads of any and all of the characters so that the reader has a comprehensive exposure to the people and events depicted in the work.

one-person cross section In this journalistic bias technique, one person is positioned as representative of a larger group—which may not be the case.

opiate theory of media violence A theory of media violence that holds that after watching enough programming people may become passive and incapable of feeling anything.

pace Pace refers to the rhythm or rate at which information should be assimilated.

panoramic point of view In a panoramic point of view, the perspective is constantly shifting.

parallel action Filmmakers use the narrative strategy of parallel action to create the illusion that events on screen are occurring simultaneously. This can be accomplished by the editing technique of cross-cutting, in which footage from different locations is juxtaposed to give the impression of events occurring at the same moment.

parasocial relationship A dynamic in mass communication in which the media communicator creates the *appearance* of a personal relationship with the audience.

parity statement An ad strategy in which ads are worded in a way that suggests that a product is unique when in fact it is indistinguishable from its competition.

participatory response This phrase refers to a form of mass communication feedback. Individuals can respond directly to programs through laughter, anger, and even personal boycotts of programs and products. Some audience members also participate through call-ins, community productions, and the like.

passive catchphrase A journalistic bias technique. Omitting the subject of a sentence (the person/thing responsible for the action) creates the impression that an opinion is common knowledge.

passive-negative personality Political scientist James David Barber devised a formula for predicting presidential performance, based on distinct character types. Barber has identified four character patterns based on his or her levels of activity (activity-passivity) and enjoyment (positive-negative affect). The passive-negative figure "does little in politics and enjoys it less." Withdrawn by nature and possessing a low sense of self-esteem, this personality type regards politics as a civic duty, often serving his term of office with reluctance.

passive-positive personality This is part of political scientist James David Barber's formula for predicting presidential performance based on character type. A passive-positive president is a compliant figure who combines a low self-esteem with a "superficial optimism." As a result, this personality is looking for acceptance, which can interfere with an aggressive approach to the implementation of policy.

performance This function of communication refers to occasions in which the purpose of the conversation is to create a favorable impression.

persuasion In this communications function, the objective is to promote a particular idea or motivate the audience to action.

photo opportunities Events which are staged in order to give photographers the opportunity to snap pictures.

platform (political) ads A political ad that outlines a position on a specific issue.

plot A plot is a series of actions planned by the artist to build on one another, with an introduction, body, and conclusion. The foundation of plot is *conflict*. Characters are initially confronted with a dilemma, which is resolved by the end of the story.

plot convention A plot convention is a storyline that can appear within a number of genres. Examples include the wedding at the end of the story, and the "boy meets girl" scenario.

point of view Point of view refers to the source of information—who tells the story.

political action committees (PACs) The Federal Election Campaign Act (FECA) of 1971, amended in 1974 and 1976, permits corporations, labor unions, and religious organizations to support political candidates through the formation of political action committees (PACs).

popular culture Popular culture describes those productions, both artistic and commercial, designed for mass consumption, which appeal to and express the tastes and understanding of the majority of the public, free of control by minority standards. They reflect the values, convictions, and patterns of thought and feeling generally dispersed through and approved by American society.

preferred conclusion When examining the logical conclusion of a presentation, it can be beneficial for audience members to consider how they would have preferred for the story to end. This response can reveal a great deal about their personal belief system.

premise A premise refers to an identifiable situation that is characteristic of individual programs falling within a genre.

preproduction editing process Preproduction editing process refers to the decisions regarding both what to include and what to omit from a media presentation. These decisions have been reached before the presentation reaches the public, so the audience is not in a position to make a critical judgment about the selection process.

presentation of opinion as fact In this journalism bias technique, reporters present opinion disguised as fact in news stories.

process Process refers to the dynamics of communications, including function, comparative media, media communicator, and audience.

production values Production values refer to the *style* and *quality* of a media presentation. Production values often create a mood that reinforces manifest messages or themes. Production values include editing, color, lighting, shape, scale, relative position, movement, point of view, angle, connotation, performance, and sound.

product placement Product placement refers to a process by which advertisers pay a hefty fee to film studios to ensure that their products are displayed in a commercial film.

profit An underlying function driving the American media industry is profit. Of course, advertising and commercial television are geared to generate income. However, journalists are also torn between serving the public's right to know and making a profit.

propaganda Propaganda refers to the systematic development and dissemination of information to propagate the views and interests of a particular group.

psychographic research Psychographic research identifies the attitudes, values, and experiences shared by groups.

pyramid style The pyramid style of American journalism refers to a construct in which the most important information should be included in the first paragraph. Readers should therefore expect to find the answers to the following questions in the first paragraph: *who, what, when, how,* and *why.*

qualifier words An ad strategy in which phrases such as "some restrictions apply" are added inconspicuously, signaling that this information is insignificant.

reception theory Reception theory refers to a school of thought that acknowledges the unique perspective of the individual audience member in the interpretation of media messages. According to this construct, audiences may have entirely different constructions of meaning than the "preferred" reading. The audience assumes an active role in interpreting the information they receive through mass media. Different groups make sense of content in different ways.

relative position Relative position refers to where a character or object appears on the screen (or page). Objects appearing toward the front attract immediate attention, whereas things in the background are generally considered of secondary importance.

rhythm Rhythm refers to the rate or pace at which movement occurs.

ritual As it pertains to communication, a ritual is a verbal or written exchange that has a social significance beyond the surface.

romantic ideal An ideal worldview that often appears in media presentations. This ideal presumes an ordered universe that operates according to absolute values: truth, justice, beauty, faith, and love.

scale Scale refers to the relative size between objects. The larger an object appears, the more important it seems.

second-person point of view The second-person point of view makes the reader the primary participant in the story. This perspective makes use of the pronoun *you*.

selective exposure A category of audience interference. Selective exposure refers to the programming choices that individuals make, based on their personal interests and values. For instance, sports fans may watch ESPN, while people disinterested in sports will tune in something else.

selective perception A category of audience interference. The phenomenon by which people's interpretation of content is colored by their predispositions and preconceptions.

selective quotes A journalistic bias technique. Reporters can color a story by choosing when to use quotes, whose quotes to include, and which parts of the person's interview to extract into a quote.

selective retention A category of audience interference. Selective retention occurs when people mentally edit what they see or hear by remembering (or forgetting) selected information.

sidebar In journalism, a story appearing on the same page with a larger, related story. Often, a sidebar story presents specific information related to the topic of the main story, i.e., background information or personal anecdotes. A typical sidebar might be about how a labor strike has affected a particular town or family.

simile An ad strategy that makes a direct comparison between the product and something else; such comparisons are introduced by *like* or *as*.

slanted sample A journalistic bias technique, in which the sample of the public asked for their response to issues and events is chosen in an arbitrary fashion and therefore is not representative of the public at large.

slogan (political) ads A political advertisement in which a candidate expresses an emotional response toward an issue.

soft news Soft news is not necessarily timely, has minimal societal consequence, and is primarily designed to entertain.

sound bite An excerpt of a political figure's speech broadcast by the news media.

sound effects Sound effects consist of sounds that are added to broadcast presentations for dramatic emphasis.

spin control This information strategy is employed by political communications teams to manage how information is presented, reported, and received by the public.

stereotypes A stereotype is an oversimplified conception of a person, group, or event. This term derives from the Greek word *steros* (hard or solid), which underscores the inflexible, absolute nature of stereotypes. Stereotype is an *associative* process; ideas about groups are based on a shared understanding about a group.

stock characters A stock character refers to a character who appears so frequently in the media that he or she has become a conventional and recognizable type.

structured motion Structured motion refers to the ways in which a print ad is designed so it dictates the order in which the audience looks at the layout.

subjective camera techniques Filmmakers can create a literal first-person point of view by employing a subjective camera technique. In this technique, the camera assumes the perspective of the protagonist, so the audience sees the world through the eyes of the main character.

subplot Some narratives contain secondary stories, called subplots. Subplots often may initially appear to be unrelated to the main theme. However, the subplots may tie together at the conclusion, underscoring the themes of the primary plot.

temporal and spatial inferences Through editing, media communicators are able to manipulate time and space in order to establish relationships between people, locations, and events.

third-person point of view The third-person point of view describes the activities and internal processes of one character. The third-person point of view commonly employs the pronouns *he* or *she*. The author is privy to the thoughts and activities of this character but retains some critical distance and is therefore not accountable for the behavior of the character.

transformational words Transformational words are employed in advertising; they promise new levels of experience (e.g., *sensational, startling, amazing, remarkable*).

undefined function This refers to instances in which the communicator does not have a clear intention of what he or she intends to say. Consequently, the presentation of information can be muddled, directionless, and ineffective.

unfinished statements Unfinished statements make implied claims by leaving it to the consumer to complete the statement (e.g., "Magnavox gives you more").

vague authority In this journalistic bias technique, reporters use undocumented and generalized groups to impose a particular point of view.

values hierarchy Values hierarchy refers to the value system operating within the worldview of a media presentation.

vector In film or television, every moving object has a vector, or *implied* direction of movement.

verbal performance skills Verbal performance skills refer to the media communicator's voice quality and delivery. Verbal performance elements include volume, tone, clarity, and pacing.

verisimilitude Verisimilitude is defined as the appearance of truth. In its ability to instantaneously preserve a moment of time in space, photography creates an illusion of verisimilitude, or lifelike quality.

worldview Popular artists construct complete worlds out of their imaginations. The premise, plot, and characters of fictional narratives are based on certain fundamental assumptions about how this world operates. Even when we watch nonfiction content like the news, we receive overall impressions about worldview. Media presentations establish *who* and *what* are important within the worldview of the program.

SUGGESTED READING

Altheide, David L., and Robert P. Snow. *Media Logic*. Beverly Hills, CA: Sage Publications, 1979.

Altschull, J. Herbert. *Agents of Power*. New York: Longman, 1984.

Berger, Arthur. *Seeing Is Believing*. Mountain View, CA: Mayfield, 1989.

Berlo, David K. *The Process of Communication*. London: Holt, Rinehart and Winston, 1960.

Bogart, Leo. *Strategy in Advertising*. 2d ed. Lincolnwood, IL: NTC Business Books, 1986.

Bolen, William H. *Advertising*. 2d ed. New York: John Wiley and Sons, 1984.

Cantor, Joanne, and Barbara J. Wilson. "Helping Children Cope with Frightening Media Presentations." *Current Psychology: Research and Reviews* 7 (1988): 58–75.

Cole, Susan G. *Pornography and the Sex Crisis*. Toronto: Amanita, 1989.

Cundy, Donald T. "Political Commercials and Candidate Image." In *New Perspectives on Political Advertising*. Edited by Lynda Lee Kaid, Dan Nommo, and Keith R. Sanders, 210–34. Carbondale and Edwardsville: Southern Illinois University Press, 1986.

Curtiss, Deborah. *A Guide to the Visual Arts and Communication*. New York: Prentice-Hall, 1987.

Dondis, Donis A. *A Primer of Visual Literacy*. Cambridge, MA: MIT Press, 1973.

Downing, John; Ali Mohammadi, and Annabelle Sreberny-Mohammadi, eds. *Questioning the Media: A Critical Introduction*. Newbury Park, CA: Sage Publications, 1990.

Ewen, Stuart. *All Consuming Images*. New York: Basic Books, 1988.

Gates, David. "White Male Paranoia." *Newsweek*, March 29, 1993, 50.

Gates, Max. "The Subliminal Message: It's All in Your Mind." *Newhouse News Service*, June 24, 1991.

Germani, Clara. "Bloodhound on the Press's Trail." *Christian Science Monitor,* June 27, 1991, 2.

Germond, Jack W., and Jules Witcover. *Whose Broad Stripes and Bright Stars? The Trivial Pursuit of the Presidency, 1988.* New York: Warner Books, 1989.

"Get Ready for Election '92." *PBS Video News,* September–October 1992, 1.

Gilmore, Susan, and Ross Anderson. "Public Sours on Political System." *Seattle Times,* November 4, 1990, A1, A6.

Goffman, Erving. *Gender Advertisements.* New York: Harper & Row, 1976.

Griessman, Eugene B. *The Achievement Factors.* New York: Dodd, Mead, 1987.

Hall, Stuart. "Culture, the Media, and the 'Ideological Effect.' " In *Mass Communication and Society.* Edited by James Curran, Michael Gurevitch, and Janet Woollacott, 315–48. Beverly Hills, CA: Sage Publications, 1979.

Hirsch, Robert. *Exploring Color Photography.* Dubuque, IA: Wm. C. Brown, 1989.

Holtzman, Linda. *Content Analysis Tally Sheet.* St. Louis, MO: Webster University, 1993.

Jamieson, Kathleen Hall. *Dirty Politics.* New York: Oxford University Press, 1992.

Kaid, Lynda, and Dorothy Davidson. "Elements of Videostyle." In *New Perspectives on Political Advertising.* Edited by Lynda Lee Kaid, Dan Nommo, and Keith R. Sanders, 184–209. Carbondale and Edwardsville: Southern Illinois University Press, 1986.

Key, Wilson Bryan. *Subliminal Seduction.* Englewood Cliffs, NJ: Prentice-Hall, 1985.

Krauss, Clifford. "Gingrich Takes No Prisoners in the House's Sea of Gentility." *New York Times,* March 17, 1992, A18.

Kumar, Keval J. "The Cultural Perspective." *Communication Research Trends* 6 (1985): 6–7.

The Learning Seed. *Why You Buy: How Ads Persuade.* Lake Zurich, IL: The Learning Seed, 1988.

Leo, John. "Multicultural Follies." *U.S. News & World Report,* July 8, 1991, 12.

Levy, Steven. "The Selling of the Subliminal." *Popular Computing,* April 1984, 75–78.

McLuhan, Marshall. *Understanding Media.* New York: McGraw-Hill, 1965.

McNeilly, R. "The Power of the Word; Computer Content Analysis Reveals Hidden Meaning of Food Service Language." *Restaurants and Institutions,* September 17, 1986, 139–46.

Maynard, Robert. "Bush Tries to Douse Electronic Prairie Fire." *St. Louis Post-Dispatch,* February 28, 1992, B3.

"Media to the Left." *Television/Radio Age,* October 27, 1986, 20–24.

Mickelson, Sig. *From Whistle Stop to Sound Bite.* New York: Praeger, 1989.

Nelson, Harold L.; Dwight L. Teeter, Jr.; and Don R. Le Duc. *Law of Mass Communications.* 6th ed. Westbury, NY: Foundation Press, 1989.

Pfaff, Daniel W. *Joseph Pulitzer II and the Post-Dispatch.* University Park, PA: Pennsylvania State University Press, 1991.

Randall, John Herman. *The New Light on Immortality.* New York: Macmillian, 1921.

Real, Michael. *Super Media.* Newbury Park, CA: Sage Publications, 1989.

Saltzman, Joe. "Commercials Defy Logic." In *Mass Media Issues*. Edited by George Rodman, 149–51. 3d ed. Dubuque, IA: Kendall/Hunt, 1989.

Schudson, Michael. *Discovering the News*. New York: Basic Books, 1978.

Shulman, David. *Race Against Prime Time*. New York: New Decade Productions, 1984.

Smillie, Julia. "Content Analysis of *New York Times*." Paper delivered at Webster University, St. Louis, MO, 1990.

Smith, Robert Ellis. "Privacy's End." *Utne Reader* 49 (January–February 1992): 64–68.

Solorzano, Lucia. "Why Johnny Can't Read Maps, Either." *U.S. News & World Report*, March 25, 1985, 50.

Sontag, Susan. *On Photography*. New York: Farrar, Straus and Giroux, 1977.

Stanley, Harold W., and Richard G. Niemi. *Vital Statistics on American Politics*. 3d ed. Washington, D.C.: Congressional Quarterly, 1992.

Stroebel, Leslie; Todd Hollis; and Richard Zakia. *Visual Concepts for Photographers*. New York: Focal Press Limited, 1980.

Taylor, James W. *How to Write a Successful Advertising Plan*. Chicago, IL: NTC Publishing Group, 1989.

Thomas, Bob. *Walt Disney: An American Original*. New York: Simon and Schuster, 1976.

Toner, Robin. "Bush Campaign Scrambles to Put Forth a More Caring Candidate." *New York Times*, January 19, 1992, 14.

Turner, Graeme. *Film as Social Practice*. London: Routledge, 1988.

Weaver, David H., and G. Cleveland Wilhoit. *The American Journalist*. 2d ed. Bloomington: Indiana University Press, 1991.

Weiss, Richard. *The American Myth of Success: From Horatio Alger to Norman Vincent Peale*. Urbana and Chicago: University of Illinois Press, 1988.

Wolman, Benjamin B., ed. *International Encyclopedia of Psychiatry, Psychology, Psychoanalysis & Neurology*. New York: Aesculapius, 1977.

Woodruff, Judy. "Can Democracy Survive the Media in the 1990's?" *USA Today*, May 1990, 24–26.

INDEX

About the Author

ART SILVERBLATT is Associate Professor and Chair of the Department of Media Communications at Webster University in St. Louis, Missouri. He earned his Ph.D. in 1980 from Michigan State University.

ISBN 0-275-94830-7

9 780275 948306

HARDCOVER BAR CODE